From Slave Girls to Salvation

From Slave Girls to Salvation

Gender, Race, and Victoria's Chinese Rescue Home, 1886–1923

SHELLY IKEBUCHI

UBC Press • Vancouver • Toronto

23 22 21 20 19 18 17 16 15   5 4 3 2 1

Printed in Canada on FSC-certified ancient-forest-free paper (100% post-consumer recycled) that is processed chlorine- and acid-free.

Library and Archives Canada Cataloguing in Publication

Ikebuchi, Shelly, author
    From slave girls to salvation : gender, race, and Victoria's
Chinese Rescue Home, 1886–1923 / Shelly Ikebuchi.

Includes bibliographical references and index.
Issued in print and electronic formats.
ISBN 978-0-7748-3056-0 (bound). – ISBN 978-0-7748-3057-7 (pbk.)
ISBN 978-0-7748-3058-4 (pdf). – ISBN 978-0-7748-3059-1 (html)

    1. Chinese Canadian women – British Columbia – Social conditions – Case studies 2. Japanese Canadian women – British Columbia – Social conditions – Case studies 3. Chinese Rescue Home – History 4. Methodist Women's Missionary Society – History 5. Rescue missions (Church work) – British Columbia – Victoria 6. Church work with women – British Columbia – Victoria 7. British Columbia – Race relations I. Title.

FC3850.C5I34 2015   305.48'8951071128   C2015-904845-1
                                                          C2015-904846-X

Canada

UBC Press gratefully acknowledges the financial support for our publishing program of the Government of Canada (through the Canada Book Fund), the Canada Council for the Arts, and the British Columbia Arts Council.

This book has been published with the help of a grant from the Canadian Federation for the Humanities and Social Sciences, through the Awards to Scholarly Publications Program, using funds provided by the Social Sciences and Humanities Research Council of Canada.

UBC Press
The University of British Columbia
2029 West Mall
Vancouver, BC V6T 1Z2
www.ubcpress.ca

This book is dedicated to Crystal Ikebuchi Mandryk, who taught me to dream, to believe, to aspire, and to risk.

Contents

Tables and Figures

Acknowledgments

Over the years that it has taken to write this book, I have often likened its writing to the care, nurturing, and disciplining of a child. This book, like a child, has given me joy, delight, heartaches, and many sleepless nights. But most of all, this book has changed me as I have watched it grow and evolve. This book is a part of me, just as I am a part of it. Yet, this book is much more than me. Writing a book, like raising a child, is never a completely solitary experience, despite the fact that it often feels that way. I am deeply grateful to all those who guided and supported me along the way, who have carefully and tenderly helped me with this large task. To all those who contributed to *Slave Girls and Salvation,* either directly or indirectly, it carries with it your hard work, commitment, and wisdom.

My first thanks must go to Renisa Mawani, who read far too many iterations of this book, providing valuable feedback and guidance along the way. I cannot imagine a better mentor. Your compassion, dedication, and encouragement not only made my journey easier but also continues to inspire me to offer the same to others I meet along the way. Heartfelt thanks also go to Jennifer Chun and Henry Yu, who both encouraged and challenged me throughout the writing of this manuscript. Your thoughtful comments have made this a better book and have made me a stronger writer. Thanks also to Dr. Thomas Kemple, who read and commented on an earlier draft. *From Slave Girls to Salvation* would not have been possible without the support and guidance of archivist Blair Galson at the Bob Stewart Archives at the University of British Columbia. I would also like to thank both Jay Smith, for reading and editing an earlier draft, and my research assistant Jorie Soames, for bringing to this project her enthusiasm and her keen attention to detail.

I am especially grateful for my family, whose endless support and encouragement have sustained me throughout this long process. A special thank you goes to Eric Ketchell and Takara Ketchell, who have been loving, giving, patient, and understanding, believing in me even when I stopped believing in myself. It has always been a source of great comfort to know that my sister, Crystal Ikebuchi Mandryk, and parents, Barbara and Tom Ikebuchi, have always been just a phone call away. I am also indebted to Stephen Braham, Jacqueline Schoemaker Holmes, Rachael Sullivan, Brandy Weibe, and Bonar Buffam. Steve, you are my best friend. It was your confidence in me that started me on this journey, and my thanks goes to you for walking alongside me and offering me love, laughter, and good food. Jackie, you are my inspiration, my friend, my shelter in the storm, and, most of all, a true sister at heart. It gives me such comfort to know that I can always count on you to challenge and encourage me. Thanks, Rachael, for reading early drafts, for being a good friend, and for always being willing to offer your support. Brandy, you continue to inspire me through your great example, boundless energy, and wonderful insights. Bonar, it has been a wonderful gift to have you as my academic sibling and friend. You always offered great advice and kind encouragement.

From Slave Girls to Salvation was also motivated by earlier lessons from inside the classroom. I am grateful for the inspired teachings of wonderful professors both at Okanagan University College and at the University of British Columbia. Their teaching has inspired me not only in my academic research but also in my own teaching. Thanks especially to Dr. Patricia Tomic and Dr. Ricardo Trumper for teaching me to love sociology and to believe in its transformative power. Thank you also to Dr. Becki Ross for inspiring in me a passion for historical research.

From Slave Girls to Salvation would not have been possible without the academic and financial support offered by the UBC Department of Sociology. Additionally, I am grateful for the financial support of the Social Sciences and Humanities Research Council of Canada. This book has been published with the help of a grant from the Federation for the Humanities and Social Sciences, through the Awards to Scholarly Publications Program, using funds provided by the Social Sciences and Humanities Research Council of Canada.

From Slave Girls to Salvation

INTRODUCTION
Breaking Ground

FIGURE 1   New Chinese Home.
Source: Ridsdale, G.F. / Library and Archives Canada / PA-122651.

On November 29, 1896, at the age of fifteen, "Emily" entered the Chinese Rescue Home (the Home).[1] The Chinese Rescue Home, later called the Oriental Home and School, began as a project to rescue Chinese prostitutes and slave girls from those who held them captive. When the Home was started in 1886, nearly three thousand Chinese lived in Victoria, British Columbia, making up about 18 percent of the total population of 16,841.[2] While the vast majority of Chinese immigrants during this period were men, the women who did immigrate were targets of both suspicion and concern. According to McLaren, "in a minority community that was overwhelmingly male and in which women were regularly bought and sold, it was assumed by their detractors that, with limited exceptions, any Chinese girl or woman who came to Canada must already be a prostitute or destined for that role."[3] Although the Home's mandate was initially to rescue prostitutes, it quickly expanded, and, between 1886 and 1923, over four hundred women took shelter there. The number of women who passed through the Home suggests a significant minority, and in the early years likely the majority, of Chinese women and Japanese women stayed there. Emily was one of these women.

According to the Home's records, Emily had grown up in an orphanage after having been placed there by her "Indian" mother, her father being Chinese. After leaving the orphanage, she lived with her sister for a time; however, after quarrelling with her, Emily entered the Home. Over the next two and a half years, Emily would run away from the institution on numerous occasions, prompting those who operated it to propose installing a wire screen on the window of her room. Although her multiple entries into the Home were explicitly framed as voluntary, Emily was, at least on one occasion, escorted back to the institution by police. In fact, despite the many references to the voluntary nature of her stay, her multiple attempts to leave are evidence that Emily was, in fact, not as free (or as grateful) as the records seemed to imply.

The first time Emily left the Home was in March 1897. In April of the same year, Emily returned to the residence on an errand. Although the purpose of her visit was not clear, she did not have any intention of re-entering the institution as a resident. She was brought in before the advisory committee, which happened to be holding its monthly meeting at the time, and "the Chairman addressed to her some wholesome advice." According to the minutes, however, she seemed "not to be much affected by the advantages of the training she would receive in the Home, and the fact that Miss Bowes [the matron] was willing to receive her and forgive her for the past did not seem to make the slightest impression upon her." While Emily was then allowed to leave, the minutes went on to state that the advisory committee was "fully alive to the importance of retaining such girls in the Home where they are under good influences but how to manage it against their will is the difficulty."[4]

The following month, the minutes of the advisory committee showed that Emily had returned again "of her own free will."[5] A month later, she was once again the topic of discussion. The report states that Emily "is now giving 'good satisfaction' and is working cleaning rooms for 1.50/month." By September of the same year, Emily had left once more. This time she went to her sister's home, which was located four miles from the Home. When her sister refused to take her in, she was taken in by the reverend "and in his house was served tea. A lady being there who had seen Emily before recognized her as one of the girls of the home and offered to accompany her and the Police to the House the evening of the same day."[6] This time, Emily stayed in the Home only two months before again running away. Each of Emily's attempts to flee was met with an increasing amount of intervention, and this time was no exception. The day after she left the Home, "Mrs. Chapman had made very diligent search for her but [she] was nowhere to be found."[7] The "next day one of the House board ladies rode out with the Chinese Police to see if she was at her sister's but she had not been there." They then visited the homes of some of the married women who had previously resided in the Home, but Emily was not to be found.[8]

Although the searchers were unable to locate Emily, the following day the matron received a postcard from a local convent requesting that she call on them. Finding Emily there, the matron was unable to convince her to come back to the Home. The matter, however, was not dropped. The matron informed the members of the advisory committee of the circumstances, and they then discussed what their next course of action should be. According to the minutes, it was the committee's opinion that Emily *belonged* "to the Home, [and that] the Convent should not have detained her, accordingly it was proposed and carried that Mrs. Chapman as representing the Home immediately write to the Convent demanding the return of Emily to the Home, and emphasizing [their] authority in the matter."[9]

One week later, the advisory committee called a special meeting to discuss a letter regarding Emily that had been received from Sister Superior at the convent. The minutes do not mention what the letter said, only that it should be answered in "as conciliatory manner as possible."[10] Further, the committee appointed a subcommittee to consult with a lawyer "as to what steps if any, should be taken to bring Emily back to the home."[11] The lawyer subsequently informed the committee that it had no recourse other than to use "persuasive measures." He indicated that "he thought it wise to call on her once more to see if she had changed her mind," which the committee did, but to no avail.[12] Despite the convent's plan to send her to an orphanage in Cowichan, Emily rebuked all attempts to persuade her to return to the institution. However, in July 1898, the matron once again brought Emily back to the Home, this time from Vancouver.

A special meeting was once again called to consider Emily's case, and it was at this juncture that "it was decided to put a wire screen to the small front bedroom and have Emily occupy that room till further arrangements be made."[13] It is clear that the advisory committee was unwilling to take any more chances where young Emily was concerned. These measures, it seems, were successful as Emily did not leave the mission again until her marriage in April of the following year. The last entry for Emily was found in a journal that bears the title "Bad Women" and that lists by name certain women who were considered to be immoral. Emily's name was on this list, followed by the date of her marriage, with a note on the opposite page explaining that she had "left her husband and lived with [a] white man."[14]

The story of Emily highlights the Chinese Rescue Home's three related mandates. In keeping with its name, these were race, rescue, and domesticity. First and foremost, the purpose of the Home was to deal with a particular racial problem. That the word "Chinese" (and later "Oriental") was part of the Home's name is not surprising as managing race was one of its primary goals. The institution's claim to Emily was based on her (partial) Chineseness. It was this that led the Home to insist that Emily "belonged" to it, not to the convent or the orphanage. Here, racial concerns are expressed not by exclusion, which was the case throughout much of the province, but, rather, by inclusion. Although Chinese women and men were, at different periods, excluded from Canada, the Home's mandate was to include – to transform and to domesticate these women so that they could eventually be assimilated. This leads us to the Home's second mandate – rescue – which was premised on notions of benevolence and transformation through moral regulation. Clearly, the relationship between race and religion is a complex one. On the one hand, the mission saw its focus on race as a matter of benevolence; on the other hand, it wanted to dissolve race by transforming the women under its care. When Emily ran away, she was repeatedly welcomed back to the fold. The matron and the advisory committee may have gone to extreme measures to keep Emily in the Home, but they did so because of their faith that she could be saved and transformed. Sarah Bowes was the matron of the institution during a particularly troubling time for Emily. Of Emily, she wrote: "I continue to bear her up on the wings of faith and prayer trusting that the labor and care bestowed may yet bear fruit for Jesus. In every way I endeavored to be a mother to Emily."[15] In fact, motherhood and family were common themes in the Home's records.

Transformation and moral regulation were to be achieved through the Home's third mandate – domesticity. The role of white women was paramount here as it was in the *home* that the work of transformation was to be accomplished. As a gendered project, the transformation of Emily was to be measured by her adherence to proper domesticity. The success of her transformation was measured first by her domestic service and later by her marriage to a Chinese man. Despite the many times she ran away, Emily's ultimate failure occurred when she left her Chinese husband to live with a white man. Here, Emily displayed her rejection of both Christian values and the racial boundaries that such values implied. Thus, whiteness and domesticity are seen to be intertwined with religious values, informing and producing the cross-racial relationships that were forged in the Home.

This case study of the Chinese Rescue Home provides an important analysis of an institution that, although iconic in British Columbia's history, has yet to be fully explored. Although other historians and historical sociologists have pointed to its significance in Victoria and in British Columbia more generally,[16] none has offered a sustained or detailed analysis. *From Slave Girls to Salvation* offers a detailed empirical study of the Home, thus adding to the historiography of British Columbia. Uncovering the organizational hierarchies, the institutional schematics, as well as the religious and racial tropes that infused the Home is crucial to understanding how it came to hold such an important place in the historical imaginings of the province. Further, these hierarchies and inner workings also illuminate how whiteness and domesticity came to be imagined and asserted in relation to and through interactions with a racialized Other.

By viewing domesticity as spatial, psychic, and corporeal, and the Home as a geographically situated site and embodied practice of moral regulation, *From Slave Girls to Salvation* moves beyond explanations that focus primarily on racial exclusion. Domesticity is central to these more inclusionary processes as it informs how space was conceived, how identities were forged, and how bodies were disciplined. Foregrounded, then, is the importance of domesticity both in its material and in its imaginative geography.[17] The Home might be likened to the hearth of the nation. Not only does the hearth represent the home and domesticity and their association with women, but it is also a symbol of welcome. It is a space for those coming in from "outside." In the case of the Chinese Rescue Home, the welcome was not unconditional. Yet the hearth offered a space for some outsiders to find openings into a world in which they were otherwise seldom welcome. The hearth also represents a place of transformation: it is here that the fire turns a cold room into one filled with warmth. It is a space where outsiders are not only welcomed but also affected and transformed. The transformation of the Other through regulation threads itself materially and discursively into the very fabric of the Chinese Rescue Home. Deconstructing the processes and practices of its benevolent work uncovers the complex relationship between whiteness, domesticity, and religion.

As a religious institution, the Home straddled the public/private and national/global divides. Run by women, the mission was a space informed by gender hierarchies, just as it was informed by racial ones. It occupied a unique space in which (gendered and racialized) national and domestic spaces overlapped; thus, a critical discussion of the institution offers us a clearer understanding of how these relationships informed institutional practices while also providing us with insights into the state's investment (and interventions) in the domestic realm. Although my analysis focuses on a single institution, as Sangster argues, the treatment "accorded a small number of women reveals a much broader web of regulation shaping the proper definitions of sexuality, the family, and gender roles for *all* women."[18] Prioritized here is a discussion of the tensions and contestations that arose from the overlap between the national and the domestic, and between the public (which was largely the domain of men) and the private (which was largely the domain of women).

The examination of these tensions is exemplified in the photo that opens this chapter. Although this photo was taken approximately twenty years after the first "rescue" of a Chinese woman from what was assumed to be a brothel, I chose it because of its symbolic and material significance. It was taken during the construction of a new home for Chinese and Japanese women and children. The new building is evidence of both the success of a twenty-year project and a promise for the future. This photo represents the building of a local home and domestic space, but it also represents citizenship and nationhood – and the challenges that Chinese and Japanese people posed to them. The significance of this photograph lies not only in what it shows but also in what it conceals. It is the white women who ran the Home who pose on its veranda, while the Chinese and Japanese women, without whom there could be no Home, are absent. Although the stories of Japanese and Chinese women and their recollections of the Home are an important piece of Asian Canadian history, this is not the history that I address. Rather, I address the history of an institution, of the intersections between whiteness and domesticity, and the ways in which these were produced through the Home. By focusing on spatial metaphors and material spaces, I theorize the Home as an active site of production. This includes the production of racialized and gendered spaces, behaviours, discourses, and ideologies.

The relationships that were forged within the material spaces of the Home were neither strictly familial nor economic but both. Building on insights from geography, sociology, and history, I use a spatial focus to analyze these spaces as embedded in, constructed through, and productive of power relations. The Home is a unique and rich site for reconsidering women's roles both inside and outside the home. As it existed at the interstices of the public and the private, and of the foreign and the domestic, the Home offers a productive space for exploring how and why Japanese and Chinese women were discursively constituted as domestically delinquent. This discursive constitution materially and imaginatively contributed to the construction of the domestic realm that "housed" the Home as well as to how these material spaces themselves contributed to the practice of power. Those who ran the Home interacted with and produced imaginative geographies that were informed by gendered and racial hierarchies. Those outside the Home, including judges, police officers, and the public, also drew upon domestic discourses in the regulation of "foreign" and female bodies and in the disciplining of white men who dared to interfere with or intervene in the domestic relations of the Home. State practices informed and shaped the types of cross-racial domestic relations that were possible inside the Home and outside it, as discourses of domesticity were taken up by state institutions (such as the courts) in ways that both undermined and cemented the legitimacy of the domestic workings of the Home and the authority of the white women who staffed it.

This book explores an institutional space that took the form of a domestic space, troubling both the binaries of private/public and of foreign/

domestic. In order to consider the material and imagined geographies of the Chinese Rescue Home, I build upon a recent body of work in geography that examines the "house and home, the household and the domestic world."[19] Geographers take many approaches to studying the home. For instance, structuralists and phenomenologists are particularly invested in delving into the relationship between the house, the mind, and emotions. This relationship is captured in Tuan's "notion of 'topophilia,' or love of place."[20] The links between the home and emotion are not limited, however, to love. In fact, many scholars productively take up the links between home and loss, fear, and danger.[21] The domestic realm is also a site of intervention for geographers and others who are interested in the material ways that the home informs gender and gender relations. Many who take this approach view the domestic as part of the "private" realm and juxtapose it with the male-dominated public realm. Others chart women's movements both inside and outside the domestic realm, troubling the boundary between the private and the public in significant ways.[22] While some postcolonial scholars trouble the space of the home as itself a site of exclusion from which the Other is debarred, others show that colonial relations and exclusions occur *within* the home as well. Most of these studies focus on how white women gained authority and autonomy through their relationships with the racial Other both inside and outside the private spaces of the colonial home.

The Chinese Rescue Home and those associated with it comprised a very small portion of the work carried out by the Methodist Missionary Board and the Woman's Missionary Society. While it had a small constituency, the Home presents a compelling case study for a number of reasons. First, while missions that were undertaken abroad strove to improve the spiritual lives of those they evangelized, racial "problems" were seen to originate (and thus to remain) outside the West. Occupying a space that was between the inside and the outside of the nation, the Home was a space not only of evangelism but also of assessment and appraisal.[23] Second, a spatial analysis of the Home provides insight into the ways in which it was situated between the public and the private. Third, by moving outside the space of the Home, I provide a valuable study of the disparate ways in which moral regulation functioned. While an analysis of the Home interrupts binaries of gendered realms, moving outside the Home further extends our understanding of how moral regulation functioned in other ways. While many scholars argue that moral regulatory projects function as technologies of social control (and the work of the organization certainly supports these claims) the Home did not exist in a vacuum.[24] In fact, it was its positioning as an in-between space that gave it its legitimacy. It was situated on the edge of the nation and yet was firmly within it. It was a space of domesticity that functioned in the public realm. It was also a site that blurred the lines between state and non-state institutions. It is these tensions and ambivalences that make the Home an ideal point of departure, allowing for a deeper discussion of the private/ public, state/non-state, and national/domestic than these binaries, in and of themselves, allow.

It is important to understand the (often spatially defined) gendered private/public divide in moral reform projects. The women who ran the Chinese Rescue Home were able to do so precisely because their mission was seen as an extension of the private realm. Thus, it is imperative to move beyond this public/private dichotomy in two ways. First, I challenge the notion that moral reform was about reinscribing the divide between private and public spheres. I do this by arguing that the Home was a place where both white women and their Chinese and Japanese charges could aspire to something more than domesticity. Second, I challenge the public/private divide by subjecting it to a spatial analysis, thereby locating the Home in its physical form, as a space that was situated on the threshold between the public and the private, infringing on both but totally inhabiting neither. Analyzing both spatial and discursive concerns means relying on a large number and array of sources (despite which many stories remain untold). For this reason, I now discuss these as well as my methodology.[25]

METHODOLOGY AND SOURCES

From Slave Girls to Salvation explores the intersections of race, gender, religion, and nation in Victoria, British Columbia. Although my analysis focuses on Victoria, I also refer to relevant material from other cities in the province, including Vancouver. Both Vancouver and Victoria were entry points for Japanese and Chinese populations coming from the United States as well as directly from Japan and China. The period of study begins in 1886, when John Vrooman Gardiner and Reverend John Edward Starr first began "rescuing" Chinese girls, [26] and it ends in 1923. This closing date is significant for two reasons. First, the bulk of the records from the Methodist Woman's Missionary Society, British Columbia Conference Branch Fonds, are dated from 1904 to 1923. Second, it was in 1923 that the Chinese Immigration Act shifted from exclusionary policies such as the head tax to an even more expansive and systematic process of exclusion. Although the Chinese Rescue Home continued to run until 1942, the objectives and the demographics of its mission changed significantly during this period. More Japanese women and children began to enter the residence, and the focus, while still largely evangelistic, shifted to education, especially of young children. This shift in demographics and concern is important and worth further investigation, but it is not my focus.

What I offer is a case study of the formative period of Victoria's Chinese Rescue Home. The Home, as a case study, offers the opportunity for an in-depth analysis of relations of power that often (but not always) mirrored those in Canadian society. As Iacovetta and Mitchinson argue, case studies "offer us a rare window on human interactions and conflict. Complex power relations play themselves out at the local level, sometimes with unpredictable outcomes."[27] With all of its diversity of artefacts – from formal reports to letters, to legal documents and carefully worded press releases and beyond – this case study offers a wealth of information about institutional practices, especially as they were applied to "deviant" women. The case study, according to Berg, "aims to uncover the manifest interaction of significant factors ... But in addition, the researcher is able to capture various nuances, patterns, and more latent elements that other research approaches might overlook."[28] Thus, as a case study, the Chinese Rescue Home opens up possibilities for studying institutions both as they affect personal relations and as they are informed by them. The Home provides a compelling study not only of race relations but also of the complex relationship between the national and the global, the state realm and the domestic realm, and the roles of race and religion in each of these. Many case studies are concerned with "deviant" populations. As such, they shed light on the intricacies of disciplinary practices and forms of surveillance. The documents that I uncovered provide interesting insights into the experiences of and relationships between white, Chinese, and Japanese women that transpired inside the Home as well as how these were perceived outside it. I also pay attention to the Home's material form as the experiences and relationships that were forged within it were solidified through its physical/institutional/domestic space.

Borrowing from cultural geographies of the home, I attempt, as Alison Blunt suggests, to move "beyond binaries such as public and private space and imaginative geographies of 'self' and 'Other'" in order to investigate the "interplay of home and identity in terms of spatial politics."[29] Gendered discourses of domesticity informed the type of physical space that was built and from within which the institution operated. Instead of working from a strictly institutional space, those who ran the Home created it as a domestic space within which they could domesticate their charges. These spaces were determined by religious and gendered discourses of domesticity, and they also *reproduced* discourses of domesticity as they dictated the acceptability of only certain types of practices. Thus, a case study that focuses on material spaces illuminates how domesticity, as a discourse, was reaffirmed through the spatial organization and performance of feminine roles and practices such as sewing, cooking, cleaning, and mothering.

As a historical project, *From Slave Girls to Salvation* is informed by the debates over voice and history. In "The Selectivity of Historical Representation," David Wishart explains that "the historian does not have access to that past, only to accounts of it, and that those accounts describe only a fragment of what took place." What is most often lost are the "accounts of the people most directly affected."[30] This is certainly the case with respect to the Japanese and Chinese women who lived in the Chinese Rescue Home. It would be a grave mistake to claim that I have compiled a history of Japanese and Chinese Canadian women as only glimpses of their stories are evident through the narrow lens of formal institutional records, letters, meeting minutes, official reports, Royal Commissions, and newspaper accounts. Motivations for entering the Home are recorded only from the perspectives of the white matrons who painstakingly catalogued each entrance and exit. While we may never know the motivations of the Japanese and Chinese women, especially those who entered the Home voluntarily, throughout I attempt to draw on secondary sources, including literature and biography, that may provide some spaces from which to consider their stories. At best, however, this attempt is piecemeal and incomplete. While it is likely that most of the women who entered the institution during the period studied have died, future studies might yet uncover the stories of residents who entered and left the Home between 1924 and 1942.

I rely on a framework that Foucault refers to as "effective history."[31] Jennifer Terry explains that effective history "involves what Foucault calls 'historical sense' – a strategic awareness of points of emergence or 'possibilities' existing at particular historical moments in the formation of particular discourses."[32] My goal is to provide a systematic and historical account of the Chinese Rescue Home and to point to the ways in which racial and gendered truths and practices were formed and challenged through this site. As Foucault explains, "History becomes 'effective' to the degree that it introduces discontinuity into our very being – as it divides our emotions, dramatizes our instincts, multiplies our body and sets it against itself."[33] The discontinuities that I trace here are found in the interstitial positioning of the Home and in the ambivalences of the private/public and national/global divides.

Given that archival records are often written by those in positions of power or authority, I adopt two strategies to lessen the "top heaviness" of the sources. First, I use multiple and diverse sources. For instance, Chapter 2 draws extensively on two Royal Commissions, a report/letter compiled by Reverend Starr, and numerous Methodist reports and publications. Chapter 3 focuses largely on records of the Methodist Woman's Missionary Society, but it also includes architectural, document, and image analysis. Chapter 4 relies heavily on newspaper accounts of court cases that reference "friends" of the Home and explores the multiple roles of the press in documenting and (re)framing court cases. Chapter 5 focuses on both Woman's Missionary Society records and court documents in order to examine "custody" (habeas corpus) cases and the state's role in determining guardianship over Chinese girls placed in the Home. This approach offers a multifaceted and more nuanced understanding of not only the form and function of the Home but also the social, legal, and national context in which it was constructed. Although this still offers a "view from above," it is, nevertheless, a more nuanced view. While the history I offer is in no way complete, it is an institutional history of the Home that is able to provide important insights into the functioning of power.

I also endeavour to uncover points of emergence, or Foucauldian "possibilities," by providing a subversive reading of history and questioning how these dominant accounts come to stand as truth. In this operation, an archivist/reader reveals that the dominant account is never fully capable of containing the subaltern it launches, nor is it fully able to stabilize itself.[34] Reading subversively, or "against the grain," is a strategy that offers a richer analysis than does reading "with the grain," but it is not a substitute for the latter. As Stoler, in her discussion of the colonial archive, contends, we also need to read the archive "for its regularities, for its logic of recall, for its densities and distributions, for its consistencies of misinformation, omission, and mistake – *along* the archival grain."[35]

Building on Stoler, I submit that all archival collections depend to a greater or lesser degree on hierarchies of power and therefore can and should be read as not only reflecting power hierarchies (such as hierarchies of race, gender, class, and sexuality) but also as producing them.[36]

Church archives, for instance, are littered with official reports made by missionaries and church officials at various levels of church governance, most of whom are white, upper-middle-class men. The misinformation, omissions, and mistakes that Stoler refers to are important indications of existing power hierarchies both inside and outside church structures.[37] Not all of the sources in church archives were penned by men, however: women's missionary groups most often reported directly to male supervisors, which means that there are many extant reports written by these women. Despite the fact that many of these women had more autonomy than did many other white women, their claims to power were often limited to supervising or reforming those who were perceived as racially or culturally inferior. Reading these texts both with and against the grain can tell us much about the complex interplay of race, gender, and class.

Providing a critical and systematic analysis is imperative, as I rely on a diverse corpus of documents that includes published texts, photos, maps, official documents of churches and religious governing bodies, personal letters, record books, newspapers, court documents, and Royal Commissions. Although these texts are largely from British Columbia, a number of reports and texts also deal with missionary work in China and Japan. Chang and Mawani offer detailed discussions of the ways in which racial knowledges are routinely transported within and across national borders.[38] Thus, it is not surprising that my sources highlight the ways in which the "Chinese and Japanese problem" was always already outside the nation. Therefore, even within "home missions," missionaries and church organizations often borrowed from racial knowledges and practices that were imported from other national contexts.

The archives themselves, as well as the documents held there, are the products of cultural, social, political, economic, and moral influences. I draw from a number of sources to uncover how religious discourse intersected with racial and gendered discourses to produce specific understandings of Chinese and Japanese women as foreign and as potentially transformable through practices of moral regulation. Given that racial and gendered discourses played such a central role in the Chinese Rescue Home, discourse analysis is an important method for understanding how one comes to make sense of race, sexuality, and gender.[39] Critical discourse analysis sees discourse as forming a dialectical relationship with the social world, and it strives to understand the relationship between both the concrete material world and the abstract discursive world. For example, the physical (material) structure of the Home was embedded

in – indeed constructed through – gendered, racial, and colonial discourses, and these material structures fed into and reproduced these same
discourses within the Home.

Thus, discourses affected white, Japanese, and Chinese women's lives
in material ways. Discourse and ideology are neither neutral nor static.
Ideology is embedded in social and cultural practices, and, just as these
practices change and (d)evolve over time, so also do the knowledges
that they produce. These discourses, therefore, shape the everyday lives
of individuals through shaping both social identity and social relations.
The archival sources used here must be understood as both material evidence of discursive practices and as the discursive practices themselves.
Jorgenson and Phillips contend that "discourse is both constitutive and
constituted."[40] In other words, discourse not only shapes social meaning
and identities but is also shaped by the social world. The texts that I chose
are not separate from the historical and social specificities that informed
them, nor are they distinct from the policies and practices that resulted
from them. Further, religious discourses cannot be understood as singular
or cohesive but, rather, must be understood as developing out of and in
response to counter-discourses. Discourses of race, nation, regulation,
and domesticity are central to this book. As such, it is necessary to discuss
how these discourses informed and were informed by the spaces of the
Home.

RACE, PLACE, AND NATION

As a racial project, the Chinese Rescue Home must be understood as a
productive space. Here, race itself was produced in complex and ambivalent ways. Taking a critical approach to race means acknowledging that
both race and whiteness are social constructions and not biological facts.
Three points are important here. First, race and whiteness are socially
constructed through processes of racialization, whereby meaning is
assigned to biological manifestations of "race": these meanings, in turn,
help to shape institutions and structures so that racialization is not only
concerned with racial bodies but also with the institutional practices that
govern and create them.[41] Omi and Winant argue that "racial formation
is a process of historically situated *projects* in which human bodies and
social structures are represented and organized."[42] The Home was just one
of many racial projects, and, as I show, racial projects in this case both

sustained and interrupted hegemonic ideas and practices for, as Omi and Winant claim, hegemony "is tentative, incomplete and 'messy.'"[43]

The shifting meaning of race can be seen as a part of racial projects that arise out of and inform state practices. The state does not simply define race: rather, the state and race are in a constant (in)formative dialogue.[44] Thus, understandings of race are understandings of the ways in which state and non-state institutions build upon and produce racial knowledges.[45] I rely on understandings of race as intrinsically tied to space. Influenced by the work of Lefebvre, Anderson, Razack, and Mawani in particular, I view race as both constitutive of and constituted by space.[46] Buildings and landscapes are not just objective and neutral; they are also subjective representations of past and present beliefs and practices.[47] Thus, my focus on space is attentive to ways in which race was always already constituting and constituted by these spaces and how values and social relations became embedded in buildings and landscapes. Although race, as a set of relations generated by the state and other institutions, informs space, it does so in distinctly relational ways that intersect and produce gendered, classed, and sexualized meanings.

Race is relational in the sense that the racialized Other is constructed as raced *by* the white subject and in the sense that he or she is raced in opposition to a seemingly unraced (white) subject.[48] Thus, in order to understand the process of racialization and its effects, one must also consider how whiteness itself is a product of racial institutions and state practices.[49] Although whiteness studies have become prominent in recent years, Fanon's work reminds us that the study of whiteness was always a part of anti-colonial and anti-racist scholarship and activism.[50] The recent studies of whiteness, however, reemphasized its importance. Twine and Gallagher argue that it is often at the local level that "whiteness as a form of power is defined, deployed, performed, policed, and reinvented."[51] Drawing from this literature, I understand whiteness as historically grounded and socially produced. This allows for an analysis that is attentive to the slippages that take place in defining not only the "racial problem" but also the instability of whiteness itself. A critical assessment of the ways that whiteness is itself constructed allows for a destabilization of the binaries of self and Other by exposing the instability and fluidity of both.

Power relations based on race, gender, class, and sexuality do not occur in isolation from each other. For this reason, I take an intersectional approach to analyzing the Home. Thus, I interrogate not only how white women, as well as Japanese and Chinese Canadian women, were framed in terms of their "race" but, in particular, how they were also, at the same time, framed in terms of nationalism, citizenship, sexuality, class, and gender. In addition, white women were also subjected to gendered and racialized forms of power, and an examination of the Home highlights some of the ways these facilitated and constrained their aspirations. Whiteness, like other racial categories, is produced on multiple registers and thus is not monolithic. Central to my argument is the understanding that the Chinese Rescue Home was a space that both challenged and interrupted discourses of white (national) superiority. Whiteness, here, must be understood as relationally formed. For instance, global constructions of whiteness informed (and were informed by) local discourses. National discourses that privileged whiteness did not exist in isolation from other racial taxonomies. Therefore, it is important to take into account the ways in which national discourses of whiteness (and other racial categories) were themselves transnational processes.[52] National discourses and processes of inclusion and exclusion were often influenced by discourses from inside the nation as well as by imperialist relationships that were forged outside the nation.

Understanding how racial and religious projects functioned in Victoria during this time necessitates an understanding of the complex processes of colonization and nation building that were then ongoing. "Nation building," as used here, refers to an ongoing and always incomplete process that includes, but is not limited to, formal state processes, "settlement," and hegemonic ideation, which, in British Columbia, included at its core anti-Asian racism. Speaking of the relationship between First Nations and anti-Chinese racism, Timothy Stanley argues: "Local anti-Chinese racism grew out of the racism that was behind colonization. Both racisms established the power and privilege of the same people: those of European origins. Racism against one group was often even expressed in conjunction with racism against the other, and racist restrictions on people from China were often simultaneously enacted against First Nations people."[53] The making of a nation was about much more than settlement: it was also about the construction of a people. That the term "Canadian" was often equated with whiteness is well documented by Stanley and others. Although Canada has often been imagined as a settler society, this notion must be *un*settled. The making of Canada as a nation was not simply a process of settlement; rather, it was a process that required both the dispossession and the disenfranchisement of Indigenous peoples and non-white settlers.

The colonization of what is now British Columbia was unique in that it was one of the "last territories to be earmarked for European settlement."[54] Thus, the logics and processes of colonization were already deeply entrenched and well-practised. However, the colonization of this territory was also unique because of the numbers of Chinese that were also entering the area. In 1855, the white population of the Colony of Vancouver Island was 509, while a "conservative estimate would place the First Nations population at the time at 100,000."[55] When, during the Fraser River gold rush (1858), some thirty thousand Chinese entered the area, the white population was certainly outnumbered. However, as Stanley points out, "despite the seeming tenuousness of European resettlement, the political, cultural, economic, and demographic transformation of the people and the lands that became British Columbia was already underway." Further, Stanley argues that power continued to be "created through a combination of statecraft (diplomacy, alliances, use of First Nations customs and culture), economic incentives (trade goods, gifts), and military force (gunboats, punitive expeditions, collective reprisals, police actions)."[56] In this way, nation building and colonization were linked to global and imperial power relations outside the territory. In fact, empire, as I argue in Chapter 3, was literally built into the structures that would become home to the Chinese and Japanese women who would reside in the Chinese Rescue Home.

Exploring the relationality between the national and the global is necessary if one is to examine how inclusion and exclusion worked during this period. Chinese and Japanese women were neither fully incorporated into the nation nor entirely excluded from it. Situated within the borders of the nation, they continued to be framed as foreign. This being the case, discussions that rely on binaries such as inside and outside cannot fully explain how it was that women missionaries could remain within the nation at the same time as they evangelized women who were always already "foreign." While other scholars trouble the relationships between religion and nation, both in terms of foreign mission work and (more narrowly) with regard to home mission work, the vast majority of studies of home mission work focus on the nation as the site of intervention and analysis.[57] Pascoe, for example, takes such an approach.[58] She examines a mission in San Francisco that was similar to Victoria's Chinese Rescue Home, and her discussion revolves largely around how Chinese women were regulated so that they might be assimilated into the nation, especially through education.[59] But Victoria's Chinese Rescue Home cannot be adequately explained through a focus on the nation alone. In British Columbia, the process was much more complex than it was in California. While the goal of the institutions in both Victoria and San Francisco was assimilation, the former also became a site within which some women were expelled from the nation. For example, immigration officials placed women in the Chinese Rescue Home while their claims were being assessed. The matron of the institution provided these officials with her recommendation as to the fitness of the women to remain in the country. Those who were categorized as unable or unwilling to undergo the transformations that were deemed necessary were, accordingly, expelled from the Home and, upon the matron's recommendation, sometimes from the nation.

I hope to trouble the nation as an ideology that relies on inside/outside binaries but that is never capable of fully sustaining them. By theorizing the Chinese Rescue Home as both inside and outside the nation, it becomes clear that it challenged national/global boundaries and also threatened race/whiteness binaries as central to defining the nation. This "borderland" approach provides a more nuanced analysis of the policing of racial boundaries, the crossing of these boundaries, and their re-entrenchment.[60] For if nations are defined by their borders, then understanding the processes that take place at these borders can provide us with a greater understanding of how the nation itself is defined. This approach provides a more nuanced understanding of how the Chinese Rescue Home became both a place that facilitated the integration of some "foreigners" into the nation (by teaching them the value of domesticity) and a place that expelled others.

It is not enough to say "We let them in" or "We kept them out." Binaries of inside and outside are not sufficient to explain how, once inside the nation, Chinese and Japanese women were framed as both incompatible with their new home and integral to its definition. Without Japanese and Chinese women, Victoria's Chinese Rescue Home would have had no foundation. Without these women, Victoria's Woman's Missionary Society would have had no mission. If whiteness was to define the nation through its moral superiority and its benevolent paternalism (and maternalism), then it needed an inferior and a subordinate Other. While it might be claimed that this inferior and subordinate Other was always a part of the national imagining, that this inferiority simply marked a hierarchy within the nation, this does not fully explain *how* the subordinate came to be defined, in the first place, through the production and mobility of racial knowledges.

Mawani and Stoler inform this discussion regarding the mobility of racial knowledges.[61] Stoler contends that racial discourse evolves out of and through its attachment to prior cultural representations.[62] In fact, these are not only localized representations: they are also built on and mobilized by forms of representation from outside the nation. For instance, racial discourses were mobilized through reliance on examples from the United States as well as from prior missionary contact in China and Japan. Race cannot be understood as singular or static; rather, it must be understood as having the potential to change, evolve, and transform as it attaches itself to other discourses and representations. These representations include narratives of Christian transformation, which can transgress but not fully overturn the boundaries of race. Domesticating Japanese and Chinese women interrupted racial discourses of non-assimilability, yet the need for transformation was contingent on understandings of racial inferiority and white superiority.

In the period under study, whiteness was a central defining component of the nation. White women, in particular, were able to use Christianity to reinforce their moral authority.[63] Although the inclusion of racialized populations within the framework of Christianity interrupted the discourses that equated whiteness with superiority, it did not open the door to full equality. Instead, racialized bodies were re-constructed as in need of transformation before they could be included. Paradoxically, in order for racialized bodies to be seen as in need of transformation, they had to be framed as inferior or subordinate. Thus, Christian missionaries often opposed biological racism, but their Christian project produced another form of racism that, just as effectively, rendered Chinese and Japanese as inferior. The discourses that made this construction possible were not to be found within the nation; rather, they had everything to do with how the nation was formed through processes that were always already in conversation with racial knowledge from outside the nation.

Racial knowledge informs the types of exclusionary processes that are a common theme in previous discussions of Chinese and Japanese immigration. The Chinese Rescue Home provides evidence that racial power also operated through inclusion. Many have documented the varied and multiple technologies of racial exclusion that existed in British Columbia, especially with regard to Chinese and Japanese populations. This has sometimes "led to a portrayal of racialized peoples as victims without voice or as people whose identities were externally imposed."[64] Recent work has begun to take into account the active role of Chinese and Japanese populations in resisting and challenging governmental and societal exclusions.[65] My study of the Chinese Rescue Home examines a context within which government and institutional work took a less exclusionary form. While many in the province were decrying the menace of the "Yellow Peril" and calling for the expulsion of Chinese and Japanese populations – if not always from the nation then certainly from white society and white labour interests – white women were taking a different approach. Although many Christians (and non-Christians) during this time argued that Japanese and Chinese men and women could not (or should not) be assimilated into the nation, the women of the Woman's Missionary Society (WMS), who would eventually run the Home, were of a different mind. Certainly, the WMS women considered these populations to be inferior; however, rather than focusing only on exclusion, they engaged in what they believed to be transformative projects of inclusion.

The Chinese Rescue Home was a site where white women exerted their moral authority in ways that enhance our understanding of how racial projects functioned in early BC history. The centrality of whiteness and its performative significance is exemplified within the Home, and it is this foregrounding and privileging of whiteness, its assertion and maintenance amidst challenges made by many, both inside and outside the Home, that is of primary concern. Although this was, in part, an assimilatory project, it was not *only* about inclusion; rather, its goals included sending converted women back to Japan or China as missionaries – an indication that racism was more than a way of delineating between self and Other. Racism worked through a contradictory process of inclusion, exclusion, and regulation. Race was used to identify inferiority, as the Other was defined in opposition to the white self. Here, whiteness was deployed as both authority (superiority) and as a model to emulate. Yet, as Constance Backhouse argues, race was impermanent and transmutable. It was also malleable and subject to transformation through domesticity.[66]

The Home illustrates how whiteness was also central to both the state and the domestic realm. *From Slave Girls to Salvation* explores how whiteness was deployed through national and global imaginings, and how these relationships intersected with religious discourses. Thus, my discussion focuses on the Chinese Rescue Home as a religious (Methodist) institution. However, it is important to note at the outset that Methodism, including its roots, factions, and relations to other Christian denominations, is not central to my discussion. Although the records of the Methodist Missionary Society have much to say with regard to how evangelical missions were conceived, internally as well as in relation to other denominations, I take into account only a very few of these concerns as they comprise a huge field in and of themselves. For those who are interested, others, such as Rhonda Ann Semple, provide comprehensive overviews of the history of Canadian Methodism.[67]

The links between race and religion are central to my concerns. Both race and religion had an uneasy relation with questions of Chinese and Japanese immigration as constructions of the former were formed through national and religious discourses. For religious leaders, discussions around race were complex as they revolved around both global and local concerns. Race was concretized as a target of religious interventions, yet it was also malleable enough to be transformed. Shifting away from a singular focus on exclusion allows for the exploration of the complex relationships between race, religion, and citizenship and how these came together and combined to form discourses of inclusion. Early "contact narratives" have overwhelmingly characterized white/Asian encounters through the lens of racism and anti-Asian sentiment. By focusing on race as an exclusionary project, such work uncovers important functions and consequences of discourses of race. Recently, other scholars have taken a more nuanced and critical approach to cross-racial contact in British Columbia. Renisa Mawani, in *Colonial Proximities,* deals with encounters between whites, Aboriginal peoples, and Chinese migrants and explores how these contacts were informed by and through spatial practices and legal strategies.[68] Like other postcolonial scholars, Mawani critiques and disrupts the binaries of colonizer/colonized, self/other, and metropole/colony. By moving away from a unitary focus on contact to a discussion of *how* contact(s) informed racial knowledges and spatial and legal practices, Mawani is able to uncover the ambivalent effects resulting from cross-racial contacts.

Timothy Stanley's *Contesting White Supremacy: School Segregation, Anti-Racism, and the Making of Chinese Canadians* and Alison Marshall's *The Way of the Bachelor: Early Chinese Settlement in Manitoba* both offer complex and compelling narratives of racial exclusion and resistance in a Canadian context. Turning to the United States, Nayan Shah draws attention to the links between state bureaucracies and racial formations/constructions as they were applied to the Chinese and how these were informed by discourses of public health.[69] His attention to the role of the state in producing racial discourses is a useful model for understanding the complex relationships between national institutions, the discourses they produced, and the actions and reactions of Chinese Americans and other public citizens. Here, Shah also points to the complex ways in which the state intervened in matters of intimacy (the family and the body), which have often been thought of as confined to the private realm.

The state was not the only force governing intimate realms: churches also intervened. How religious institutions approached race differed significantly from how public institutions did so. My focus on religious missions is not meant to imply that white/Asian contact was free from exclusionary discourses and practices; what I show is that contact between white women, Japanese women, and Chinese women was more complex than many have suggested as white women attempted to bring Japanese and Chinese women into a nation that was at once hostile and ambivalent to their presence. In particular, I explore the roles and importance of white women because they provide insight not only into the discourses that informed these relationships but also into the complex relationships between state and non-state institutions. In so doing, I examine the ways that both Christianity and citizenship were projected onto the bodies of Asian women by white women who, themselves, were marginal to national projects. While much of my focus is concerned with white women's roles, I also discuss Japanese and Chinese women's responses to religious interventions. Marshall, in her study of Chinese bachelor societies, argues that religious affiliations between Chinese and whites were about much more than spiritual enlightenment. She explains that many Chinese men converted to Christianity because of the opportunities that this afforded them.[70] As I discuss in Chapter 3, Chinese and Japanese women were also cognizant of the benefits that conversion might offer.

Building on Mawani's approach, I address the legal and spatial manoeuvrings that informed and shaped relationships between whites, Chinese, and Japanese in British Columbia.[71] By focusing on a single case study, I am able to provide a detailed and systematic study of the ways in which gender and religion coalesced with and undercut state-sanctioned boundaries of both race and domesticity. Like Shah, I emphasize how various levels of government intervened in the domestic realm and how this intervention intersected and collided with/against religious narratives and discourses.[72]

The Chinese Rescue Home was not only a regional project but also a national one as it sought to include and exclude Asian women not only in and from British Columbia but also in and from the nation. It was a site shot through with discourses of race and gender, which borrowed from global missionary tropes as well as from imperial and national discourses. Numerous scholars, who have studied the work of women missionaries and other moral reformers both in their home countries and abroad, look at how gender intersects with religion and citizenship.[73] In *Relations*

of Rescue: The Search for Female Moral Authority in the American West,
1874–1939, Peggy Pascoe explores the role of women missionaries in the
development of women's moral influence on what she calls "female moral
authority."[74] I offer a narrower but more in-depth approach, which allows
me to consider how women gained moral authority through their work
in the Home and how they used discourses and spaces of domesticity
to achieve their goals. If women's status as second-class citizens meant
that they reaffirmed their worth through claims to white superiority, it
also meant that these claims, and the practices that accompanied them,
were curtailed by the dominion of white men. The nation, largely the
domain of men, thus significantly curtailed women's public engagements
and opinions. The domestic realm, as a site of state intervention, also
fell under the nation's dominion as the courts and other state authorities
weighed in on who might be allowed within the walls of this domicile.
White women created spaces of autonomy that were also shaped by the
white- and male-dominated Methodist Missionary Society. By focusing on a "foreign" mission located on Western soil, I examine how the
domestic realm was produced on three scales: the local, the national, and
the global. Examining these scales together allows me to simultaneously
examine local practices, national imaginings, and global discourses as well
as the practices that threatened and sustained them.

Evangelical nationalism relied on discourses of race, which were predicated on cultural differences.[75] Whiteness was contrasted not only to
those who were non-white but also to *foreignness* itself. Thus, the Chinese
Rescue Home not only marked off the public and private as gendered
realms but also marked off the domestic and the foreign, which made it
crucial to defining the nation and citizenship. It was precisely the mission's form as a domestic space that allowed for the transmission of Christian morality and its attendant transformative practices. These practices
and discourses of morality must also be understood in the context of
raced and gendered moral regulation.

MORAL REGULATION AND DOMESTICITY

Domesticity was central to the regulation of Japanese and Chinese women
within the spaces of the Chinese Rescue Home. The relationship between
race, gender, and domesticity was not only spatial: domesticity also functioned as psychic and corporeal practice of regulation. Understanding
domestic spaces as constitutive of discourse *and* of practice, especially as

these discourses and practices relate to moral regulation, is a central goal of my research. According to Alan Hunt, moral regulation projects are a "form of politics in which some people act to problematize the conduct, values or culture of others and seek to impose regulation upon them."[76] This regulation operates on local, national, and global scales. While taken up by ordinary citizens, these projects are deeply enmeshed in state practices that are informed by colonial discourses, especially around race.

Due to the complexity of regulating the racial Other, it was important that I adopt an approach that views the nation as contested and contradictory. The discourses that fed this particular strand of moral regulation must be understood as located within larger discourses of gender, race, and religion, which, in turn, drew from knowledges existing outside the nation. The Royal Commission on Chinese Immigration (1885), for example, drew on global knowledges about race from San Francisco and Melbourne. Religious discourses, while largely Western in origin, also built on missionary narratives from Japan and China in ways that informed not only their understandings of Asian populations but also how and where they would evangelize them. In its yearly reports, the WMS, for instance, often discussed strategies for evangelizing Chinese women in China, seeing them as useful models for evangelizing Chinese women in Canada. In addition, religious discourses were also modelled upon British traditions and borrowed from (and sometimes rejected) approaches that had been adopted in the United States.

Within these discourses, the racialized Other is, in many ways, viewed as ungovernable. This meant that, in order for moral regulation to take place, transformative work needed to be done. Thus, transformative work must be seen not as a precursor to moral regulation but as part of the practice of moral regulation itself. Like Nayan Shah, I am concerned with how missionary women worked to transform Asian populations from being inassimilable into being cultural citizens. Shah, for instance, shows how racial boundaries of exclusion were transgressed when missionary women trained Chinese women "in middle-class domesticity." This "simultaneously made 'fallen' women 'respectable' and served to transform Chinese society in the United States."[77] In the Canadian context, religious missions such as the Chinese Rescue Home were less about bestowing cultural citizenship on their charges than about global citizenship. Proper transformations were as much about the entrenchment of Christian values globally as they were about the transformation of the individual and the nation. The regulation of Chinese and Japanese women was primarily concerned with producing "Bible Women" to spread the gospel in China and Japan and only secondarily with integrating Japanese and Chinese women into the Canadian cultural community.

Moral regulation was, thus, a complex, spatial project. According to Hunt, moral regulation requires the following elements: a moralized subject, a moralized object or target, knowledge, a discourse within which knowledge is given a normative content, a set of practices, and a "harm" to be avoided or overcome.[78] While it was clear that the state, the media, and the WMS women all acted as moralizing agents in the Home, and residents were moralized objects, other considerations were also at play. It was not just the "immoral" *practices* – namely, the sexual behaviours of Chinese and Japanese women – that were being targeted. Despite the fact that the institution was meant to be a rescue mission for prostitutes and slave girls, sexuality, while certainly a concern, was not the primary target of regulation. Because white women viewed Japanese and Chinese women as having been largely coerced into prostitution, once freed from their lives of sin, the regulation of their sexuality was seen as largely unnecessary (except in cases in which women were resistant to their interventions). Instead, white women focused their attention on providing Japanese and Chinese women with skills that were in line with (white) classed and gendered expectations. Teaching women to dress, sew, cook, or build a fire the "English way" was intended to teach them to cultivate and to take on their new roles as transformed and whitened subjects. These behaviours were a form of discipline that took place within a domestic sphere. The Home produced Chinese and Japanese women as "docile bodies" who could be "transformed and improved."[79] These practices were also lessons in social hygiene.[80]

Although the teaching or controlling of certain practices was linked to a harm that was to be avoided or overcome, in the case of Japanese and Chinese women, this harm was quite diffuse. If it were only prostitution and sexual "licentiousness" that had to be curtailed, placement of the women in the Home would certainly have meant an end to, or overcoming of, potential harm. But the practices and behaviours that were regulated within the residence were about more than simply ending prostitution. Assimilation through moral regulation was seen as inherently unachievable except through transformation: changes in behaviour (regulation) would never be enough. Thus, the WMS approached the problem more broadly as the "Chinese problem."[81] In other words, moral regulation needed to be not only about the regulation of practices (and the avoidance of harm associated with those practices) but also about transformation. The Home's mission was not only to transform practices and behaviours but also to domesticate the objects of regulation. In addition to cultivating new behaviours, mission work was also designed to produce and to cultivate domestic *subjects*.

To be clear, the transformation of racialized bodies into models of whiteness was not a transformation of the Other into the self but, rather, of the Other into another Other. Japanese and Chinese women might be encouraged to aspire to *models* of whiteness, but they would, at best, only inhabit a space between the white self and the Other. If Japanese and Chinese women were able to transgress race and *become* white, this would jeopardize the missionary project itself as it would call into question the superiority of the white self. The *emulation* of whiteness reaffirmed its value. Transformation first meant the removal of the women from their places of domicile and their admission into the Home. Once in residence, the women were then able to become part of the "family of God." This was a practice in domesticity as evidence of this transformation was to be seen in the women's ability to learn and to embody not only Victorian moral values but also Christian ones. Thus, the Home was concerned not only with providing training to Chinese and Japanese women so that they would not have to return to lives of immorality but also with (1) transforming them from racial outsiders into "family members" and (2) socializing them into their rightful positions within their new "family" – the family of God. However, this transformation, once complete, did not guarantee their acceptance into Canadian society. Although some were allowed to return to their own communities and others even entered white homes as servants, successful transformations did not always translate into a presumed fitness for assimilatory projects. For some, in fact, successful transformations were not seen as evidence of their fitness to stay within the nation at all but, rather, as evidence that they should be expelled from the nation to be missionaries in China or Japan.

Canadian histories, to the extent that they have included Japanese and Chinese populations, have often framed them as inassimilable or as subjects of white discriminatory practices and policies. In what follows, I use a plethora of sources not to deny such exclusions but to explore how racial power worked through exclusions *and* inclusions and how these processes took place simultaneously, often operating in tandem. By constructing the Chinese Rescue Home as an active space and site of production, I utilize a series of housing metaphors to theorize the domestic and domesticity as practices and processes of power. Chapter 1 begins by building the "foundation" of the Home by providing some historical and geographical context.

In Chapter 2, I identify and explore the four "pillars" of the regulative power of the domestic and domesticity by examining the discourses of nation, whiteness, Christianity, and gender as they operated in the Home. These pillars not only provided the support for the Home but also created it as a necessary intervention, a solution that existed as a space both outside and inside the nation. It was precisely the intersections of the religiosity of the mission and the imaginary of the home that allowed for the transformation of (female) racial bodies into *domestic* bodies (both in a national and in a gendered sense). In Chapter 3, I cross the "threshold" into the Home to examine how domesticity was tightly bound up with motherhood and maternalism. The "threshold" metaphor highlights how domesticity blurred the public/private binary as, in the Home, moral regulation was always acted out on or at the threshold between the private and the public, thus facilitating the constant crossing over between these two domains. The domestic was both materially and ideologically framed through gendered discourses of "home" and "family." Yet, as an institution, these domestic spaces were used by white women, and to a lesser degree by Japanese and Chinese women, to cross the threshold from the private to the public realm.

In Chapter 4 and Chapter 5, I shift the lens, pointing it outside the Home. In Chapter 4, by focusing on "walls," I consider how the parameters of the Home were (re)defined not only from within the institution but also from beyond it. I examine newspaper accounts in order to discuss high-profile civil and legal cases that involved key players in the Home. These cases show the importance of domesticity in the moral regulation of Chinese and Japanese women, and they also highlight the importance of state and citizens as moral regulators of those who dared to remove domesticity from the transformation process. In Chapter 5, I use "roofs" and "rafters" as metaphors to complete my "reconstruction" of the Chinese Rescue Home. Here, I explore the state's role as protector and arbiter in habeas corpus cases. In these instances, the state provides the Home and its charges with a protective covering (roof) that enables it to function as *parens patriae* while also providing the framework (rafters) that enables the institution to take on this surrogate parenting role. The state thus reframes the Home as a site of refuge rather than of "rescue." The habeas corpus cases enable a deep analysis of the state's role in delineating the boundaries of cross-racial contact and in defining (national) familial relations. I conclude by returning to the themes of nation, race, and domesticity, linking them to contemporary racial projects.

I

Foundations of Stone

Victoria and the Chinese Rescue Home

The Chinese Rescue Home might be understood as originating in the desires of two men, Reverend John Edward Starr and John Vrooman Gardiner (henceforth referred to as Gardiner), to rescue Chinese women from prostitution and slavery. Yet, even though these men were the founders of the Home, their roles were quite peripheral to its long history. In fact, the institution would, from its earliest days, be the domain of women: it would be run by women and its mission would be directed at women. It would be a mistake, however, to assume that its foundation was confined to the private realm; rather, the Home must be understood as part of a larger national project of "settlement." Understanding the foundation upon which the Home was constructed requires placing it within a larger context of settlement, both geographically and historically.

Histories of British Columbia in general and of Victoria in particular document the successes and the challenges faced by white settlers. Yet their focus is primarily on the lives and roles of white men. Over the past two decades, many scholars have added to these colonial histories, providing alternative histories of the Pacific Northwest and including the challenges and contributions of Japanese and Chinese men to projects of settlement.[1] However, women were also crucial to the settlement project, both through their reproductive capacity and their moralizing capacity. In fact, it was the underrepresentation of white women in the colonies of Vancouver Island and British Columbia that was blamed for the lack of civilization in these places. According to Adele Perry, Samuel Wilberforce,

Bishop of Oxford, was quite concerned with the lack of women in the area: "Without woman's restraining influence, Wilberforce warned, the young colony risked becoming a disgrace to the English race itself."[2] If British Columbia was to have a future, white women were needed, both to be the mothers of future generations and to be the moral conscience of a wild and untamed frontier. Thus, both missionary groups and feminist groups sponsored so-called "Bride Ships," each being eager to bring white women to British Columbia in order to aid in settling and civilizing the west. Settlement, thus, was not simply a project directed at the land: it was also something that required both traditional family forms and proper domesticity. Shipping white women to Victoria was meant to address the lack of each, with these women being expected to fulfill both the need for wives and the need for domestic servants (to serve white women already in the colony).

White women's reproductive and moralizing roles were certainly seen as necessary to the settlement project. Settlement was not, however, simply about the *practice* of laying claim to land: it was also about creating and maintaining a hierarchy of race that solidified white settlers' rights to the land. Discourses of white settlement arose, at least partially, to address the challenges to this hierarchy. Thus, understanding settlement requires understanding the power relations and powerful relationships that it fostered. If Aboriginal populations and non-white immigrants were seen as racial impediments to proper settlement, then white settlement depended on the taming of so-called "savage" Aboriginal populations as well as the control, expulsion, and sometimes transformation of Chinese and Japanese "sojourner" populations. Thus, the significance of white-dominant settler relations in Victoria is found not only in the relationships between white men and the land but also in the complex connections between "settlement" narratives and the relationships they produced. These relationships included those that took place within and around the domestic realm. Yet, the importance of the relationships between these white women and other women in the area – namely, Aboriginal, Japanese, and Chinese women – has largely been overlooked. Understanding white women's relationships, especially to Chinese and Japanese women, requires the application of three important lenses: (1) a settlement lens provides some national context; (2) a spatial lens provides an understanding of local realities, especially with regard to racial hierarchies; and (3) an institutional lens provides insights into the motives and aspirations of the women who ran the mission as well as of those who resided within it.

Settling Down, Settling in: Settlers, Savages, and Sojourners

Although women's moral and domestic influence on white men was seen as crucial to the project of settlement, their influence did not end there. If white women were to be the moral conscience of white men, the same was also true regarding their relationships with other populations in what would later become the province of British Columbia. Settlement relied on relationships between white women, Indigenous women, and women of colour in order to fulfill the twin goals of bolstering the importance of white women (in particular) and white settlement (in general). Although in this chapter I focus on the relationships between white women, Chinese women, and Japanese women, it is important to understand that these relationships are part of a larger project of civilization.

Given that Victoria was built on land that had long been inhabited by Aboriginal populations, the twin projects of civilization and settlement were necessary to legitimize white settlement and to control those who opposed it. Women's roles in these processes were critical for if whites were to co-exist peacefully with the so-called "savage" Aboriginal populations, then the latter would need to be literally domesticated. Religion was one avenue for regulating Aboriginal populations. As Adele Perry tells us, missionaries "were an integral if always ambivalent component of the colonial project in British Columbia during the last half of the nineteenth century."[3] So, too, was domesticity. The Crosby Home for Aboriginal girls in Port Simpson, for instance, was run by the Woman's Missionary Society and provided both a religious education and a domestic one. That many of the first residential schools were aimed at providing an education for Aboriginal girls is indicative of the importance of domesticity to projects of civilization. One of the central problems of colonialism, according to Perry, was "the creation of permanence where there had only been mobility, whether by importing sedentary peoples or by literally fixing migratory ones." One Anglican is cited as stating that it was difficult to "exercise an efficient oversight over a body of Indians so independent and nomadic as ours, divided up into so many small families or settlements, and so widely scattered throughout so extensive a range of country."[4] Permanent homes became crucial to addressing this problem. While there are a number of similarities between the Chinese Rescue Home and early residential schools, there are also important distinctions. Unlike the Home, residential schools were state mandated and were directed only at children. The Home began as a project directed only at girls and women.

Although boys would eventually be allowed to enter the Home as students, during the period of study, its focus remained primarily on women and girls. While the treatment of First Nations girls in "girls' homes" was in some ways similar to that of the women in the Home, the fact that the latter was run by religious institutions and not officially sanctioned by the state makes a comparative study difficult to sustain.

The absence of a fixed and gendered domestic realm in Japanese and Chinese communities also unsettled the dominant understandings of settlement. Because of the predominance of "bachelor societies" among the early Chinese and Japanese settlers, initially, many saw them as sojourners who were incompatible with the very notion of settlement. Victoria was the main port of entry for Chinese immigrants coming to Canada. According to Roy, the Chinese, who were the first Asians to arrive in Canada, came, initially, "from the declining California gold fields" and, after 1860, directly from China.[5] In the mid-1860s, Chinese in the colony numbered approximately four thousand, although this number declined to about fifteen hundred by 1870. In the early 1880s, the second wave of Chinese immigrants came to British Columbia to work on the Canadian Pacific Railway: an estimated sixteen or seventeen thousand came at this time. The first arrivals from Japan came later, beginning with nineteen-year-old Manzo Nagano in 1871. By 1891, there were approximately two hundred Japanese in Canada, and this number steadily increased. The 1901 census recorded 4,738 Japanese living in Canada, 97 percent of whom resided in British Columbia. In the early stages of Japanese immigration, the majority of immigrants were from the lower classes. Like the Chinese, most of the early Japanese immigrants were men who came to make their fortunes in British Columbia. Most of these men took up work in fisheries, coal mines, or the lumber industry, sometimes alternating between them.[6]

There was much ambivalence among whites with regard to the arrival of Japanese and Chinese labourers. Some in British Columbia welcomed their labour, while others engaged in formal protests, including the violent and destructive Vancouver riot in 1907. Formally, as Lai recalls, as early as "1872, the BC legislative assembly passed an act to disenfranchise both Chinese and native Indians."[7] Yet, despite the fact that exclusionary practices were in play, economic necessity dictated that Chinese and Japanese people would continue to have a place in British Columbia. It was this dependence on Japanese and Chinese labour that led many to argue that the riots and hostility were a result of increased concern over the economic threat that Asian labourers were thought to pose to white populations.[8]

Regardless of the reasons, anti-Asian sentiment resulted in legislation that greatly reduced immigration from China and Japan when the federal government imposed head taxes on the Chinese and entered into the Hayashi-Lemieux "Gentlemen's Agreement" of 1908, which greatly limited the number of Japanese labourers who could enter Canada. The enactment of such limits and exclusions significantly affected immigration, especially with regard to gender. In addition, although the reason that so few Chinese women entered the province was, in part, due to exclusionary immigration policies such as the head tax, the authors of *Jin Guo: Voices of Chinese Canadian Women* argue that it was also rooted in the familial pressures exerted on women residing in China: "Some villages were supported entirely by the remittances sent by the family wage earners in North America. Thus, most of the women and children stayed behind to make sure that the men would continue to send money home."[9]

Although very few Chinese women came to Canada in these early years, it was assumed by many in the province that those who did come were either slaves or prostitutes who needed to be "rescued." And so they would end up in the Chinese Rescue Home in Victoria. With regard to Japanese women, the Hayashi-Lemieux Agreement of 1908 had the opposite effect. Because of its focus on reducing threats to labour, the "Gentlemen's Agreement decreased the number of male immigrants, but accelerated the immigration of women."[10] Many of these women came over as "picture brides," a long-distance adaptation of the traditional practice of arranged marriages. Although parallels might be drawn between these brides and white women who came over on bride ships, because of their non-Western marriage practices, Japanese picture brides were initially seen as morally suspicious and thus, along with Chinese women, were targeted by the Home.

Although the 1871 Victoria municipal census indicates that there were very few Chinese women in the city during this period,[11] Adilman explains that accurate estimates are difficult to discern as the numbers provided by Department of Immigration records and the Canadian Census do not correspond. She also tells us that at least "100 to 200 Chinese women were imported annually from 1887 until the beginning of the twentieth century."[12] For women who did come to Canada,

the majority ... came from the Pearl River Delta region of Guangdong province in Southern China. Women from this area have traditionally demonstrated an exceptional independence. The people of this region had been emigrating for centuries, mostly to Southeast Asia. So going overseas was an accepted practise and the strength of the family allowed villages to function in the absence of men. Women in Southern China have traditionally worked outside of the home, demonstrating self-reliance by sowing and harvesting crops while the men were away.[13]

Given the long-standing beliefs about the sexual depravity of Chinese women in particular, these women became the concern of the matron and missionaries who ran the Home during its early years. During British Columbia's transitional periods, however, Japanese picture brides also became the subject of concern.

Japanese picture brides entered the province for many reasons. During the sojourner stage, which lasted until 1908, Ayukawa points out that the Japanese population residing in Canada was largely male.[14] Those few Japanese women who also migrated had been brought to assist their husbands. In the second stage (1908–24) "women began arriving and in doing so launched the settlement stage in the history of Japanese in Canada." Some of the women who arrived were educated and came from wealthy families, while others were uneducated and came from poorer areas. While the motivations for coming to Canada were as diverse as were the women themselves, most were startled by the conditions that confronted them. "Many were taken directly to remote lumber camps, sawmill towns, fishing villages, and untamed farms in the Fraser Valley, the Okanagan and southern Alberta."[15] For those who entered through Victoria, many were first shepherded by immigration officials to the Chinese Rescue Home, where they awaited their grooms. Although legally married, neither the province nor those who ran the mission recognized these marriages, at least initially. Thus, many women had to participate in marriage ceremonies at the residence before they were allowed to leave. In these early decades, the province was already deeply invested in Japanese and Chinese women's lives as it attempted to (re)enforce appropriate (white) forms of domesticity. This was part of a larger project of empire.

In 1871, British Columbia joined Canada in Confederation. While Adele Perry aptly describes life in early British Columbia as being "on the edge of empire," Victoria was located on the very outer edge, perhaps even the precipice, of empire.[16] During this period, building a white British Columbia was of primary concern in a province that was racially diverse and dominated by a resource-based economy.[17] Physical, economic, and moral development were imperatives during this period. Pethick refers to 1886 to 1901 as the "Jubilee Years."[18] In 1886, the Canadian Pacific Railway finally made its way to Victoria, bringing with it the promise of expansion and prosperity. During this period, a "small manufacturing base was established in and around Victoria, including tanneries, sash mills, a foundry, a soap factory, a shipyard, and a gas works."[19] This meant that, in addition to a large underclass consisting of manual labourers (especially miners and fur traders), many of British Columbia's wealthy elite also settled in Victoria. The result was a hierarchized and highly classed society. An "incredible amount of snobbery existed in early Victoria, and invariably it was directed toward ... those who worked 'in service'; those who were of Chinese origin; those who came to Victoria to earn a living in the theatre, in dance halls, or in prostitution; and those who worked 'in trade.'"[20] Given the city's racial diversity, it is not surprising that race (in general) and racial mixing (in particular) were of concern to Victoria's white citizens, especially to its elite.

In 1878, for instance, Victoria's representatives in the House of Commons "placed a motion on the order paper at Ottawa urging that 'no person be employed on the Pacific railway in any capacity whose hair is more than five inches long.'"[21] Although these provisions were meant to exclude the Chinese, preventing them from taking white jobs, this motion was framed without explicit reference to race. At other times, this was not the case. In 1878, for example, the provincial legislature proposed that an annual tax of sixty dollars be imposed on "all Chinese in the province." In Victoria, "the entire Chinese population ... including house servants, went on strike simultaneously, and soon afterwards Judge Gray of the BC Supreme Court pronounced the law unconstitutional."[22] The "striking" of Chinese house servants would likely have had the most significant impact on the domestic lives of white women in the province, given that many relied on Chinese labour in the home.

Living in Victoria during these early years was especially challenging for women, regardless of race and class. For those who were wealthy, challenges included finding suitable help in the home, and the lack of help due to immigration and employment restrictions meant that many upper-class women were forced to take on domestic work that they would not otherwise have performed. The lack of and need for white women during this period has been well documented by Green and Perry.[23] Both show how poor white women from England were recruited in order to change the racial configuration of settler society by bringing in a population that could serve wealthier families who would otherwise be dependent on Aboriginal women or Chinese men for domestic help.

Despite the importation of white women as domestic help, and notwithstanding the training of young Chinese women to do the same, even wealthy and middle-class women lived very demanding lives. Many, in the absence of a full staff, had to oversee the running of large homes in a city where wealth and prestige continued to matter. Some of these women were also involved extensively in charity work and in the suffrage movement. During the early 1900s, women's organizations in Vancouver and Victoria had far-reaching objectives in the area of social reform. These included hospital auxiliaries, nursing, charitable societies, and other "good causes."[24] One such charitable society was Victoria's Chinese Rescue Home.

Geographies of the Home

Evidence shows that early missions to Chinese populations began in 1861. North American churches had a long history of missionary work in Japan and China.[25] Thus, for many missionaries, Japanese and Chinese immigration to Canada did not mark their first contact with these populations. In British Columbia, the extension of this missionary work to immigrants from Japan and China was a natural progression. In the US context, Peggy Pascoe argues that Chinese rescue missions in San Francisco developed because women who were supporting projects in Shanghai wanted to develop a project closer to home.[26] In British Columbia, the same was likely true as "home mission work," which was once directed only at Aboriginal populations, was soon broadened to include first Chinese and then Japanese populations. While not all churches (or church members) welcomed these "foreigners" into their midst, some opened their doors to Japanese and Chinese parishioners, while others helped to build them their own churches and "ministered" to them through missions, rescue homes, home Bible study, or English-language classes.[27]

Located in the heart of Victoria, the Chinese Rescue Home was meant to offer a space where Chinese and Japanese women could be accepted and transformed through the intervention of white missionaries. Originally, rescued women were temporarily housed in the homes of their two "rescuers," Reverend Starr and John Gardiner; however, given that the Home's two founders were men, this could only be a temporary measure. Soon, a matron was hired and a house was rented within which to keep the women. The Home was later relocated, and eventually a new building was built to house them. All of the structures that were to house these women were located outside Chinatown but in close proximity to it, on the border between Chinatown and the white business and residential communities. These locations were likely chosen because they offered ease of access to Chinese women as well as the respectability and security of being close to the white community. By the time the work of the rescue mission began, in 1886, Chinatown comprised two full city blocks, between Store Street and Government Street and between Herald Street and Cormorant Street (see Figure 2 below). The Home's original location is just outside this map area and is marked on Figure 2. The ambivalent location of the institution is noteworthy as it was always situated in between white and Chinese settlements, this geographical reality greatly affecting both its mission and its role in Victoria.

In 1909, when the Woman's Missionary Society was building the new Home (the Oriental Home and School), Chinatown had almost doubled its size since 1891 and now included the adjacent blocks between Government Street and Douglas Street. As fire insurance plans from 1885 and 1891 show, although much of Chinatown was confined to these two (and later four) blocks, racial boundaries were not distinct.[28] In 1891, for instance, Chinese businesses and houses spilled onto the block east of Government Street, separated from white institutions such as the Masonic Hall only by a thin strip of grazing land. North of Herald Street was a mixture of business and residential areas, housing a wagon shop, an iron works, the Indian Methodist Church, as well as cabins marked off as either "Chinese" or "Chinese and Indian Cabins."[29] While the 1901 census shows the Chinese and Japanese population to be 2,978, Japanese made up only 287 of this total.[30] Thus, it is not surprising that Japanese and Chinese people lived in close proximity. Although widely referenced as "Chinatown," this area included buildings that were marked off as Chinese laundries, and, in between, there was a large building marked "Japanese." On the map, a thin dotted line separates these buildings from a community called Chatham Terrace, which was most likely composed of Victoria's white citizens (See Figure 2, especially the area north of Herald Street, on the east side of Government Street).

Located in the heart of downtown Victoria, Chinatown was almost unavoidable, and, in many ways, it became a crucial part of the city. Chinese businesses included laundry services, cigar making, groceries, and restaurants. Maps, such as the one below, show that land use was determined in racialized ways. The Home, for example, was strategically placed. Its first site was on the north side of Herald Street between Douglas Street and Government Street (see Figure 2), an area outside the boundaries of Chinatown but in close proximity to it. However, from the late 1890s until it closed in 1942, the Home was located east of Douglas

FIGURE 2 Victoria Fire Insurance Map, 1891 and Victoria's Chinatown: Land Utilization, 1909.

Source: Image VFP 1891, p. 10. Courtesy of Royal BC Museum, BC Archives; David Chuen-yan Lai, Chinatowns: Towns within Cities in Canada (Vancouver: UBC Press, 1988). Used with permission. Cartography by Eric Leinberger

Street on Cormorant Street. This area was located near Chinatown but outside it. In fact, less than a block from the residence, on the corner of Cormorant Street and Douglas Street was the Commercial Hotel and one block south on Douglas Street was City Hall. Although the Methodist Mission Church was positioned in the heart of Chinatown on Fisgard Street, the Home was not – an indication that the male-dominated Chinatown was considered dangerous for white women. Further, given that the institution was modelled upon Victorian domestic spaces, these had to be located outside the male-dominated environs that made up Victoria's Chinatown.

White Women and the Home

After the Woman's Missionary Society took it on as a project, the Chinese Rescue Home's day to day running was conducted by a matron, who was eventually assisted by teachers and other helpers as the institution grew and its population expanded. Other women were involved in an advisory capacity, chairing and sitting in on monthly meetings, making decisions on finances, seeking legal advice, testifying in court cases, assessing applications for new residents, seeing to the institution's maintenance, and later constructing a new building for the Home.

Advisory committee members were generally women from well-known, often wealthy families. For instance, for many years W.J. Pendray held the position of president of the advisory committee. Her husband founded and built an empire in Victoria by producing soap.[31] According to the *British Colonist*, Mr. and Mrs. Pendray, both originally from Cornwall, England, moved into their "palatial" home, complete with electric fountain and elaborate ceiling scrollwork, in March 1897.[32] Likewise, Emma Spencer, who sat on the advisory committee for many years and served as its president in 1905, was well connected in Victoria's high society circles, with her husband, David Spencer, having "extensive retailing interests" in the city.[33] While most of the women on the advisory committee were listed only by their surnames (e.g., Shakespeare, Grant, Adams, Burkholder, and Smith), many of these names were associated with prominent Victorian families. For instance, Noah Shakespeare and John Grant were both mayors of Victoria in the 1880s; A.J. Smith held the position of Victoria councillor; and W.H. Burkholder was a candidate for school board trustee.[34] Likely, few of these women would have taken on paid employment. Instead, they took on responsibilities pertaining to the domestic realm, in their own homes and through their participation in the affairs of the Chinese Rescue Home.

Unlike the women of the advisory committee, most of the matrons of the Home were supplied by the General Board of the WMS. This meant that most arrived in Victoria from eastern Canada or, in a few cases, if women missionaries had been on furlough, from Japan and China.[35] Thus, while some had experience working with Asian populations, most did not. During the period for 1886 to 1925, the WMS supplied eighteen missionaries to the institution. While none had university training, "five women had considerable teaching experience and others had engaged in social or philanthropic activities." Most were middle aged, the average age of the matrons being thirty-seven, "possibly because the board preferred mature women for this particular type of work, which involved contact with the more sordid side of life."[36] Finding younger women to accept the position may also have been more challenging than finding older women, given that the work in the Home was difficult and, in the early years, solitary. During the first four years, the WMS supplied only one woman, Annie Leake, to the Home. While Leake was creative in drawing on friends for help, much of the time she was left to her own devices, unable to leave the residence unless she could find someone to stay with the girls or women in her care.[37] After Leake's tenure, it was more common for the institution to employ two women, a matron and an evangelist (the evangelist was later replaced by a teacher or teachers).

That the work was difficult is evinced by the fact that only one matron, Ida Snyder, agreed to a second term overseeing the mission. Although they were trained and supplied by the same organization, each matron brought her own approach and personality to the position. Annie Leake was described by many as militant and independent.[38] Her five years at the Home were anything but smooth. On one occasion, she was publicly accused of abuse,[39] and on two occasions she was criticized by the board for her conflicts with John Gardiner. She was asked to take her furlough at the end of her five-year term and subsequently resigned.[40] Although there is very little information in the organization's files about these women, the reports they filed enable us to gain insights into them.

For instance, Sarah Bowes, who served as matron from 2 September 1895 to December 1898, signed her reports as "Home Mother" rather than "Matron," as the women who previously filled this post had done. Clearly, she was embracing metaphors of home and family. Prior to her tenure at the Home, she was an avid organizer for the Woman's Christian Temperance Union, travelling around British Columbia setting up branches in various towns and cities.[41] F. Kate Morgan, on the other hand, who started as a teacher in the school and was appointed as matron in 1899, signed her reports more formally as "Superintendent of Work."[42] Morgan's less amiable salutation might be seen as reflective of her greater suspicion of Chinese populations, for which there is clear documentation. She strongly opposed unrestricted immigration, testifying at the Royal Commission on Chinese and Japanese Immigration in 1902 that she believed they were "all a menace to the public from their ways of living, [and] the way they herd together."[43] She was slightly more generous towards Japanese women, stating: "I think the women of Japan are superior. There is no slavery in Japan."[44] She quickly followed this, however, with a condemnation of Japanese polygamy, then proclaiming that she "would not trust a young brother or sister in the custody of a Chinese or Japanese."[45] Of the eighteen women who served as matron between 1886 and 1923,[46] some left missionary work after their tenure at the Home, some due to illness and others to marry. Others continued on with their missionary work in other locations until they retired from the field.[47]

Despite its geographical location in Victoria, the Home's work extended beyond the capital city. In fact, much of the WMS's work in Vancouver began as rescue missions aimed at Chinese and Japanese women who were subsequently brought to the Home in Victoria. In addition, letters and reports of the rescue mission were frequently sent to WMS groups in eastern Canada and to the WMS's general board in Ottawa (which oversaw and funded much of this work). Although the Home was a localized and domestic project, the work that it conducted in Victoria contributed significantly to how race and gender were constructed both provincially and nationally, especially in relation to missionary work. For instance, even the commissioners overseeing the Royal Commission on Chinese and Japanese Immigration in 1901–2 turned to the matron of the Home for her expert opinion on Chinese and Japanese populations (see Chapter 3).[48]

The relationships that were forged within the Home must be understood within the broader relations of racialized and gendered power that were operating in, and that underpinned the creation of, Victoria. Power operated in a myriad of ways. First, the Home as a domestic space increased white women's power spatially within white society as it extended it beyond the private realm. Second, power functioned productively to define not only the Other but also whiteness itself.[49] The self-interests of white women as well as their deployment of racial discourse was varied and mired in ambiguity. While white interests in British

Columbia arguably involved excluding certain racialized groups (such as the Chinese and Japanese), the interests of white missionary women at the Home were served through the inclusion, or at least the partial inclusion, of these same groups. Their investment in rescuing Japanese and Chinese women and children accorded them a certain degree of power and prestige as benevolent works were viewed not only as evidence of moral superiority but also as a mark of higher social and economic class.

Within the institution itself, white women used their relatively privileged positions as part of Victoria's elite to "rescue" Japanese and Chinese women and to transform them through Christian conversion and domestic training. White women used their privilege as capital that they "invested" in charity or benevolent work and that offered returns in various forms of prestige and power. This was an investment that took the form of both time and money. The work that they accomplished not only reflected their privilege (they could afford to have others fulfill their own domestic duties) but also reinforced existing hierarchies of power. Not surprisingly, WMS records are filled with discourses of Christian benevolence. And this benevolence often manifests itself in ways that, although motivated by discourses of inclusion (especially inclusion in the "family of God"), reinforce and reify existing hierarchies of race by defining whiteness as superior.

These women used their white privilege to gain entry into the homes of Japanese and Chinese women under the guise of evangelistic missions. Here, the domestic realm was opened to white women not as an intimate familial space but as an evangelical one. Entering homes was useful not only for advancing the evangelistic work that these women were committed to doing but also for "recruiting" new residents for the Home. In reports to the various WMS advisory committees in both Vancouver and Victoria, home visits, whether welcomed or not, were seen as markers of evangelical success. In addition to home visits, workers encouraged women to come into the Home by offering English lessons and by admitting women whose husbands requested that they learn service skills or "English ways."[50] In Vancouver, the WMS sponsored cooking classes for Japanese and Chinese women as a way to ingratiate themselves with the women in these communities.[51] White women assumed that "English ways" of cooking and cleaning (and, indeed, white domesticity in general) were superior to those practised by Japanese and Chinese women. They also believed that the women who took these classes would feel compelled to learn other important lessons, specifically religious ones. For Japanese

and Chinese women, however, taking these classes had less to do with
their belief in the superiority of English cooking and more to do with
opportunities to learn skills that might benefit them materially – opening
up opportunities for other types of work, such as cooking or service work.
These types of recruitment strategies suggest that the WMS also engaged
in benevolent practices that were aimed at encouraging voluntary admittance to the Home. Yet these more "empowering" strategies, it must be
remembered, coincided with maternalistic and repressive tactics directed
at less cooperative "inmates" (it was quite common for reports and records to refer to the residents of the institution as inmates, despite the
emphasis on free will).

"INMATES" OF THE HOME

In many ways, the Chinese Rescue Home functioned as a total institution, concerned, as it was, with isolating, disciplining, and reforming its
inmates.[52] Within the Home, inmates were not afforded the autonomy
that white women claimed for themselves. As in society at large, both
race and gender determined who was deemed fit to make choices and to
what extent their free will was allowed to reign. While documents often
refer to a resident's *choosing* to be in the residence, those who entered
did so under a wide range of conditions. While some were recruited by
the WMS and thus came voluntarily, others were coerced. The power of
Home officials to make choices for, and to deny the choices of, the residents functioned at multiple levels. Power, as Foucault reminds us, is not
only coercive but also productive.[53] Admission and recruitment worked
through both coercion and benevolence, producing the desire for domestic betterment among Chinese and Japanese women. These new desires
were based on Western cultural standards of acceptable femininity and
domesticity.

In the Home, race functioned ambivalently as a discourse and practice
of benevolence. Those who ran the Home relied on common-sense definitions of race when admitting women, although these definitions were
not always straightforward. The WMS women believed that Japanese and
Chinese women could be saved – a sentiment not shared by many whites
in the province – but the fact that they saw these women as in need
of moral and spiritual salvation is evidence of their own belief in white
superiority. Understandings of race contributed to the infantilization of
Japanese and Chinese women and justified coercive and paternalistic

strategies. Although the goal of racial betterment was viewed as benevo-lent, it often came at the price of coercion.

Understanding the types of women that were admitted to the institu-tion, by whom, and under what circumstances, is important for three reasons. First, understanding who was admitted and who was refused entry provides insight into how race operated, both with respect to its limits and with respect to its possibilities. While Japanese and Chinese women as well as mixed-raced children were admitted to the Home, there was some concern about, for example, admitting a "Hindu" (at the time a euphemism for East Indian) woman. Second, knowing who brought the women to the mission provides a context for understanding not only relations of gender but also the relationships between state agencies and the institution. While the Home was run by women, many of the women who were admitted to it were brought there by men: some of these men were family members, some were clergy, and others were state officials. Third, understanding the circumstances under which women entered the Home provides context for understanding the relationship between it, the community, and the state. If some of the women did not enter volun-tarily, the relationships and practices that were forged in the Home must be understood within a broader racialized and gendered context than that of missionary and convert.

While there was a myriad of reasons that women and children were admitted, the one main criterion for admittance was racial difference. The name of the institution itself, first called the Chinese Rescue Home and later the Oriental Home and School, suggests that the race of the resi-dents mattered. Although some white women did stay at the home tem-porarily, this was rare and was usually limited to female missionaries who were in need of a place to stay during their travels or to workers in the Home who required a place of domicile. Race, although significant, did not always function in narrow or biologically prescribed ways. Mixed-race children were also admitted to the residence, suggesting that, while race mattered, racial "purity" did not. Women or children with one par-ent who was Chinese or Japanese were considered "Oriental," or at least "Oriental enough" to enter the Home. While it is impossible to know for sure how many mixed-race children or women gained admittance to the Home, its register makes explicit reference to three children who were of mixed-race parentage. Emily[54] was described as having an "Indian" mother and a Chinese father,[55] while a six-year-old girl was described as half Irish with a Japanese father.[56] The third child was admitted with her mother, Anna Lim,"[57] who was described as being Swiss. What these cases suggest is that, while race was important when it came to admission, in the case of mixed-race children or women it functioned in ambivalent ways. While the presence of these individuals in the Home suggests that they were seen as Oriental enough to gain admittance, the fact that these distinctions were made in the record books at all suggests that racial hybridity mattered. It was not enough to allow them admittance based on their "Orientalness." Their "Indianness" or "Irishness" or "Swissness" needed to be identified in admission documents. References to hybridity were, thus, a critical part of record books and suggested not the superiority of whiteness but, rather, its vulnerabilities to cross-racial intimacy in this racially diverse city.

The admittance of Lim, the Swiss mother mentioned above is, thus, worthy of some discussion. One of the few white women who stayed in the school, Lim was married to a "Chinaman."[58] The WMS report of 1906–07 explains that Lim "was in very poor health, but she finally decided to return to her husband in Vancouver. She is a Swiss woman who married a Chinese man, and the unfortunate circumstance is that he also had a wife in China."[59] After their initial stay in 1906, Lim's daughter returned three years later and lived at the Home for a seven-month period. Both mother and daughter returned again in 1932, staying for almost a year. It is clear from this case that racial criteria for admittance did not always function in a straightforward way. Lim and her daughter's residence in what was then the Chinese Rescue Home suggests that, for those who regulated admission, mixed-race children and a white woman who married a Chinese man could not be considered "white."[60] Although many cases were brought before the board prior to the women in question being allowed admission as residents, the case of the Swiss woman was handled by the matron alone. This suggests either that admitting a white woman was viewed as less dangerous than admitting a non-white woman or that, by virtue of her marriage to a "Chinaman," she was considered Chinese by association. Another possibility is that her mixed-race daughter was considered to be Chinese and thus gained them both admission (however, this seems less likely, as many children were admitted without their mothers).

While racial difference was certainly an important consideration for the admittance of women and children to the Home, how they were admitted was also significant. According to admission records, early residents of the institution were often spirited away,[61] through pretense or subterfuge, from lives of slavery or prostitution. This work was accomplished mostly by John Gardiner and Reverend Starr, with the help of "friendly

Chinamen." This trend of women being "spirited" into the Home continued over the years. Interestingly, the list of men who brought women and children to the domicile broadened to include police officers, Canadian and American immigration officials, officials from the Japanese Consul, doctors, husbands, and fathers. In all of these cases, it is likely that it was the domesticity of the Home that made it such an attractive and appropriate option. Husbands and fathers routinely sent their wives and daughters to receive training or to obtain shelter in the Home.

Records from the Home show that, in the first fifteen years, of the seventy-three women who were listed in the register, forty-seven were Chinese and twenty-six were Japanese women. Clearly, the name "Chinese Rescue Home" was not an accurate descriptor, but it remained the official name until 1909, hinting that authorities invested little in formally distinguishing Japanese women from Chinese women. Of these cases, there were fourteen whose admission records were ambiguous. Of the remaining fifty-nine, forty-seven were brought into the institution by men, three by a man and woman team, three by women, and the remainder (nine) admitted themselves. It was clear that many of the women who were admitted probably had little choice. While it cannot be assumed that they were unwilling or that they did not participate in the decision, it may be assumed that the decision was usually not solely their own as many were admitted by men. Even for those women who entered voluntarily, their choices in such a hostile climate were very limited. Leaving their own homes, whether they were escaping abusive "owners," husbands, fathers, or a life of prostitution, opened them to the risk of deportation. Thus, even for many of those who entered the Home "voluntarily," their choices were severely constrained and it was one of the few places to which they could turn.

According to the Home's records, all but one of the Chinese women were placed in the institution either as a result of a "rescue" or because they were fleeing lives of slavery or prostitution. With regard to the twenty-six Japanese women who were registered during this fifteen-year period, their reasons for admittance varied considerably. Only four were placed in the Home due to their suspected involvement in or vulnerability to prostitution. Two were sent by a doctor so that they could receive medical treatment. Ten were placed due to family-related issues such as poverty or the absence of a husband or father due to death or work-related travel. A further six women were admitted or admitted themselves for educational reasons, the most common being to learn English (see Table 1). Although the reasons for their admission differed significantly, the majority of the

TABLE 1 Reason for Admission to Chinese Rescue Home, 1886–1901

Reason for admission	Prostitution or slavery	Family-related	Education	Medical	Other	Total
Chinese	46				1	47
Japanese	4	10	6	2	4	26
Total	50	10	6	2	5	73

For the period 1886–1901

Source: "Oriental Home Record Book and Register, 1896–1914," Oriental Home and School Fonds, United Church BC Conference Archives (Bob Stewart Archives), 21.

residents were *compelled* to enter the Home. This is particularly significant for Japanese women as, in the years following predominantly Chinese admissions, immigration officials began placing many more of them in the Home. After 1909, the focus shifted away from rescue and towards education, especially in the English language and domestic training. It was not only how women entered the institution that was important but also how they were categorized.

Although race was used as a descriptive category in the Home register, it was not a prominent discourse within other institutional documents. However, there are a number of points that need to be made about how race operated as an organizational category that served to legitimize the power of white men and women over Japanese and Chinese women and children. Religious missions such as the Home can be understood as interventions whose purpose is to alleviate a threat to social order.[62] The Home's mandate was to order race and racial bodies. Although white women certainly engaged in evangelical missions aimed at other white women, the degree to which they could utilize their power to constrain them was considerably less than was the case with regard to the women in the Home. For instance, in one case in the Chinese community, people objected to the confinement of two "slave girls" in the Home. According to the matron's report, when threatened with legal proceedings, the women running the Home simply stated that they "did not bear expenses alone, and mentioned the names of [their] Advisory Board."[63] The advisory committee was clearly thought to be powerful in the community, but the Chinese men and women from whom these girls and women had been "spirited away" did not simply bend to the pressure exerted by it and the WMS women. Still, the advisory committee was able to convince the lawyer representing this community group not to take on the case. As this case and court records show, even when the seizure of women was contested by Chinese men, white women's authority usually held fast.

White women were involved in many types of benevolent work, yet racial hierarchies guaranteed that greater control was exerted over racialized populations than over other populations. This control depended not only on racial hierarchies but also on the exploitation of racial ambiguities. On the one hand, there was a seemingly egalitarian doctrine of brotherhood and sisterhood, which was meant to erase race; on the other hand, there was the assumption of racial superiority, that the "Anglo-Saxon 'race' was ... much more capable of controlling their instincts than other races" and that, therefore, any "moral regulation brought to bear on these [other races] would have to be external and coercive."[64] Moral regulation included a number of different lessons, which were applied with varying levels of force and coercion. That the moral lessons that were "brought to bear" on Japanese and Chinese women who resided in the Home arose out of concerns with their sexuality fits with common racial assumptions that associated Asian women with sexual excess. Regardless of the reasons that women entered the Home, the control that white women exerted over them often took the form of control over their bodies, sometimes through physical constraint. Barbed wire on fences and locks on windows and doors indicated that the inmates at least occasionally required this type of constraint.[65] This concern with the body was often deemed protective (e.g., the workers were protecting women's bodies from the threat of sexual exploitation), but it also took the form of coercion or constraint. Clearly, control over these women was not limited to moral instruction around sexuality.

When the WMS took control of the Home in 1888, five of the "girls" who were residents were over the age of twenty-one. All of them were considered to have been rescued or had run away from lives of slavery/prostitution. Although many of these women's ages were not indicated in the Home register, most can be assumed to have been adults. For instance, most of them had travelled to Canada alone and were married or widowed. But the fact that most residents were adults did not diminish the control exerted by white women – there was a reason residents were colloquially referred to as "inmates" of the Home. That the WMS women fought for guardianship of children left in the Home is not surprising, given the responsibility that they bore for their care. However, it was not possible to gain legal guardianship of adult residents in the same way. In many cases, the WMS women's authority over these women was legitimated by the latter's having been placed in the Home by men, who, as

husbands, fathers, or immigration officials, did have some form of legal/
social control over them. The WMS women viewed these Chinese and
Japanese women as dependents, thus justifying their maternalistic role in
relation to them. The spatial representation of the Home as a domestic
space further legitimized this role. The treatment of the residents in the
mission was based on racial and religious assumptions that held, first, that
the Anglo-Saxon race was superior and, second, that inferior races could
only mature through Christian instruction. The infantilization of these
women through discourses of mother and child meant that they were
not only expected to follow the rules of conduct set out by the Home
"mother," or matron, but also that they were expected to relinquish their
autonomy in crucial decision-making processes.

Portrayed as the product of benevolent work and as a sanctuary for
victims, the Chinese Rescue Home, by acting as *parens patriae*,[66] also
took on a distinctly paternalistic dimension.[67] Translated as "parent of
the nation," or "parent of the country," this doctrine was used to justify
the state's interventions into the family in cases of abuse. The state's role
as benevolent parent was mimicked by those who ran the Home. The
Home, however, took this role not only with children but also with adult
women. The Home's practice of treating women as children meant that
they were not afforded the freedoms that would normally be associated
with adulthood. In this way, the institution functioned paternalistically,
both in the protective sense and in the disciplinary sense of the word.

The women who ran the Home prided themselves on *freeing* the
women they saved from lives of prostitution/slavery, even though some
of the latter saved themselves by running away from their "masters" or
"mistresses," sometimes in the dead of night with nothing but the clothes
on their backs. However, once liberated, these women were subjected
to a different type of master and to new rules and regulations. This in
itself was not necessarily problematic as voluntary compliance with rules
was an expectation of all institutions. However, at the Home, the line
between voluntary compliance and coercion was not always clear. While
isolation and incarceration were not among the Home's formally recognized objectives, a number of incidents highlight the use of coercion and
constraint. First, courts, police, and immigration officials placed women
and children in the Home, thus calling into question the voluntary nature
of the residency of at least some of the women. Second, records and minutes contain multiple references to inmates "running away," "escaping,"
and "slipping out" of the institution. Third, physical measures were taken
to secure the Home and the women within it.

Even those who entered the Home of their own accord did not always find leaving easy. The records do not reveal whether residents were required to stay for any set length of time, only that stays were described as voluntary. Certainly, garnering support for the Home would have been difficult if it came to light that many of the women did not wish to be rescued or that, once in the institution, the types of lessons being taught were not welcome. The following examples from Home records clearly indicate that, for some at least, Christian transformation was not as welcome as the WMS often suggested. In August 1897, Elsie,[68] a sixteen-year-old woman, was rescued from Vancouver by police and brought to the Home. Despite the fact that this case was described as a "rescue," Elsie did not easily adapt to her new life in the institution. In the following year, she was reported to have "run away" from the Home on three different occasions. Notwithstanding the considerable effort that the WMS made on her behalf, including fighting for her legal custody and filing a subsequent appeal, Elsie continued to run away. When she grew tired of her "freedom" she would send a message to the matron, who would, upon the promise of better behaviour, come and retrieve her and bring her "home."

While it was not always clear where Elsie went or why she left, she was, at least on one occasion, harboured by "Laura's husband" under circumstances that the WMS deemed "peculiar."[69] This story belies common narratives that positioned Chinese women and girls as virtual prisoners of Chinese masters or mistresses. Elsie, while rescued by police from her "master," ran to another *woman's* home, suggesting that she had ties to this woman, her husband, or both, prior to her entry into the Home. These ties were discouraged once Elsie was in the Home, as is evinced in later advisory committee minutes. When "Laura" sought admission into the Home, the advisory committee stated that, given her and her husband's involvement in harbouring Elsie, "it was thought best not to permit her to come, except on very short visits."[70] Thus, although it was clearly not easy to keep women in the Home, the advisory committee used whatever tactics it could to have them returned or to prevent other escapes, including severing their ties to their communities and relying on police or other officials to bring them back into the fold.

In yet another case, a Japanese woman was placed in the institution by her husband and was "to remain [for] one year."[71] For Japanese men, the Home offered a way to dispose of or discipline errant wives. While the records only show that her husband placed her in the Home for a one-year period, during which he would pay for her board, it is likely that he placed her there due to his suspicions of infidelity. The woman, however, was able to use the Home as a means of escape. According to the institution's register, three weeks after having been admitted, she escaped through a window with the help of a man who had "before twice decoyed her from her husband."[72] It is clear that, whatever the motives of the WMS women, Japanese men and women had their own motives for using the Home. Dealing with these many motives meant that the women who ran the institution felt that they had to keep a tight rein on those who stayed within its walls. This is evidenced by the lengths to which residents needed to go in order to leave. Had this woman been permitted the freedom to come and go as she pleased, there would have been no need to escape through a window. Clearly, some women chose to enter the Home and were likely aware of the rules that would structure their movements. But what these examples show is that women were not free to leave of their own accord, which raises important questions about voluntary admissions and the basis of consent.

There are other indications that suggest that residence in the Home was not based on the consent of the women involved. For instance, in November 1898, the advisory committee passed a motion to "replace the fence and put two or three strands of barbed wire on the top to prevent the girls escaping."[73] In January of the following year, it was reported to the board that the fences were repaired, as were the doors and locks.[74] This emphasis on security and on preventing escape is suggestive of the carceral nature of the institution. It is also evidence that the women and girls who stayed in the Home did not readily comply with the wishes of those who ran it. Moreover, the women who ran it were not above using coercive measures to either obtain or to retain their residents. In May 1908, the advisory committee met to consider whether to allow two young girls to enter the Home. The mother "came to the Chinese Home bringing with her the eldest and youngest daughters [aged fourteen and four] and asked permission to leave them saying she could manage the other two at home. She promised to pay for their board if possible at the rate of $50 each per year."[75] It was only after the woman signed a paper agreeing that, should she be unable to pay the board, she would leave the girls to help in the Home for two years after they "had attained the age of 14" that the advisory committee agreed to admit them.[76] No one considered the rights of the girls to consent to these measures; rather, a possible two-year sentence of labour was imposed upon them. Despite having signed the contract, however, the woman came back one year later and removed her children from the residence without interference.

Clearly, the Home functioned on more than the idea of rescue alone. The assumptions that motivated it were clearly evangelistic, but these do not explain why such extreme measures were often necessary to constrain the residents. Drawing on the work of Uday Mehta, Alison Bashford and Carolyn Strange argue that isolation and other exclusionary practices are motivated by the conflicting rationales of "protection, punishment, prevention, cure, correction, restoration, and purification."[77] Many of these rationales certainly underwrote the interventions that took place in the Home. Rescue work was designed to protect Chinese and Japanese women from the evils of prostitution/slavery, with the added benefit that this also protected vulnerable white populations. As Bashford and Strange contend, "forced isolation ... was implemented both to protect the confined and to provide *protection from* the confined."[78] In addition, as one record book labelled "Bad Women" suggests, the institution also had a distinctly punitive function that necessitated the distinction between vulnerable victims, reformable women, and "bad women." Further, Home registers show that many women were admitted as a way of preventing them from falling into prostitution. For instance, one record states that the woman in question "came into the home to escape going to San Francisco into an immoral life."[79]

While these records may suggest that those who ran the Home acted to prevent immorality by participating in "confinement-as-prevention,"[80] they may also suggest that many of the residents were put into the Home because they were viewed as potentially dangerous.[81] Japanese and Chinese women and children were viewed as posing a potential threat to the social fabric, and this threat had to be stemmed. While it is true that some of the women and girls who were rescued had been living as prostitutes or slaves, this was certainly not the case for all or even most of the residents. Given that Japanese and Chinese women and children came to the Home for many different reasons, only racial difference can explain the perceived threat that they posed. Ideas of Oriental excess or deviance marked Japanese and Chinese bodies off as potentially dangerous. Thus, even women who came to the Home to learn English or domestic service skills were subjected to moral scrutiny.

Some women came into the Home to escape the threat of domestic violence, while a few Japanese women were placed there by the Japanese Consul, the only explanation being that they "needed the help and training of the Home."[82] Others were placed in the mission by the Department of Immigration until it could be determined whether they were to be allowed to stay in the country. Usually they were released only after they were married (in the Home) or deported to Japan. Still other women were accepted at the request of husbands or brothers, either for educational purposes or to avoid the danger of possible or perceived immorality. All of these women were seen as potentially dangerous, some by virtue of their ignorance but most by virtue of their sexuality. This threat was best addressed through domestic interventions, Christian conversion, or, in some instances, legal marriage. Sometimes, however, training, conversion, and marriage were not deemed to be sufficient forms of regulation. According to the Home's register, one woman was deported after having been married in the Home because she was thought to be "living a doubtful life."[83] In all likelihood, she was suspected of being sexually promiscuous and/or unfaithful to her husband.

Some children were placed in the Home because of the danger that their mothers were thought to pose to them. For instance, several children were admitted by fathers who explained that their mother was "bad," thereby putting the children at risk of also becoming bad. The assumption was that, if left to their own devices, Chinese and Japanese women were potential (sexual) threats not only to themselves but also to their children and to the wider society.[84] In her study of the Chinese rescue mission in San Francisco, Pascoe found that mission workers ignored evidence that some Chinese women entered prostitution knowingly, preferring to believe that these women were "powerless victims of evil men."[85] However, the records of the Chinese Rescue Home are more ambivalent than what we find in Pascoe. While the "victim" discourse is a common one, so, too, is that of the "bad woman." Descriptions of the "bad woman" or "bad mother" were evident both in the Home's lists of these types of women and in its descriptions of those who refused help or ran away. The links between proper domesticity and morality were evident in that "improper" sexuality was often equated with the inability to properly mother.

The Home, in some ways, parallels the sanatoriums that Bashford discusses in "Cultures of Confinement: Tuberculosis, Isolation and the Sanatorium."[86] In the sanatorium, those confined were both infected patients and carriers – both those who were infected and suffered from the ailment and those who showed no sign of disease. Like the sanatorium, the Home confined both the dangerous prostitute and the potentially dangerous women – the morally and sexually "fallen" but also those who were deemed by courts, police, husbands, or immigration agents to be *at risk* of becoming prostitutes. This risk referred not simply to the risk that a prostitute posed to herself but also to the risk she posed to the wider community and the nation. Like tuberculosis, immorality was viewed as a disease. The danger of contagion, for instance a bad or immoral mother, posed enough of a risk to justify confinement (i.e., isolation of contagion). Once in the Home, women and children underwent treatment for (i.e., inoculation against) immorality not through medical but, rather, through religious and domestic interventions. The disease of immorality was associated with so-called "inferior races" but was understood as treatable through the transformative powers of the Christian faith coupled with domestic training of the body.

As one of the Home's journal entries explains, residents were brought to church each Sunday and "morning worship opened the school" each day.[87] Here, "correction, restoration and purification" were that matrons' central goals.[88] Even the mentally ill were thought to be curable through the religious ministrations of those who ran the mission. In the minutes of December 1913, for instance, the advisory committee describes what it calls a "great case" in which "a girl ... had been brought down from Chilliwack suffering from some mental trouble, [and] we decided to keep her for a few months in order to do her good and reclaim her."[89] Clearly, Christianity was deemed an antidote to the gendered and raced threats that Japanese and Chinese women were seen to pose. This spiritual antidote was paired with physical domestic training to further inoculate these women against future immoral behaviour.

The historical foundations and organizational context for the Chinese Rescue Home, along with a brief history of Japanese and Chinese immigration, show how immigration policy provided the bedrock upon which the Home was built. Historical and geographical context dictated not only where the institution would stand but also who would build it and inhabit it. Geography alone does not sufficiently explain the power relations within the Home. Understanding the institution's objectives provides insight into how (and by whom) Japanese and Chinese women were admitted and how they were ultimately received. Having laid the historical and geographical foundation for this book, Chapter 2 begins the discussion of the gendered, national, and global discourses of domesticity and delinquency that legitimized and grounded the work of the WMS. These discourses would eventually become the pillars upon which the Home would rely for strength and support.

2

Pillars of Domesticity and the "Chinese Problem"

> A free people will never be constituted or held together by any iron band. They must be held together by something that is powerful enough to assimilate and purify and elevate and unify all those discordant elements that may come within its range.
> – Lemuel Moss, Baptist minister

Although Lemuel Moss (above) is referring to religion, one of the tools of assimilation and elevation was to be found in something much more mundane – domesticity. This was certainly the case for a young woman known as Katie. Katie stayed in the Chinese Rescue Home for two years before leaving to marry a man named Ah Lou. According to the *British Colonist*, which described the wedding, Katie had met Ah Lou while she was "leading a life of degradation in one of the dens of Fisgard street." However, she steadfastly refused to marry unless she could have a "neat little home in the 'white part' of town, and unless she got such a home where she could receive company and invite her English friends to tea." Her demands were met when her husband-to-be provided her with a "cosy little five-roomed cottage on Quadra street ... well furnished in European style." The couple was subsequently married at the Home. By this time, according to the *Colonist*, Katie had been thoroughly "civilized." She had turned her back on all that was Chinese, instead preferring five o'clock teas and the "kindred dissipations of polite society."[1] What this article implies is that Katie's reward for having been "civilized" was not only escape from a life of shame but also association and communion with white society. In a city in which anti-Asian sentiment was common, and in which it was routinely argued that citizenship should be reserved for whites, this communion was made possible because of Katie's successful domestication. Understanding this racial ambivalence necessitates an examination of how the domestic informed cross-racial relationships both inside and outside the Home.

Discourses of domesticity and the domestic realm were enmeshed in the relations and the regulatory practices within the Home. Yet the Home did not exist in isolation. The state, in its various forms, was deeply concerned with the relations between the "foreign" and the domestic, and in many ways it underwrote and informed the work that would be carried out in the Home. Drawing on two Royal Commissions and a letter written by Reverend John Edward Starr, one of the founders of the rescue mission, I show how the term "domestic" is used in two ways, signalling connections between state concerns and religious concerns. First, an analysis of the two Royal Commissions highlights the perceived domestic delinquency of Chinese and Japanese men and women. Here, the term "domestic" is used to consider the nation as a domestic space that was juxtaposed with the foreign bodies of Chinese and Japanese women. Both the Royal Commission on Chinese Immigration (1885) and the Royal Commission to Investigate Chinese and Japanese Immigration into British Columbia (1902) investigated concerns raised by white community members about Japanese and Chinese populations, the threat they were seen to pose to the (white) nation, and the growing hostility towards them. The report of the 1885 commission was 731 pages and included testimony from many of Victoria's clergy and missionaries. The report of the second commission was 430 pages and, like its predecessor, included transcripts of evidence taken during a two-and-a-half month inquiry. These commissions provide some crucial context for an intriguing proposition sent by Reverend Starr to Elizabeth S. Strachan, president of the Woman's Missionary Society.

Second, by analyzing a letter by Starr to the WMS, in which he asks the society to take control of the Home, I show how, in it, the domestic takes on a gendered and more localized veneer than it does in the Royal Commissions. Much like the commissions, Starr's letter highlights the "four pillars" of the Home: religion, nation, whiteness, and gender. These pillars provided the Home with its strength and support. Starr's elucidation of the goals of the institution provides entry into how the same discourses that were prevalent in the Royal Commissions also came to inform the moral regulation of racialized bodies. Within the institution, these pillars were tethered together by domesticity. Those who ran the Home were keen to transform the lives of domestically delinquent Chinese and Japanese women through religious imperatives that would allow them to be assimilated into the "family of God" and, in some cases, into the nation itself. Gender played an important role in defining these goals and in prescribing who should carry them out. Although the Home had initially been the vision of two men, John Starr and John Gardiner, it was crucial that the promise of this work be fulfilled by women. Thus, it was the women of the WMS who ultimately defined the "moral citizen" and applied this definition, in both an evaluative and a regulatory way, to Chinese and Japanese women's bodies. The very subjects who were framed by the Royal Commissions as domestically delinquent were to be domesticated within the domestic realm of the Home and the nation. Reading these three documents in tandem enables us to make connections between and among global discourses, national imperatives, and local practices.

Domestic Delinquents

In their discussion of nineteenth-century global mobility, Marilyn Lake and Henry Reynolds explain that, "although the freedom to 'dwell in any country' was ... a privilege increasingly reserved for whites, more than 50 million Chinese embarked for new lands in these decades, an equal number of Europeans and about 30 million Indians."[2] In their groundbreaking book, *Drawing the Global Colour Line,* Lake and Reynolds track the transnational circulation and movement of racial discourses, and in this chapter I focus on the sedimentations and settlings of these discourses. The types of racial discourses that appeared in the Royal Commissions dealt with "foreign" bodies both within Canada and beyond it, and the distinction between foreign bodies and domestic bodies is important. As Lake and Reynolds remind us, "White men's countries" were created not only by *barring* "foreign" bodies but also by *defining* them as foreign. Assimilability was a question of whether the foreign could be made domestic.[3] In the two Royal Commissions there is considerable disagreement regarding how to deal with foreign bodies. While many believed that Chinese and Japanese populations were inassimilable, those who ran the Home believed that domestication was possible. Here it must be remembered that the Home was built on and engaged with national and global questions of moral character similar to those found in the reports of the Royal Commission on Chinese Immigration and of the Royal Commission on Chinese and Japanese Immigration.

Domestic compatibility was measured through national and global discourses of race. The first commission, the Royal Commission on Chinese Immigration (1885), drew extensively on discourses of "racial problems" such as the "Chinese problem," which were transported from other national jurisdictions. The second, the Royal Commission on Chinese and Japanese Immigration (1902), built on these same types of discourses. However, there was considerable ambivalence regarding whether Canada should allow continued immigration from China and Japan. Two rationales underwrote support for continued entry. First, it was argued that "foreign" bodies should be allowed entry into Canada so that white missionaries could continue to enter foreign lands. Second, foreign bodies were deemed acceptable within domestic borders under certain conditions, none of which included assimilation into white society. Even those who supported Chinese and Japanese immigration to Canada did not support their assimilation.

Commissions of inquiry have recently become an object of social, historical, and legal investigation. As Mawani argues, Royal Commissions were part of "legal-knowledge production and of juridical power," identifying Chinese as internal and external enemies.[4] By 1914, Chinese "prostitution had been newly conceptualized as a racial threat that was both *internal* and *external* to the settler regime ... The biopolitcal concerns of the colonial state became increasingly fixated on the (foreign) yet internal enemies."[5] Chinese prostitutes were framed as domestic insurgents and as domestically delinquent. The foreignness of these internal enemies was borne out in the approach adopted by the 1885 Royal Commission. It framed the "Chinese problem" as a national problem, one with which Canada was forced to deal but whose origins were to be found outside the nation. In fact, although the Royal Commission's first three considerations were concerned with social and trade relations in British Columbia, concerns that were of a global nature, its fourth and final consideration is illuminating in that it related to "the moral considerations which arise out of the residence and contact of the white people with Chinese here and *elsewhere*."[6] These moral considerations, especially as they related to the "residence" of Chinese, centred on their perceived (in)assimilability. If they could not be assimilated, the commissioners argued, the Chinese must be dealt with in such a way that would not obstruct the work of missionaries who travelled abroad. Thus, the Royal Commission on Chinese Immigration defined the Chinese as both a national and a global problem.

As the preface to the 1885 Royal Commission on Chinese Immigration indicates, commissioners consulted with governments and witnesses from across the world. During "the enquiry at San Francisco in 1876, evidence was taken respecting the Chinese immigrant in all parts of the world from San Francisco to Melbourne; the subject literally surveyed 'from China to Peru'; and the Commission of the Canadian Commissioners called for all information attainable respecting it."[7] This commission was quite clear that the so-called Chinese problem was not solely a Canadian issue but one that spanned the globe. Given their presumed similarities, the Chinese problem in the United States was to serve as a model and pre-scription for Canada "for the present of California may prove the likeness of the future of British Columbia."[8] The United States was a model that was often referenced in both Royal Commissions as well as in missionary literature. The US response to Chinese immigration was seen both as a series of mistakes that needed to be avoided and as a model that needed to be emulated. The distinction between a domestic and a foreign problem was blurred for, although the Chinese were viewed as a Canadian racial problem, they were also viewed as a global problem.[9]

That Chinese bodies were problems even in China is evidenced by both the discussion of Chinese "character" and by discourses that main-tained that it was the duty of whites to improve the moral character of the Chinese people. The 1885 Royal Commission contains a large sec-tion that describes in detail the "character of the Chinese in China."[10] Especially relevant here are discussions of Chinese women as victims of the tyrannical "Chinaman." The commission argues that the Chinese problem was not uniquely Canadian but, rather, had been transplanted or imported. According to the commission: "The position of women in China is deplorable; the oppression of the system of concubinage ... is so great that affianced maidens have committed suicide to save themselves from marriage with its tyrannies and jealousies ... They can be discarded; sold; and made the slaves of keepers of houses of prostitution."[11] Although it was in March 1887 that the plight of Chinese girls and women was first brought to the attention of the readers of the *Missionary Outlook,* a publication of the Methodist Church of Canada, it is clear that the 1885 Royal Commission on Chinese Immigration had already anticipated that such a problem would eventually emerge. In fact, its report seems to foreshadow the circumstances that led to the eventual publication of the *Missionary Outlook* story. The commissioners had warned the Canadian government that the "Chinese are the only people coming to the contin-ent the great bulk of whose women are prostitutes [*sic*]."[12] According to the Royal Commission, the "evidence is that Chinese prostitutes are more shameless than white women who follow the same pursuit, as though the former had been educated for it from the cradle."[13] The innate immorality of Chinese women was especially evident in mothers, something that ensured even their children's immorality. Referencing San Francisco, the Royal Commission framed Chinese prostitutes as threats to white populations both in terms of disease and in their corruption of "little boys."[14] Women were clearly a concern to the commission not only because of their supposed immorality, domestic delinquency, and lack of conformity to white standards but also because of the threat they posed to the sexual propriety of white families and homes.[15]

Although Chinese women's bodies constituted a problem inside the nation, an even larger problem was believed to exist outside the nation. The state was concerned with foreign bodies within the nation and with facilitating global moral suasion. The global nature of the Chinese problem arose in a different context in the 1902 Royal Commission on Chinese and Japanese Immigration. Discussing the "moral and religious aspects" of immigration, the commissioners drew on testimony from a number of witnesses belonging to the Christian community, including ministers from the Presbyterian, Anglican, Methodist, and Baptist churches in Vancouver and Victoria as well as from a teacher at the Chinese Rescue Home. The commission found that "the ministers and clergy ... with very few exceptions were opposed to further immigration of Chinese or Japanese labourers."[16] Given that most of these men and the sole woman were interviewed precisely because of their long histories working with Chinese men (and sometimes women), this was somewhat surprising.

What is most notable, however, was not their rejection of would-be Chinese and Japanese immigrants but how the discussion was framed around global issues of white mobility and dominance. The concern with borders was not limited to who could be admitted but also included the free movement of white bodies. Thus, the moral issue of refusing entry to Chinese or Japanese immigrants stemmed not from questions of racial exclusion but, rather, from how missionaries could then justify their own excursions into China and/or Japan. After going on record to say that, "as a matter of self-preservation, some steps ought to be taken immediately to limit their coming or to prohibit them altogether,"[17] Reverend W. Leslie Clay, minister of the Presbyterian Church in Victoria, was questioned by the commissioners as follows:

Q. Would not the whole race be much better off if the Chinese were left alone and kept within their own walls in China?

A. I do not see how we could keep them within their own walls and seek to enter within those walls ourselves. ...

Q. Would they not be justified in asking us to leave them alone when we exclude them?

A. I think they would.

Q. Would it be desirable in the interests of the white race to have the Chinese remain within their own walls and have no intercourse with the white people in any shape or form?

A. No, I do not think that would be desirable. I do not think we would be working for the best interests of the world at large in adopting that course.

Q. I should like to know how you can reconcile the one thing with the other; that is how you can expect to go into China unless in justice you should allow them to come into your country.

A. Certainly. I say we cannot stop them coming in when we wish to go into their country. I have suggested that the whole matter might be arranged by a treaty between the two Empires; that the number of labourers passing from one country to the other should be limited to a certain number in each year.[18]

Clay's testimony illustrates that the issue of Chinese immigration had to be considered not only in terms of domestic interests but also in terms of global ones.

Clay's suggestion that limits be placed on immigration in *both* directions was framed as one of justice and fairness. However, it was also firmly entrenched in classed and raced assumptions. The Chinese labourers who were to enter Canada from China were clearly of a different sort than were the white labourers who proposed to enter China from Canada. In both cases, the Chinese were framed as a population in need: in the case of Chinese immigrants, the need was for moral and economic sustenance *in* the West; in the case of Chinese nationals, the need was for spiritual nourishment *from* the West. Thus, the policing of borders was tightly bound up with concerns regarding global racial dominance and white superiority – concerns that were also prevalent, although on a smaller scale, in the Home.

The testimony of Reverend Elliot Sproule Rowe, a Methodist minister in Victoria who advocated the prohibition of Chinese immigration, also focused on global concerns. When asked: "Do you think having regard to the same amount of labour expended that you are any more likely to get converts here than in China?" Rowe responded, "I think there is as much chance of converting the Chinese in China as there is for converting them in Victoria."[19] In other words, if Chinese could be easily converted in China, there would be no reason to allow them entry into the country. Bishop Perrin of Victoria took a similarly global approach to the issue. While he did not advocate outright prohibition of Chinese immigration, he explained that he thought "the present immigration [was] ... not a desirable one for the country, because they [were] not the best representatives of the race."[20] Here, the issue of immigration was framed not only as a racial problem but also as a class problem. Perrin continued: "We have a distinct mission to go to China because our religion is the universal religion. If they are here we have a duty to perform. The majority of white people are higher in morality than the Chinese."[21] Equating whiteness and Christianity with morality served to set the Chinese population apart as immoral and in need of white intervention.[22] Neither Rowe nor Bishop wanted China and Canada to lose contact with one another; rather, they wanted Canada to breach the border between the two nations for the moral betterment of China.

Although this was an opinion that was shared by many clergy, for those who worked with Chinese in Canada the global possibilities of home missions were, in fact, particularly important considerations. While it was clear that many felt that they had a global obligation with regard to the conversion of non-Christian peoples, this did not prevent them from viewing Chinese immigration as a problem. Even F. Kate Morgan, a teacher and evangelist in the Home, agreed: "I don't think immigration unrestricted is advisable. It is not so to the Chinese, and I know it is bad for the country. From what I know of Oriental character, I think better Christian teachers can be made in China than here."[23] Again, recommendations to limit Chinese immigration were linked to something in the *character* of Chinese immigrants – something that dictated that they were better left in China. That Morgan continued to work in the Home, however, suggests that Chinese *women* might have been viewed as more amenable to domestic interventions.

Reverend Canon Beanlands of Victoria, although he did not oppose immigration, had a similar view. However, while he believed that more success might be found in converting Chinese populations in China, he did not oppose their coming to Canada and, in fact, advocated a very distinct type of immigration. Like Morgan, he was also concerned with the domestic realm. When asked if it was "in the interests of a country to have an immigration of her people here who will not assimilate,"

Beanlands replied that it was as he "should always like to see them as a servile class."

Q. From which you could draw help?

A. Yes.

Q. No intention of elevating?

A. I do not see it is our business in the least.

Unlike Perrin and Rowe, who saw it as a Christian duty to elevate the Chinese, at least in terms of their religious training, Beanlands was less concerned with this aspiration. However, when asked if he thought this servile class could go to heaven, Beanlands magnanimously replied, "Oh, yes; we have no class distinction there."[24]

That Chinese should be allowed into heaven clearly did not mean that they should be allowed full citizenship within Christian nations. These discussions were more than discursive interventions into how Chinese and Japanese populations were to be understood: they would eventually become part of a larger project, which tested such claims upon Chinese/Japanese bodies. In the case of Japanese immigrants, this larger project included limiting immigration; in the case of Chinese immigrants, it included head taxes and outright prohibition.[25] The roles of the state, especially when they took the form of Royal Commissions, were crucial in shaping how those who ran the Home and how those who worked outside it functioned as agents who contributed to the shaping of moral geographies.[26]

PILLARS OF DOMESTICITY

The Royal Commission on Chinese Immigration took place just two years before Reverend John Edward Starr wrote his September 1887 letter to the Woman's Missionary Society requesting its help. Starr was a married Methodist minister living in Victoria, and he had contributed financially to the Home and had helped in the "rescue" of at least one girl who resided there at the time this letter was written. His involvement in the founding of the Home was only the beginning of his advocacy work on behalf of children. Starr was appointed as the first commissioner of Toronto's juvenile court in 1911. Hogeveen describes him as "a large bodied man with a sympathetic heart who was a friend to all who knew him. Given the court's mandate and the novel principles of social welfare inspired justice embedded in the JDA [Juvenile Delinquents Act], it is fitting that a minister would be appointed judge."[27] Although Starr would eventually become a representative of the state, prior to this he was "the pastor of the Berkeley Street Methodist Church. He had been interested in children's work for most of his life. In addition to his pioneering efforts with organizing Toronto's Children's Aid Society, Starr was actively involved with the YMCA."[28]

Intertwined throughout both Royal Commissions are discourses of religion, nationhood, and whiteness. Gender is also central. As mentioned, these discourses became the pillars that strengthened and supported the Home. Although based on ideologies similar to those displayed in reports of the Royal Commissions, in the Home, these discourses were explicitly united by a common element: domesticity. In the Royal Commission reports' discussion of immigration, the nation is juxtaposed with a foreign threat – the so-called Chinese problem. The nation was also one of Starr's concerns, but he believed that the clash of foreign and domestic could be bridged through processes of domestication. This domestication took whiteness as its model. Thus, although the Royal Commission reports privileged whiteness as a basis for *exclusion*, the Home privileged whiteness as a basis for *inclusion*. In order for Chinese and Japanese women to embody whiteness, a (racial) transformation needed to take place through the process of religious conversion. Certainly, religious considerations were also of paramount importance in the Royal Commissions' discussion concerning the opening of borders in order to support evangelistic endeavours. Within the Home, Christian evangelism was a fundamental imperative, but it was an imperative that both began within and challenged Canadian borders. While many of those who were interviewed by the Royal Commissions did not view Chinese and Japanese as compatible with the nation, Starr believed that Chinese and Japanese women could be transformed through religious conversion. Thus, gender was crucial to the Home's success. If the Royal Commissions viewed Japanese and Chinese as incompatible with the domestic, the Home had the corrective. Domestication was tied to gendered ideologies of proper domesticity, which were instrumental in creating domestic citizens. And women were indispensable in this process.

Just as the origins of the Chinese problem became fodder for public debate, so, too, did potential remedies. While many, including a missionary who worked in the Home, called for the expulsion of Chinese prostitutes from the nation, others were committed to overseeing their redemption and transformation within the nation. As in the Royal Commission reports, the nation was a theme that took on primary importance in defining the Home. Starr's letter highlights two important assumptions that underpinned the founding and the maintenance of the Home. First, by locating the Chinese problem outside the nation, it signals the foreignness of this mission, despite its location in Victoria. Second, it suggests that possible solutions to the Chinese problem included expulsion and/or transformation and domestication through the powers of God. The institution was posited as a site of transformation, capable not only of saving the souls of this "heathen" population but also of domesticating their minds and bodies. These religious interventions would guarantee at least partial entry into the nation for, once domesticated, Chinese and Japanese women could presumably find spaces of belonging. The goals of the Home provide insight into what it meant to be properly domestic as the institution was seen as one solution to the problem of foreign bodies.

Unlike some "home missions," which were directed at white women or white communities (such as missions directed at the French or at "delinquent" women), the Chinese Rescue Home addressed questions of foreignness. Its work offered the women of the WMS an opportunity for cultural "travel" and engagement with Otherness without ever leaving home. Although the Chinese problem was conceived as global, the WMS women were afforded opportunities to deal with "foreigners" within their own communities. The significance of foreignness was evident in early WMS reports, which initially included local work with Japanese and Chinese populations under the headings of "The Chinese Work" and "The Japanese Work" – headings that were previously reserved for work in Japan and China. It was not until 1902 that the reports listed this work under the heading "Chinese Work, British Columbia."[29] Often mission work undertaken with Chinese and Japanese populations was sandwiched between "foreign" work and "Home missions," which also included French and "Indian" (First Nations) populations. Given that the Home was located in Victoria, missionaries did not constitute it as foreign. Yet, unlike missions to the French or First Nations populations, missions to Chinese and Japanese populations were not seen as home missions, likely because these populations were deemed foreign. In other words, the Home occupied an ambivalent space between the national and the domestic.

Starr's letter also provides ample evidence that Chinese women who were housed in the Home were viewed as inherently foreign. Unlike the Royal Commission reports, however, his letter expresses some ambivalence regarding their perceived inassimilability. In the Home, discourses of the domestic, as both home and nation and as opposed to the foreign, were intertwined. In her discussion of the antebellum United States, Amy Kaplan argues that "the *domestic* has a double meaning that not only links the familial household to the nation but also imagines both in opposition to everything outside the geographic and conceptual border of the home." She contends that the domestic, in both senses of the word, is defined against foreignness, in particular against "racial demarcations of otherness."[30] However, the Home was a much more ambivalent domestic space. While it defined itself in opposition to foreignness, it also housed the very foreignness that it defined itself in opposition to. In order to address this contradiction, Chinese and Japanese women were required to undergo processes of domestication, which were deemed possible only through the transformative powers of God.

Domestication, according to Kaplan "is related to the imperial project of civilizing, and the conditions of domesticity often become markers that distinguish civilization from savagery." She suggests that, in addition to demarcating the foreign from the domestic, the home also "contains within itself those wild and foreign elements that must be tamed."[31] Civilizing the "savage" and making the foreign body into a domestic one means engaging processes of assimilation. While many argued that Chinese and Japanese were not assimilable, once in the domestic realm these processes of assimilation had to be engaged. In some cases, the success or failure of these processes was used to determine whether Chinese and Japanese women would be allowed to stay in Canada. Their suitability was determined not by Canada's willingness to accommodate foreign bodies but, rather, through assessments of whether these bodies could successfully be transformed into domestic subjects. Japanese and Chinese women in the Home were evaluated on their domestic (national) compatibility according to their willingness to embody familial domesticity. However, successful transformations did not guarantee that the women could, or even should, stay within the nation's borders.

An important goal of the Home, according to Starr, was to "train and educate such of these girls as evince an aptitude for the work to become Bible Women among the Chinese Women either here or in China."[32] Here, Starr focuses on the important role that Chinese "Bible Women" might play both in their home communities and in China. The journey from prostitute to Christian missionary, in this case, was not a journey towards domestic citizenship. It was clear that these new Christian missionaries would take a circuitous and global journey that would return them to their communities in China and Japan, albeit in a new form.

There was no question of their evangelizing in white communities. Despite their transformation, Chinese women could only evangelize in foreign (i.e., in non-white) fields. While her ability to perform missionary work was evidence that the transformation of the Chinese prostitute was complete, Chinese women could never aspire to the moral authority afforded to white women. The initial transformation of the Chinese prostitute or slave girl was only possible through the interventions of white men and women, including Starr and the WMS. The suggestion that Chinese and Japanese women could now be trusted to take on this important evangelical work (albeit in a limited way) was clear evidence of their having been accepted into the "sisterhood" of God, if not necessarily into the nation.

The privileging of whiteness was evident not only in the Royal Commission reports but also in the segregation of Victoria. That the Home, which openly promoted cross-racial contact, was able to exist in such a racially and economically divided city was not due to a weakening of white privilege: on the contrary, it was a direct result of it. Certainly, the institution was a site where the everyday regulations of race were suspended, at least partially. However, cross-racial contact was only tolerated so that Chinese and Japanese women could be remade according to a white image. It is for this reason that the work of the mission demands an understanding of the malleability of race.

Although prostitution and slavery were framed as gendered and racial problems associated with Chinese women and with their domestic delinquency, in the Home's documents and reports race rarely appears in obvious or straightforward ways. While it could be argued that the actions of the WMS originated in racist beliefs about Chinese and Japanese populations as inferior and in need of saving, very rarely were Chinese and Japanese women explicitly described as *racially* inferior to whites. Yet the absence of such discourses does not mean that race was absent from the work of female missionaries in the Home. While the Royal Commissions' reports present race as an immutable category that justified claims that Chinese and Japanese populations were foreign and incapable of assimilation, the WMS was concerned primarily with domesticating Chinese and Japanese women and including them in the family of God. One tactic for dealing with this incommensurability involved claiming that race did not matter in God's family. At the same time, religious missions arose out of a belief in the cultural and religious inferiority of other "races." In other words, their work was shot through with fundamental tensions as the missionaries sought to subvert, to transform, *and* to reify race. Home missionary discourse on racial questions focused upon changeable socio-cultural factors. For this reason, biological racial discourses were seldom employed. Yet, because differences from whiteness could be resolved only through transformation, missionary work continued to reinforce racial difference, with biological understandings of race morphing into a focus on cultural behaviours.[33]

If cultural behaviours could be transformed or reformed, then racial inferiority, while it would not and perhaps could not be fully erased, could at least be somewhat ameliorated. Cultural differences, as racial differences, were mobilized to mark the inferiority of Chinese and Japanese women. While the term "cultural difference" did not appear verbatim in the Home's records or in the Royal Commission reports, it was clear that missionaries preferred a distinction that focused on culture and environment over a distinction that focused on biological racial difference. For instance, Reverend Alexander Brown Winchester, in his testimony to the Royal Commission on Chinese and Japanese Immigration, explained that making comparisons between Chinese and whites was difficult because any differences were due to different moral standards and to the conditions under which they were expected to survive in British Columbia, especially conditions involving "isolation and social ostracism."[34] Further, he explained that the superiority of Chinese immigrants in Toronto to those on the west coast was due largely to their being better treated by white society.[35] In other words, moral superiority was, for him, environmentally determined. It was, however, largely measured against white, Western standards.

That white women were chosen as the racial model to be emulated was based on the unquestioned assumption of Eurocentric privilege.[36] Even when Chinese or Japanese women went on to careers as missionaries, this was seen as a simple continuation of the original work overseen by white men and women. Japanese and Chinese women were characterized as a new generation of missionaries. In this way, the work of white women could be seen simply as an extension of their reproductive labour: they were producing a new generation of Christ's children. It was whiteness that guaranteed women's fitness to be mothers of the nation. And it was this whiteness that was to be the model emulated within the Home.

Even in the Home's earliest incarnation, transformations were already evident. The changes in the residents were initially described as physical transformations. Dressing the girls in European clothing was one of Starr's earliest suggestions to the WMS. According to Starr, the women's original clothing was exchanged for donated "European" clothes. Their physical masquerade as white women was the first step in their moral and cultural domestication. According to Starr, the girls in the San Francisco Chinese Mission Home were not dressed in European clothes. He insisted that the girls in Victoria preferred European clothes and that these clothes were both cheap and had the added benefit of disguising Chinese/Japanese wearers. He seemed to think that race could be transformed through the adoption of Western clothing. When Gardiner "took them the other day thro [sic] The City for a row on 'Th Arm' ... their own people did not recognize them in their European clothes," he wrote.[37] Thus, the goal of physical transformation had two important effects: first, the emulation moved the women closer to white domesticity and, second, it severed them from their former selves and their former lives. If they could no longer be recognized, they could not easily return to the "foreignness" of the Chinese community. Western clothing became a tool of domestication, marking the boundaries not only between the foreign and the domestic but also between the private realm of female domesticity and the public realm of predominantly male activities.

The privileging of whiteness was also apparent in another way. As Starr reveals in his letter, the first goal of the Home was concerned with how it would protect the white community from the corrupt influences of Chinese men. It was to strike at the economic system that supported slavery and prostitution and was aimed at bankrupting the procurers (or procuresses) – specifically, the Highbinders – who subjected these women/girls to such conditions. This allegedly criminal organization, according to the 1885 Royal Commission report, was particularly sinister, as it "[was] disposed to aid the law, protect the keepers of brothels, and undertake ... for money, assassinations."[38] The undermining of the Highbinders was to be accomplished by removing the source of their income – their slaves and prostitutes. According to Starr, the "cash value of the girls we have now in the Home to their procurers is over $10,000.00."[39] "Rescuing" the girls not only reduced the procurers' cash flow but also depleted their inventory. Starr's initial focus on the effects as they were felt outside the institution was an indication that the Home's most important goal was to rid white Victoria of the racial threat posed by the Chinese. That Chinese women might be transformed into national citizens was a by-product of this process.

While the privileging of whiteness was the basis for racial transformation, Christianity was the tool for ensuring its success. With this second goal, Starr shifts his attention away from economic matters and directs it instead towards religious ones. Here, he focuses on the transformations that had already taken place in the Chinese women and girls in the Home. According to him: "In their habits they are clean – in their tastes even refined and quick to learn alike household duties and the English language," and their gratitude "is enough to wring tears from a stone."[40] Although their being moved to the Home was crucial to the beginning of this process, changes were brought about not only through a change in geography but through religion and, as Starr's focus on "household duties" suggests, through domestic training. Christian love was what was believed to offer the potential for change, while training was thought to solidify it. Missionaries saw the Chinese, and later the Japanese, as assimilable only through Christian faith. Only once Japanese and Chinese women embraced Christianity could they enter into the family of God and, as domestic citizens, become part of the nation.

Religious language of brotherhood (and sisterhood) is prevalent throughout Starr's letter.[41] On the third page, he refers to the rescued girls as "Christ's sisters and mine"; in the following page he refers to them as "our Almondeyed [sic] sisters"; and, in the final paragraph, he appeals to the WMS as follows: "The god who is Your father and the father also of your yelloskinned [sic] sisters guide you in your deliberations upon this new pressing work, stimulate your faith and nerve you to sturdier efforts and grander endeavors on behalf of Heathen Womandom."[42] Although in two of these three comments Starr refers to race when describing these new "sisters," it is clear that, once in the Home, their move from "heathen" to "sister" would require a religious transformation from foreign to domestic.

It was only through religious conversion that the racialized body could become transformable, controllable, and easily subjected to moral regulation. Without moral regulation, there would be no way for these women to enter into the family of God or the nation. While the change that was to take place was a spiritual one, physical transformation was also important as changes to the body made it more amenable to its place in the family of God. True sisterhood was only possible once both physical training and spiritual conversion were complete. Much as a pet is "domesticated" into the family home through physical training, so too is the foreign body domesticated through physical, religious, and spiritual training. As one might expect, the second goal of the Home was to Christianize girls/women who were rescued. This goal highlights two important and sometimes contentious issues: consent and free will. Central to the transformation was the girl's/women's *desire* to be converted. According to Starr's letter, "they are all anxious to hear about Jesus."[43] Christian conversion and Godly transformation, then, had to be desired by the subject and not simply imposed on her. With their desire assured, the field had been ploughed and transformation was simply a matter of planting the seeds.

The Christian metaphor of sowing seeds that would later bear the fruits of one's labour is a common one. In her 1923–24 report, for instance, the matron referred to the Home as "part of the Master's vineyard."[44] This metaphor also appears in the WMS minutes both in Vancouver and in Victoria. In the context of a domestic and familial space, this metaphor takes on distinctly sexual undertones as WMS women planted the (male) seed of Christianity into the passive and receptive (female) bodies of Japanese and Chinese women. The WMS women vigilantly watched for signs that their "seed" had borne fruit. The seed here, of course, is Christianity; the soil is the mission field (in general) and Japanese and Chinese bodies (in particular); and the fruit are new Christian subjects. The planting of seeds was only the beginning of a process whereby the eventual fruits of mission labour would themselves plant seeds that would, in turn, bear fruit. In this way, the work of the Home became global: the seeds that the WMS women planted were expected to bear fruit and to reseed not only the Chinese and Japanese communities in Victoria and British Columbia but also in China and Japan.

Another poignant example of the harvest metaphor is found in an obituary published in 1898, a clipping of which was found in the Home Register, 1888–1908. It began with the following: "There is always something especially interesting in the first flowers, first-fruits of any season. But when the Master walks in his garden, and selects from among those he has given us to tend, how our hearts thrill and our heads bow in worship and wonder! Christ has chosen Daisy from among the 'Chinese girls' in Victoria."[45] Here, the mission field is represented as a garden that white women have been chosen to tend, and Daisy and the other Chinese girls are the fruits (or flowers) of their labour. Even the name "Daisy," which had been given to the girl by an agent of the Home, is significant. Such language indicates that white women considered themselves to be authorized by God to tend to and to cultivate these Chinese girls.

Once the seeds of Christianity were planted, the Home would have to evaluate whatever they produced. As alluded to earlier, this evaluation was legitimized and required by the state, especially if it had been instrumental in placing Japanese and Chinese women in the residence. Here, candidacy for citizenship (social, if not legal) was measured through two of the "sacred performances" of religion, both of which were of great concern to the WMS women:[46] baptism and Christian marriage. Baptism, perhaps one of Christianity's most prominent metaphors of transformation, was clearly a marker of success for the WMS. For believers, baptism signalled the washing away of sin and the clean (and pure) body that arose (symbolically, if not always literally) from the water. As applied to Chinese and Japanese women, this symbolic cleansing may have had even greater nationalistic implications as it was a marker of Christian brother/sisterhood. It involved a washing away of colour (and race) in an attempt to unite all believers into a colourless (i.e., white) family. That baptism was one of only seven categories used to identify residents and to track their progress indicates its importance to those who ran the Home. Interestingly, of all of the categories that were used for this purpose, baptism was perhaps used the least. In the Home's first fifteen years (1886–1911), only fifteen of the 156 residents were baptized. The rejection of baptism suggests that, while they were in the institution, Chinese and Japanese women were not simply passive subjects. They made significant choices, perhaps chief among them their rejection of baptism, despite its importance to Christianity and to the women who ran the Home.

Although the number of baptisms was relatively few, when they did occur, they were celebrated as markers of success and were used to justify requests for increases in funding to missions and missionaries themselves.[47] After two baptisms were reported in Vancouver, for instance, the advisory committee for the Home recommended a grant be given to hire a "native worker" in this area.[48] The Vancouver WMS group also focused on baptisms as markers of success. Again referencing the seed sowing metaphor, one report states: "first fruits are being gathered at Steveston and Sap [Sapperton], a woman having been baptized at each place."[49] Clearly, baptism signalled the maturation of the Other into the brother/sisterhood of Christ.

Baptism and Christian marriage, although markers of success, were also a form of mimicry. According to Bhabha, "in order to be effective, mimicry must continually produce its slippage, its excess, its difference." Baptism marked the Other as "almost the same, but not quite" at the same time that it marks the triumph and superiority of whiteness.[50] Japanese and Chinese converts could, as Bhabha suggests in another context, repeat the rituals of Christian baptism and marriage, but they could not represent them.[51] Domestication was always a partial project. Chinese and Japanese women might learn English and "English ways" but they could never *be* English, nor could they be considered fully Canadian, even if they were allowed to enter or remain within the nation's borders.

Despite the fact that Chinese and Japanese girls and women could never achieve or embody true whiteness, the success of mission work was measured according not only to the degree to which they could and did mimic Christian beliefs and the sacred performance of religion but also to the degree to which they could attain the trappings of "Canadian" (i.e., white) domesticity and citizenship. And so religious conversion continued to be the primary concern of those who ran the Home. Of those who were raised there, some went on to become missionaries in their own right, and it was often reported that young children who attended the kindergartens in Vancouver and the school at the Home influenced their parents' beliefs. In Vancouver, for instance, it was reported that "good work had been accomplished, perceptible in one way by the interest taken by the Chinese Mothers where formerly they seemed entirely indifferent."[52] In Victoria, "some of the parents [were] ready to acknowledge the Christ's love, as seen in their little ones."[53] Not only were children fertile grounds for the seeds of Christianity, they were also a way to gain access to parents – particularly mothers.

Norman Knowles documents a similar situation in his discussion of Japanese missions. He explains that the "superintendent of Japanese missions, Rev. F.W. Cassillis-Kennedy, viewed the arrival of women and the creation of family units as an ideal opportunity for evangelization." The superintendent is cited as saying that the children "will in ten years time be the parents of the new generation and if the Canadian church does her duty by the oriental [sic] children entrusted in her care now, the future generation will have a strong leaven of Christianity. Through the children the present day mothers and fathers can be influenced and some of them Christianized."[54] Here, the family unit is seen as a key site of intervention for the *Canadian* church to gain access to and to shape new domestic citizens. The Canadian church is feminized as it intervenes into the familial/domestic realm in order to reach these children who might not only influence their parents but also sow the (biological) seeds to produce a whole new generation of Christian Canadians. The seed-planting metaphor may be understood as indicating the ultimate transformation – that of barren soil into fruit. Thus transformation was not only about the overcoming of a congenital deviance but about the giving of life itself.

While missionaries routinely used the seed-planting metaphor, it took on a particularly gendered meaning when used in relation to women. The planting of seeds is reproductive work that is tied to the domestic realm. Given that this work was concerned with Chinese and Japanese *women,* domestic spaces were integral to these endeavours, as were the white women who would reign over them. The late nineteenth century, as well as the early twentieth century, marked a time in which clear gendered lines were drawn in public space. Especially in urban environments, men occupied the public sphere and women, for much of their adult lives, were restricted to the private sphere. As Barbara Riley argues, the idea of a "domestic science" was introduced as early as 1900 as a way to ensure not only that women remained in the home but also that they took their role there seriously.[55] Clearly the state was invested in policing the boundaries of the home as well as the behaviour within it. For many women, the only years in which they were able to work outside the home were those between finishing their formal education and getting married. Acceptable careers for these women were often limited to teaching, nursing, and other "caring" professions. Thus, becoming a missionary was, for some women, an opportunity to travel and to acquire independence that they might not otherwise have experienced. The Methodist WMS provided this opportunity for some.

The intention to form a missionary society for women was made public in the periodical known as the *Missionary Outlook* in January 1881.[56] The Methodist women made their intentions clear both here and, later, in the WMS constitution: they would bow to the authority of the male-dominated Missionary Society and "raise funds in such a way as [would] not lessen the General Income. Conflict of authority would be disastrous."[57] It was suggested that "any Branch Society ... devote its funds to the support of some existing interest" and that only when "the Branches become sufficiently numerous to warrant the organization of a General Society [could] the objects of such Society ... be widened and the funds be more completely at its own disposal."[58] In other words, only after the women proved themselves through grassroots organizations were they to be permitted to formalize their own. That the Methodist women in Canada were anxious to gain this autonomy was clear. In April of the same year, the "Woman's Work" section of the *Missionary Outlook* contained the following missive:

> We are waiting, as patiently as we can; for tidings that Women's Branch Societies have been established in many of our Circuits. What are the women of our churches doing in this matter? Almost every denomination in the United States has its Woman's Missionary Society. The Baptists and Presbyterians in Canada are following suit, and the Methodists are lagging behind. We utter no needless warning when we say that unless the Methodist Church bestirs herself, her pre-eminence in missionary zeal

and liberality will soon be a thing of the past. Other denominations will outstrip us in the race.[59]

This call to action highlights the women's desire not only to gain autonomy and formal recognition but also to establish denominational supremacy. Thus, the missionary "race" provided women with an outlet both to fulfill their desire for autonomy and to participate in the global race for souls.

Only one month later, the waiting was over. Although their grassroots organizing was not initially successful, the women were not willing to abandon their hope of forming a Woman's Missionary Society. They resolved that: "*Whereas,* experiment has proved that Branch Societies are not likely to be formed to any large extent, until there is a General Society through which they can operate directly in the Mission-field ... That immediate steps be taken to organize an Association to be known as The Woman's Missionary Society of the Methodist Church of Canada."[60] Despite hopes that branch societies would, for some time, fall under the purview of the larger missionary society, the WMS was formed to "employ suitable female labourers for Mission work as occasion may require; [and to] apportion the funds of the Society for the support of its agents."[61] Power was not to be absolute. According to Article 6 of the provisional constitution: "[The] Society shall work in harmony with the authorities of the Missionary Society of the Methodist Church of Canada and be subject to their approval in the employment and remuneration of Missionaries or other Agents, the designation of fields of labor, and in the general plans and designs of the work."[62] The WMS, its decisions and its finances, would come under the purview of the male-dominated Missionary Society. The gender segregation of missionary societies would influence the types of work that could be accomplished by each group.

The goals of the WMS, according to its constitution, were to "engage the efforts of Christian women in the evangelization of heathen women and children; to aid in sustaining female missionaries and teachers, or other special laborers in connection with mission work, in foreign and home fields; and to raise funds for the work of the Society."[63] Further, separate auxiliaries were to be formed with the same goals, with all money sent directly into the coffers of the General Society. Women's missionary societies, according to Henning, "counted more members than any other mission-movement and were among the largest reform organizations of the nineteenth century." In the United States, the "Methodist Episcopal Church alone counted 50,817 auxiliary members in 1878 and

123,488 in 1894." Likewise, in Canada, the WMS would soon have an active membership, and, like their American sisters, Canadian women would find in these organizations "important new professional opportunities. In mission boards and auxiliaries, women drafted constitutions, elected officers, raised funds and published magazines."[64] While many women were content to participate in auxiliary work at the local level (raising funds through membership drives or fundraisers, writing to and receiving letters from missionaries overseas, or putting together gift hampers for various home missions), others took on more active roles in the women's branch of the General Society. This sometimes afforded them opportunities for extensive travel to oversee Home mission work across Canada and to report to the board. Still others took on the role of missionary, travelling extensively to foreign fields with the goal of evangelizing the "heathen races."

But foreign missionary work was not a career that was accessible to all. Potential candidates had to meet several stringent requirements. According to the WMS constitution, a missionary candidate had to meet seven criteria: (1) she had to believe herself to be called by God into foreign mission work; (2) her ability to work as a missionary in a foreign field had to be demonstrated through her "Christian usefulness at *home*";[65] (3) she was required to "declare her intention to make foreign missionary work the service of her *effective years*, and agree to give at least five of these years of continuous service, as a *single woman*, to the work of the Woman's Missionary Society, unless prevented by ill health";[66] (4) she was required to provide references regarding her scholarship, and it was preferred that she have experience in either medicine or teaching; (5) she had to be between twenty-two and thirty years of age, although "intellectual training, with facility in acquiring languages, a remarkable ability for Christian work, may be considered as a sufficient deviation from this rule";[67] (6) she must show "financial and executive ability and power of adaptation to circumstances"; and (7) she must be deemed healthy.[68]

It is clear that becoming a missionary through the WMS was neither an easy nor a straightforward process. Its requirements meant that only women who were young, healthy, and formally educated (or at least have demonstrated intelligence) could apply to the missionary field overseas, and all of its criteria were in line with societal expectations regarding women's work. For instance, because only single women could apply, missionary work would not disrupt a woman's "natural" calling – that is, her home and family (yet, at the same time, women's missionary work was to be modelled on their "natural," or biologically endowed, abilities, which were also associated with home and family). Given these requirements, only a few privileged women were afforded the opportunity to travel overseas and to engage in WMS missionary work. For those who did not qualify, membership in a WMS auxiliary or advisory committee was often a way to participate, albeit from a distance. Participation in home missions also provided opportunities to women who did not qualify for foreign missions. For those who were not in excellent health or who were already past the age that was considered ideal for women missionaries, less glamorous and arguably less prestigious opportunities were to be found in home missions. The WMS sponsored a number of home missions before Reverend Starr approached it about taking on the Chinese Rescue Home.

In his entreaty to the WMS, Starr emphasized the importance of domestic spaces. He began with a description of the physical structure itself. The Home was to be "a one-story 8 room frame building situated upon Fredrick St. in close proximity to the parsonage ... This plainly and only partially furnished but withal comfortable and as rents run cheap."[69] So the Home was a plain and unremarkable place but one that was presumed to offer safety, hope, and, most important, domesticity. Despite its humble aesthetic value, the domestic realm was to be a safe haven, insulated from the dangerous conditions outside it.[70] It was only as a domestic space that the Home could fulfill its goals.

It was important that the Home prepare the girls/women for "household duties in case of marriage."[71] Starr reported that there were seven girls in the domicile between the ages of eight and nineteen and that there were two more, ages seven and nine, whom he hoped would be re-rescued. Another woman had been married to an "industrious Christian Chinaman who helped to rescue her" and had provided her with a good home. [72] Training the girls/women in household duties was meant to prepare them for their hopeful destinies as wives of "Christian Chinamen," but it also had the added benefit of making them more marketable as domestic servants. Inclusion could only come after conversion – a change manifest not only by a profession of faith but also by the subject's adherence to Christianity *and* middle-class values.[73] In the Home, these values were feminized as they came in the form of domesticity. It is impossible to discount the usefulness of this training to the institution itself as it meant that the Home would have no need to hire someone to do household chores.

Given his focus on the domestic realm, it is not surprising that Starr appealed to women to run the Home. In his letter, Starr implores the WMS to take an active and important role in the running of "'The Home' for rescued Chinese girls in Victoria." The outlook of this fledgling work, he said, was "dreary enough unless the Women of the Methodist Church in Canada come to the Home's Help."[74] It is significant that Starr did not appeal to the General Missionary Society but directly to its women's branch. Although the Home was founded by Starr and Gardiner, it was clear from the outset that reforming women was women's work. Even before the WMS took over the management of the Home, a matron had been hired to deal with all aspects of the domestic realm and of domesticity itself.

Not only would white women significantly affect the lives of women in the institution, they would also influence the type and degree of state support the Home would receive. In his letter, Starr describes the withdrawal of state support to the Home. The first "rescue" was accomplished by Gardiner, whom Starr described as a deeply religious man, a son of missionaries, and himself a "missionary of the Methodist Church among the Chinese."[75] This rescue was of a nine-year-old slave girl, who "had her wrists broken, her back whipped until it ran sores and the sores irritated and burned with lighted tapers by an old hag of a procuress because the girl failed to bring in as much money by soliciting and prostituting herself as her procuress or keeper thought she should."[76] Gardiner, with the help of the chairman of the Police Committee, rescued both the nine-year-old and a second girl. As a result, word spread of a "'Jesus Man,' ... who would help them away from their slavery and protect them." However, after this first rescue, police refused to assist Gardiner and he was forced to rely on "friendly Chinamen" to "make an appointment with the girls and spirit them away."[77] Once the women of the WMS took over, however, the state's support of and interventions into the Home increased, indicating the state's protective stance towards white women and its support and recognition of women's authority in the domestic realm. Their moral reach, however, extended beyond the domestic realm.

For many women engaged in this type of outreach, benevolent work was not only about imposing moral order on other women but also about providing moral guidance to white men.[78] In the West, home mission projects, as Pascoe maintains, "began to symbolize, not just female benevolence, but also female opposition to the male-dominated social order that characterized emerging western cities."[79] Starr's discussion of the chief of police's refusal to help likely would have signalled a need for the moral authority of women and, therefore, may have encouraged the participation of women in the administration of Chinese rescue. Thus, through the fracturing of the moral authority associated with whiteness, white women were interpellated by a call for their special brand of moral authority.[80] By shifting the domain of morality to the domestic, Starr raised the moral authority of Christian women over that of men. This provided the WMS women with an opportunity to increase their authority both inside and outside the private sphere.

The job of matron was a highly responsible position: as an institutional setting the Home required a keen manager. Instead of emphasizing her managerial role, however, Starr described the matron in distinctly gendered language. The requirements for the matron were linked to professions that were deemed suitable for women; mothering, teaching, nursing, and missionary work. As mother of the Home, the matron was to act as both housekeeper and moral authority, training the young girls and women to be "good women." As teacher, she was required to ensure that the female residents were schooled in the English language, and her missionary work would require her to Christianize and then train interested residents to become Bible Women. Not only was the role of matron limited – if not in actual power then certainly in definition – to traditional female roles, but these roles were to be transmitted with alacrity to the Chinese and Japanese residents. It was not just any white woman who could fill this position: she would have to be someone who fulfilled religious, racial, and gendered expectations. If the matron was to be the citizen after whom Chinese and Japanese bodies were to be modelled, then she had to be the epitome of Victorian womanhood.

This chapter discusses the investment in building a white province and nation, as illustrated through my discussion of two Royal Commissions. However, Starr's letter compels us to consider that the influence of whiteness, Christianity, and gender upon the nation was much more complex than readings of the Royal Commissions reports might suggest. In his letter, Starr offers several suggestions for running the Home, should the WMS agree to take control of it. The first suggestion regards the selection of a "good Matron," the current matron being "not as tidy as she might be and ... not [having] the ability to give the girls even the rudiments of English education."[81] Instead, Starr contends, the Home requires a "whole souled warm hearted consecrated Christian woman ... [so that] these girls could be speedily Christianized and converted."[82] In this single suggestion, it is clear that the institution is to be defined by four important pillars. The privileging of nation is evident in Starr's discussion of how Chinese girls and women were to be transformed from foreign into domestic. This required a "whole souled" woman who was fully devoted to the Home. The institution, therefore, was to be not simply an employer but also a calling. This is further emphasized through Starr's use of the word "consecrated," implying not only Christian belief but also a deep commitment. The matron's ability to educate the "girls" in English is an indication of the privileging of whiteness and hints at a hierarchy and fracturing of whiteness itself. Further, the future matron is required to be warm-hearted, signifying for her an emotive, and thus feminized, role.

In Victoria, the interventions of white men and women into the lives of Chinese and Japanese women were directed at their domestication. First, Chinese and Japanese women, through Christian salvation, were to be made into domestic citizens. Although no one offered them full or unconditional acceptance into the nation, Christian salvation, it was argued, would transform these women into models of white Victorian womanhood and thus allow them to stay within the nation. Second, women were also domesticated in another sense of the word. Japanese and Chinese women were initially viewed as domestically delinquent. Seen as sexually deviant, they were constructed as existing outside proper (domestic) womanhood. Their presence in the (sexual) marketplace needed to be controlled and managed through their re-placement and training within the domestic realm. The Home was a project that would both challenge and reinforce what it meant to be a woman in British Columbia. As the next chapter suggests, the physical spaces of the Home constructed the type of work that women could pursue while also shaping the various aspirations of white, Chinese, and Japanese women.

3
Crossing the Threshold

Interrogating the Space and Place of Victoria's Chinese Rescue Home

In April 1908, the proposed construction of a new building for the Chinese Rescue Home was discussed at length in the *British Colonist*. The building, it was suggested, would be "modern in every respect." It would be impressive and, of paramount importance, it would be a domestic space. The building, it was proposed, would have a large laundry, a kitchen, a parlor, a playroom, a sewing room, and dormitory-style bedrooms for the "girls."[1] Although it was to be constructed as a domestic space, the Home was seen by those who ran it as much more than a private home. According to Ida Snyder, the matron of the Home in 1908, the work done in the institution was more effective at stemming prostitution trafficking than were the laws found in the United States. A representative of the Home explained to the press that, when members of the Royal Commission on Chinese and Japanese Immigration (1902) had visited the home they had "admitted that we have checked the traffic far more efficiently than could possibly have been done by any paid agent for the government, in as much as we train the girls and women to be useful members of society."[2] The Home's physical form was crucial to the success of this work.

While the Chinese Rescue Home built on and challenged contemporaneous discourses of the "foreign body" and its relation to domestic spaces, its physical structure supplemented it, especially with regard to the ways in which it challenged the binaries of foreign and domestic. Crossing the threshold of the Home allowed white women access to foreign bodies within the national (domestic) context. But it did more than this. The Home constituted a threshold *between* the foreign and the domestic in much the same way that it challenged the public/private binary. Although the Home was formulated as a domestic space, it was also an institutional setting. The material spaces of the house produced the Home as what Blunt refers to as both a "material and an affective space."[3] Because of this, the Home provides space for an analysis of how gender, especially as conflated with motherhood and family, acted as a discursive viaduct through which its spatiality was transformed into embodied practice.

According to Shelley Mallett, "home is variously described in the literature as conflated with or related to house, family, haven, self, gender, and journeying."[4] Inspired by her observations, in this chapter I tease apart several of these concepts as a way of foregrounding the importance of the domestic realm in the work of the Woman's Missionary Society. I use both structuralist and poststructuralist approaches to examine the spaces of the Home as material and symbolic spaces of reproduction and resistance, both of which were bound up with women's moral authority. I analyze both house (physical space) and home (discursive space), making connections between racialized and gendered spaces and discourses. An analysis of four images of the Home and those who lived within it grounds my later discursive analysis in a more material one. I examine not only photographs but also the architectural design of the house in order to elucidate the links between meaning making and material practices. By examining Home record books, advisory committee minutes, and official WMS reports, I draw links between these physical spaces and the types of discourses and practices found within them.

I offer a genealogy of the Home that operates, as Foucault describes, "on a field of entangled and confused parchments, on documents that have been scratched over and recopied many times." These documents are used to record events, "not in order to trace the gradual curve of their evolution but to isolate the different scenes where they engage in different roles."[5] My goal is to trace the disjuncture, discontinuity, and multiple meanings of the Home. Instead of tracing a linear narrative through time, I interrogate connections and ambivalences through an examination of multiple sources.

As a material and symbolic space, the Home was certainly neither a new nor a unique type of institution. Protestant women in the American West joined together in the 1870s "to try to establish female moral authority."[6] Rescue homes were one of the projects that allowed white women a degree of power and moral authority that could not be obtained elsewhere. Modelled after an idealized notion of the Victorian Christian home, these rescue homes did not openly disrupt the notion of separate spheres; rather, they simply extended the "natural" influence of women as wives and mothers. In this manner, these homes extended women's power in ways that did not challenge the power or authority of white men. White women's power was mostly limited to the power they had over racialized women and, to a lesser extent, racialized men. In order to understand how this power played out in real spaces, I use Lefebvre's spatial triad of conceived, perceived, and lived spaces to frame my discussion.[7] Although each theorization of space is unique, they must be understood as being in dialogue with one another during the production of material and symbolic spaces.

Conceiving Mother-land: "Constructing" the Home as a Signifying Mechanism

Over the last decade, the home has become a site of intervention for many scholars, including cultural geographers, historians, anthropologists, and sociologists. Duncan and Lambert describe the home as "perhaps the most emotive of geographical concepts, inextricable from that of self, family, nation, sense of place, and sense of responsibility toward those who share one's place in the world."[8] This was certainly the case with regard to the Chinese Rescue Home. The house, as a physical manifestation of home, was tied to family, empire, and nation. It was a conceived space, planned and ordered in very particular ways. How the institution was constructed was important as it was the space of the Home that allowed for the crossing of both physical and symbolic thresholds. The house itself stood as a gendered material site and metaphor of empire (motherland) and of family (mother). Although it is impossible to completely separate "house" from "home," house refers to the physical building (structure) in which members of a home (usually a family) reside. In defining "home," I build on a standard definition: "[the home is] the focus of one's domestic attention."[9] The home is simultaneously the space towards which one's domestic attention is directed and the *act* of directing that attention. A house (the structure) only becomes a home once domestic attention is directed towards it through action (agency) and/or through language or ideas (discourse). Although it is clear that home and house are mutually constitutive and thus impossible to fully separate, an analytical distinction can identify the ways in which structure shapes discourse and action and how these, in turn, helped to shape the "construction" of the structure.

Pascoe argues that "home mission women interpreted the 'home' as the ideal Christian home of Victorian rhetoric" and that "women had a special 'mission' to sustain Protestant moral values by rescuing female victims and teaching them to emulate the family and gender roles of white, middle-class Victorian culture."[10] Building on this point, I examine the house as the materiality of home spaces in order to uncover how the physical space of the home played a role in furthering the aforementioned goals. The spaces of the Home organized and enabled certain social practices, allowing possibilities for what could and could not take place within its walls. It was precisely its materiality that influenced how and by whom it would be run as well as who could reside within it. In other words, the building produced *meanings* for those who encountered and resided within that space, including the emotive and affective ties that the idea of "home" elicited at this time.

Little is known about the first structure that accommodated the Home. The only information available pertains to its size, indicating that the initial structure was a small, "one-story 8 room frame building situated upon Fredrick St."[11] In January 1888, the WMS moved its residents to the house shown below (see Figure 3). It was from this house, at 100 Cormorant Street, that the WMS would operate the rescue mission for the next twenty years. Although very little was written about how this site was chosen, it is

FIGURE 3   Chinese Rescue Home.
Source: Image C-07913 courtesy of the Royal BC Museum, BC Archives

clear from the picture below that it was originally constructed as a "home." While it is probable that the WMS chose to use a house, as opposed to a more institutional type of building, because amenities such as bedrooms, cooking, and cleaning facilities would already be present, the decision to pursue this site and not another was neither inconsequential nor accidental.

In the earliest report of the institution, Reverend Starr suggested that, should the WMS take on this project, there was "a house better located and in every way better adapted for a 'Home' which the owner would divide into the compartments necessary."[12] What is significant here is that Starr does not suggest a "building" but, rather, specifically refers to a house. A house, according to Starr, is "in every way better adapted for a 'Home.'"[13] While this use of the word "Home" may not seem surprising given that, throughout the document, Starr refers to the rescue mission as "The Home," this is the only place in the document where he refers explicitly to the mission as *a home*. Here, he is not referring to the actual institution but to its function. There seems to be no question that the more appropriate space for rescued *women* was in the home. According to Adele Perry, it was not uncommon for men in early British Columbia to live in group households. However, the conditions in these households were very different from those in the Home. Men who shared a residence with other men were more likely to live in rough bunkhouses, tents, or cabins, where domesticity took the form of simple survival. Cooking was often done outdoors over fires, and cleaning took place on the river's banks.[14] A house for women, however, was always already imbued with the discourses and practices of home and domesticity as its physical structure was mobilized to produce gendered ways of behaving.

The house shown in the photo above, taken on May 24, 1906 (Figure 3), is well maintained and has a simple charm, with its wide decorative veranda and the ivy-covered posts flanking the front entranceway. The colonial style is a reminder of the historical legacy of empire, the wide veranda and decorative finishing reminiscent of Victorian values of home and hearth. The small picket fence in front of the house is most likely a later addition. In 1898, a motion was passed to replace the original fence and to put strands of barbed wire on top of the new one to prevent escape.[15] On the fence bordering the left side of the house, remnants of what appears to be this barbed wire remain. The remnants of a carceral past are abridged but not entirely erased from view – a reminder, perhaps, of how tenuous the residents' freedom really was.

While the house itself is the central feature of the photo, spilling out onto the front veranda and into the street are its residents and staff. Unlike some of the later photos, which resemble school pictures, this photo has a less formal or institutional feel. Although the women and children are properly dressed, they are lined up somewhat haphazardly, much like they might have been in an informal family photo. The children are not organized by age cohort as they would have been in a school photo; rather, they are foregrounded, with the women taking their place outside the house but always in its shadow. Thus, the photo highlights the house as a place to which the women were tied, sometimes harnessed there by the babies or small children they carried. What the photo also highlights are the possibilities embodied in the children who stand not only outside the house's shadow but outside the fence altogether. As is clear from this photo, the building that housed the Home was far from institutional in form. It resembled, in every aspect, a home space.

Only two years after this photo was taken, on December 8, 1908, the women and girls were moved to a new and larger facility, built on the same lot as the first one on Cormorant Street.[16] The new building was designed by prominent architects Hooper and Watkins and was built for the WMS for the purpose of housing the Chinese Rescue Home, which was renamed after the move. The minutes of the November 1909 meeting of the advisory committee explain: "In view of the fact that we have Japanese as well as Chinese in the Home, and that the term 'Rescue' has a tendency to prejudice certain classes, especially the merchants, against our work, it was proposed by Mrs. Snyder that the name be changed from 'Chinese Rescue Home' to 'Oriental Home and School.'"[17] Although the idea of a rescue mission had lost favour with the merchants, the word "home" obviously had not. Significantly, the word "home" was the only remnant of the original name.

If the previous house was reminiscent of colonial times, the third house, built expressly for the purpose of housing the residents of the Home, had a much grander appeal. This house, which was to become the home of the Oriental Home and School until it closed,[18] was designed in the style of the Georgian manor home. By the time the house was being planned and constructed in 1907 and 1908, Georgian architecture had long since gone out of fashion. However, it is most likely that its appeal was not just a matter of fashion, and perhaps not even of function. The appeal of Georgian architecture was emotional. Most popular during the eighteenth century, the Georgian manor not only elicited memories of colonial conquest but was also a material reference to the metropole.[19] There were different types of global connections at play within the Home: in this case, these connections had to do with its ties to England. The rescue home was certainly not the only example of Georgian architecture

FIGURE 4   Oriental Home and School.
Source: Image C-07927 courtesy of the Royal BC Museum, BC Archives

in Victoria, but the symbolism of its design was, in some ways, unique when compared to that of other Georgian houses.

Another Georgian-style house located in the area was the historic Craigflower Manor (See Figure 5). Built in Victoria in the 1850s as part of the Hudson's Bay Company's (HBC) commitment to supporting colonization, this Georgian manor house had direct ties to British colonization. Built almost fifty years after what is now recognized as the end of the Georgian era of architecture, this house was styled to reflect strong ties to the metropole as evinced through the HBC's colonial ties to England. Although Victorian architecture, the architectural "fashion" during this period, would also have signalled the HBC's ties to the metropole, the use of Georgian architecture was most likely the result of both cultural and aesthetic factors. First, a certain amount of architectural "lag" was to be expected in Canada as much of Victoria's architectural aesthetic was influenced by American and English design. As Segger notes, design was often borrowed from the United States through the transplantation of American and British architects as well as through their architectural travels, especially to the south.[20] Second, this lag may reflect more than a reluctance to embrace changes in architectural styles. The shift to Victorian

FIGURE 5   Craigflower Manor.
Source: Image A-01435 courtesy of the Royal BC Museum, BC Archives

architecture in the United States was reflective of a period of "explosive change. ... the growth of democracy and nationalism, technology and the transformation of old agricultural economies, the movement of people to cities and across oceans."[21] It was a reflection not only of change but also of prosperity. "Stick Style" homes, popular across the border in Seattle during this period, were deliberately more decorative than were Georgian-style homes. In Victoria, however, it seems that nationalism was less about prosperity and independence from the metropole than was the case in Seattle. An infant city, Victoria depended on the motherland in ways that cities such as Seattle did not. Thus, Craigflower Manor's architecture reflected the colonial moment as embodied by Georgian architecture.

That the Chinese Rescue Home, built over fifty years later, was also styled after a Georgian manor home seems more surprising. The Home was funded by a charitable organization, not a colonial company. One must ask, then, why the same style of architecture chosen for Craigflower Manor, which was now a full century out of fashion, was also chosen as the architectural design for the Chinese Rescue Home. The answer is the same in both cases: to establish links to the metropole. Architecturally, Craigflower Manor was tied to England through the HBC's economic relations with that country, while the Chinese Rescue Home was tied to England through moral imperatives. The material form of the Georgian manor was the result of WMS women's investment in establishing a Victorian moral authority. The Georgian era directly preceded the Victorian era and was a time of Christian revival. For Methodists, the Georgian era marked the period in which the denomination of Methodism had its roots. What this house represented was not only Victorian moral values associated with the home but also the values of Methodism, which predated the Victorian era. Thus, both the motherland of empire and the fatherland of religion were "married" through the physical structure of the Chinese Rescue Home. Christian aspirations, identity, and practice were manifested in the space of the Home. Investments in empire were literally built into constructions of the nation and constructions of the home. The Georgian manor house may have conjured up ties to both colonialism and to religious roots, but it also conveyed something more.

A closer comparison of these two Georgian houses also reveals a few obvious differences. While the Georgian home that was built as part of the HBC project had strong architectural features, the Home took these features and intensified them. The box-like style of the Georgian manor house was exaggerated, as was its grandeur. Instead of being constructed out of wood, the Home was constructed out of brick, perhaps signalling the strength of the commitment of those who built it. What is more remarkable, however, is how overstated the Home was, both in its size and in its detail. While the double porch, dormers, balustrades, and decorative trim did make the house more homey, these features also connoted wealth. Given that this was a Christian charitable institution, the scale was overly extravagant. The records, however, suggest that the exterior of the house was not intended to represent wealth but, rather, the scale of benevolence. In the Home's 1907–8 annual report, Matron Ida Snyder comments as follows:

> We express our gratitude for the beautiful and roomy new home and school which is being built for us, and are looking forward with pleasure to the time when it will be ready. I am sure any of you who are privileged to come west and visit our school will be proud of the building, and we workers hope that the work will grow to all the possibilities of the building.[22]

She saw this house not only as a place of hospitality but also as representing the increased potential for evangelistic work. In this way, space reflected and shaped the aspirations of the women who ran the mission.

However, this house represented far more than Christian benevolence. The Home's brick walls and high fences did more than keep the residents sheltered; they also represented safety and sanctuary. Crossing the threshold into the *house* meant entering a home. The decorative trim and the plethora of windows transformed what might otherwise have been seen as an institution into a home. Thus, the Home's spatiality functioned as both a mode of governance and a space of opportunity for white, Japanese, and Chinese women. First, the house represented the Victorian ideals of home and family – ideals that the women sought to instill in their "inmates." In this way, the Home worked to govern and to inculcate Victorian ideals of familial relationships into the residents while also reinforcing the importance of these ideals to the women in charge. Second, the construction of a home space also functioned as a mode of governance by reproducing racialized, gendered, and classed roles. This was achieved through the institution's function of training Chinese and (later) Japanese women as wives and/or servants. Last, the Home functioned as a site for housing the aspirations of both white women and their charges. It served as a sanctuary not just for the Chinese and Japanese women who sought shelter there but also for white women who sought to escape the confines of the private sphere. White women and their Japanese and Chinese charges crossed the threshold into this pseudo-domestic realm for many reasons. And, although their choices were limited by the spatial context of the Home, many found room within its walls to internalize the transformations imposed on them, learning new skills in the process.

Hearth, Home, and Motherhood Perceived

The physical space of the Home facilitated certain roles and was open to only certain residents. Razack explains that perceived space "emerges out of spatial practices, the everyday routines and experiences that install specific social spaces ... Through these everyday routines, the space comes to perform something in the social order, permitting certain actions and prohibiting others."[23] Thus, the numerous discourses of house and home allowed for the reproduction of racialized and gendered roles as well as for their potential subversion. If the Home functioned much like the private sphere, both materially and metaphorically, how did white women engage the public sphere? Metonymy facilitated the crossing of thresholds between the public and the private realms. Metonymy is "a figure of speech consisting of the use of the name of one thing for that

of another of which it is an attribute or with which it is associated."[24]
While the house signalled a deep and enduring relationship between the
metropole and the colony, its reference to *home* metonymically signalled
another gendered relationship, that of mother and child. The distinction
between house and home was complex and often difficult to make. While
these two terms are often conflated in the texts that I examined, with
both "house" and "home" representing the material building, it is the
word "home" that conjures up associations/attributes that reproduced
gendered relations. The home was an affective space that influenced and,
in some cases, dictated the types of behaviours and emotions that were
thought acceptable and that were to be cultivated.

Despite the fact that, in the records, the residents are often referred to
as "inmates," they are also considered to be part of a larger family. These
discourses of filial relations are manifest in the photograph below (Figure 6), which represents some of the early workers and residents of the
Home. The formality of the photo, with a backdrop of trees and nature,
a decorative carpet, and a plant to the right, suggests that the Home
did not mirror an institutional setting but, in fact, was modelled on a
familial/domestic setting. Taken in 1910, this photo represents the ideals
of the Victorian home and family. The modest dress of the white workers is evident on a smaller scale in the young women and children in the

Figure 6   Home and School Group.
Source: Image C-07926 courtesy of the Royal BC Museum, BC Archives

photo, thereby highlighting the influence of the former. The same holds true for the hairstyles and postures. The three white women on the right of the photo tower above their subjects, clearly representing authority. The only other white woman in the group is shown seated, with an infant cradled in her arms, representing and modelling motherly behaviours and expectations. However, this "family" also subverts the values of Victorian morality by depicting the mixing of races.

British Columbia at this time was marked by anti-Asian sentiment and fears of mixed-race contact, and this photo stands in stark opposition to this. In his influential discussion of colonialism, particularly regarding the relationship between sex, culture, and race, Robert Young describes colonialism as a "desiring machine" that "produced its own darkest fantasy – the unlimited and ungovernable fertility of 'un-natural' unions."[25] The resulting "hybrid" of such unions was evidence of the ambivalence of discourses of race, which simultaneously marked out the Other as an object of both repulsion and desire. Framing the hybrid as a product of this "dark fantasy" provides a compelling departure from contact narratives that focus on inclusion and exclusion. Here, the Other is transformed from the Other not into the self but into the hybrid, into something different. The missionary's relationship with the Other had to move beyond contact in order for such a transformation to take place. Thus, in the case of the Home, the relationships it housed were not a product of the "dark fantasy" of colonialism but, rather, of its "white fantasy." This fantasy entailed a non-sexual relationship that would (re)produce the racial hybrid in the white image not through birth but rather through a religious re-birth and transformation. The racial Other was to be introduced into the family of God through the adoption of a white mother and a celestial father. This was best accomplished within the realm of domesticity associated with a home-like institution. Domesticity was tied not only to women's moral authority but also to their (re)productive capacity. The home (and the Home), therefore, was the ideal space in which to produce new Christian subjects.

The physical space of the institution shaped the types of (familial) relationships that could be formed within its walls. Examples of this are abundant in the many familial references in the minutes of the advisory committee, publications written about WMS work, and WMS formal reports. Although the Home family may have threatened ideals of whiteness as the foundation of the Victorian (and Canadian) ideal family, heteronormativity remained its foundation. In the absence of a man, a surrogate father stood as head of the house: the family metaphor was completed by situating God as father to all. Thus, the racial Other had the potential to become reborn not through sexual mixing but through adoption. This blended family entailed a partial erasure of race, a washing of the racialized soul that made it "white as snow." Of course, adoption into the family of God certainly did not mean equality between Chinese/Japanese women and their white "sisters." Racial equality would have meant that the work of the WMS was no longer necessary. Regardless, references to God's family and Christian sister/motherhood are pervasive in WMS documents and reports. One report, for instance, claims: "We try to impress on all that this is God's Home, and that we must act as His children."[26]

That God stood as head of the house was due to the fact that the male figure in the Home was limited to a celestial one. Indeed, any adult male was seen to be out of place in this realm of domesticity. The sanctity of the home was constantly at risk from outside (male) threats to the women's sexual purity. According to Victorian familial ideals, the only acceptable male in the home was husband, father, or brother. Given that no blood relationship tied these women together, any male was viewed by the matrons as a potential sexual threat to those who were not daughter, sister, or wife. Thus, the sexuality of the girls and women was governed and protected through the institution's expulsion or rejection of male children once they were a certain age. While the WMS did, on occasion, accept male children into the Home, they did so only reluctantly and circumspectly. For instance, one father applied to have his children, "four boys and four girls between the ages of 2 months and 11 years,"[27] admitted as their mother had recently died. In the agreement that the father signed, he "promised to leave the boys in the Home two years and the girls 6 years at the close of which period he was at liberty to take them to China with him for a visit."[28] The advisory committee asked that a new agreement be drawn up, whereby "the four girls and the boys of 3 yrs and 7 yrs be admitted"; however, it was "thought unwise to admit the eldest boy, he being ten years of age."[29] Despite this, the oldest child, a girl aged eleven, was to stay in residence for six years. Likewise, in another case, Joe,[30] two and a half years old, was admitted with his two sisters after it was determined that their "mother was bad." Although his older sisters stayed in the Home until the ages of twenty-one and twenty-five, respectively, Joe was required to leave at age eleven because he was deemed "too old for the Home."[31] These gendered decisions were clearly based on the perceived need to govern and protect the sexuality of the young women. And so domestic space was preserved through the exclusion of all males, save very young children. This male threat also points to the ambivalence around Chinese and Japanese femininity. Although many painted these women as threats to men and boys, in WMS reports they are depicted as vulnerable and in need of protection, especially the younger ones.

These familial relationships should not be reduced to religious discourses of God as father and all others as His children. There is much more to these familial discourses than Christianity. To begin with, they are highly gendered. White women were aspiring to model their Victorian family values for their "inmates." Further, in all likelihood, the sense of family provided Japanese and Chinese women with a sense of community and inclusion, which may have tempered the fact that they were also being tightly regulated. The term "family" was frequently applied to the residents of the Home. The photo below (Figure 7), for instance, is labelled "The Oriental Home Family." Interestingly, as highlighted in Chapter 2, Reverend John Edward Starr, writing to the WMS, used the familial discourse of sisterhood in his petition to this group. Yet, once the WMS took over the running of the institution, there was a shift to a different type of familial discourse, that of mother and children, marking a new hierarchy of power.

Mothering, although it was of vital importance to those who ran the Home, was not a discourse that was evenly or consistently used. Nor was it grounded in common sense understandings of biology or nature. Here, motherhood was deployed as a mode of governance, affording white women a way to reproduce Victorian womanhood in their charges.[32] Maternalism was both a justification of white women's roles and a skill

FIGURE 7　Oriental Home Family.
Source: Image C-07922 courtesy of the Royal BC Museum, BC Archives

that was to be instilled into the girls and women in the Home. Discourses of motherhood, however, were not always straightforward. When one resident, Jeanie,[33] requested that her child be allowed to enter the Home, the discussion that ensued was concerned only with whether or not her husband would be willing to pay board for the child.[34] In fact, when Matron Ida Snyder "failed to make any satisfactory arrangements with Jeanie's husband about their little daughter," the child was not allowed to enter.[35]

There was no discussion of the ethics of keeping a mother from her child or of the naturalness of her desire to be near her. Perhaps this was because the Home had become surrogate mother to Jeanie, thus marking her not as mother but as child. Alternatively, it may have been assumed that motherhood was something only white women *naturally* experienced, making it necessary for them to model it to their racialized charges. What is clear is that this woman's role as mother was secondary to the cost of allowing her child to enter the residence. The final decision may have been due to the advisory committee's recommendation, but it was enforced by the determined Matron Snyder. Although she was more drawn to working with children than with the more challenging adult women, Snyder refused to let the child enter without knowing that her board would be paid.[36]

It was almost a year before records showed that Jeanie's daughter had been allowed to enter the Home: "Mrs. Snyder reported that [Jeanie's] little girl was an inmate of the Home and that her father paid $2 dollars a month towards her board."[37] Her admittance set an important precedent, and another child was soon reunited with her mother on the same terms. Although the payment of board seemed to be the deciding factor in both of these cases, the matron provided an additional rationale: "the presence of the little children made the place seem more *natural* and home like for the elder girls beside it gave them an opportunity of training them in the care of children."[38] The matron's reference to the naturalness of children in a home is interesting for two reasons. First, she did not state that the presence of children *made* the place more natural and homelike but that it made it *seem* more natural and homelike. This distinction clearly shows that despite efforts to make the house a home, the latter could only be created by the labour of Chinese, Japanese, and white women. Second, and related to the first point, the admittance of these children was intended to facilitate training young women in mothering. In other words, mothering was not understood as inherent in the biological relationship between mother and child but, rather, as a Western trait that needed to be imparted to the residents in order to complete their transformations.[39]

The familial language of mother and home is apparent in WMS reports as early as 1896. In an article entitled "Chinese in British Columbia" the author reports that the "Girl's Home in Victoria has had a year of checkered experiences, as to numbers, but has abundantly shown the value of its existence, if only as the gathering place for the spiritual nurture of those who have married from it, and who constantly need and receive a *motherly* oversight."[40] Likewise, two years later, the WMS reported that "unremitting care and toil have been the portion of the Home-Mother, but she has not been without evidence of the Lord's presence and acceptance of her labours."[41] Here, the discourses of both home and Christian motherhood are joined, bringing together the institutional and the familial. "Unremitting care and toil" echoes discourses of the Victorian wife and mother. It also makes clear that this type of mothering was not seen as natural but as a labour that required constant and continuous care.

In 1899–1900, once Ida Snyder took on the role of matron, the family metaphor was often used. Snyder, a no-nonsense woman, accepted the challenges of running the Home, often employing unconventional techniques. For instance, Rosemary Gagan recounts a story of how Snyder developed her own strategy for weaning one Chinese woman off opium. Her approach was to substitute cigarettes for opium, which she then rationed so that she could gradually wean the woman off the tobacco. Her strategy worked well until the woman stole Snyder's secret supply. She was punished by Snyder's consigning "the remaining tobacco to the stove."[42] Despite her abrupt and strict demeanour, Snyder refers to the women in the institution as family. In 1898, she reports that there was only one girl in residence when she arrived but that "in January, [she] had a family of nine, six of them Chinese, and three Japanese."[43] Sometimes her references to family are not so endearing. "The year began with seven and closes with eleven inmates," Snyder begins in her 1902–3 report. She continues her tallying of the inmates but exchanges her carceral language for a more familial one, stating that "there have been five additions to our *family.*"[44] The following year, Snyder again opens her report with a reference to family, reporting that "we have a family of thirteen dependent upon us for protection."[45] Here, family is certainly not about sisterly relationships but, rather, about a mother and her dependents. The family had become a site and a practice of governance. This trend of reporting family size continued to be an annual practice for many years to come. In fact, in some cases, the annual reports take on the tone of family letters, reporting the seemingly mundane and private, rather than institutional reports.

The 1906–7 report begins as follows: "We took our family of thirteen out camping for six weeks and found the tent very acceptable, and especially so as tents could not be rented here this summer."[46] The 1913–14 report, written by Matron Maggie Smith, closes with: "We have all been kept busy with our large family of happy children, and kept happy ourselves."[47] Again, the discourse of mother and children is prevalent, if not entirely clear. Although the matron refers only to the children in the Home, in 1913, of the twenty-five residents admitted, 40 percent were women over the age of nineteen. Clearly, infantilizing the residents helped to secure the metaphor of mother and children as a reality. But family was not simply a discourse that was employed to describe the residents of the Home: it was also a device used to justify regulating and placing the women and children there in the first place.

In the 1909–10 report, Matron Snyder tells the story of a young suicide victim who never made it to the Home, describing her as a "poor little homesick, motherless waif! Taken from her own family and sold from one family and city to another till death set her free."[48] The matron highlights the case of this young "motherless waif" not to emphasize the dangers and traumas she faced but, rather, to highlight the importance of the institution in sparing others from this same fate. Without the intervention of institutions such as the Home, loss of family, she implies, especially of one's mother, is tantamount to death. Having a family member to care for them is not considered to be enough for young children. A father, for instance, despite his familial relationship to his children, was not viewed as an appropriate caregiver by those who ran the Home, even when he had a home and access to the necessary financial resources for their care. A mother, particularly a "good mother," was key. In homes in which a "good mother" could not be found, the Home became a substitute. This privileging of white women as appropriate guardians is interesting given that, during this period, the courts often deemed the father to have ultimate rights and responsibilities over his children and their mothers (see Chapter 6).

The discourses of motherhood and home often went hand in hand. As the following report highlights, those who ran the Home took motherhood very seriously. Families, as Strong-Boag suggests, "have always proved sites of negotiation ... Family relationships have attracted attention from clergy, doctors, psychologists, social workers, and politicians."[49] Fitness to parent was based on a diverse set of criteria taken from experts who promoted the ideal of the nuclear family. Having (or being) a biological mother was not enough. According to the 1923–24 report, "the

Children's Aid Society placed in our Home two little Chinese girls whose mother is entirely unfitted to be their guardian."[50] While the report does not indicate why the mother was deemed unfit, Matron Annie T. Martin clearly identified having a "bad mother" as being a worse fate for a child than having a dead mother.

> Our hearts went out in a very special manner to these poor little help-less ones, who cannot yet realize the tragedy of their home. An orphan with sweet home memories is blessed indeed beside these *worse than motherless children*, whose memory of home must always bring shame and resentment – Truly the Lord is mindful of His own, for it is marvelous how pure these little ones seem to have been kept. They remind one of water-lilies growing in a stagnant pool, which, in spite of their sordid surround-ings, retain their snowy whiteness.[51]

It was only through the benevolence of the Lord that these "water-lilies" could remain pure in the presence of a mother who, like the stag-nant pool, was deemed unclean and thus unworthy of motherhood. It was the Christian God who was the true father of the child, the flower plucked from the stagnant pool leaving no ripple as it was transplanted from one home to another. The paragraph that follows this passage high-lights a more preferable scenario. Matron Martin explains: "More fortun-ate in their home life were two sweet little Chinese girls ... who if they remember at all, will think of a mother who was tender, kind and pure, though not a professing Christian at the time of her death."[52] Again, those who ran the institution considered an orphaned child to be more fortun-ate than one whose mother was morally bad. Children were considered orphaned even if they had lost only their mother because mothers were viewed as primarily responsible for the well-being of children.[53]

In 1916–17, six young girls were admitted to the Home after the death of their mothers.[54] While many children were placed there after the loss of both parents, others were admitted by fathers who had either lost their wives to illness or who deemed their living spouses to be incapable, either through illness or moral defect, of raising their children. The Home's familial atmosphere probably made it easier to convince fathers to place their children there. As the Home functioned as a surrogate home for children rather than as an orphanage, their placement there may have seemed less permanent. Other children were rescued either by state offi-cials or by Home workers. Many of the children in the Home were not orphaned, abandoned, or abused but were removed from what were deemed to be "undesirable" homes. As Alison Diduck and others argue, the "desirable" home and family is based on the "promotion of a 'model' mother" who was "performed by middle-class, and consequently usually white, women."[55] Although some "wayward" parents were able to eventually reclaim their children, many remained in residence for most or all of their childhood and/or adolescence.

The following passage from the WMS report of 1920–21 highlights the successes of one such orphaned child, Abby,[56] who had been in the Home since she was ten months old. Her mother had been admitted by her husband in March 1901, while he was trying to secure enough money to travel to San Francisco. She stayed only one month but returned with her six-month-old daughter in January of the following year and remained four more weeks. In May of the same year, the baby was placed in the Home when her mother was taken to hospital, where she died the same night. Abby's father paid her board until his death, when she was nine years old. The following report was written when Abby was approximately twenty:[57]

> [Abby]…, who graduated from the Normal School in May, has entered upon her duties as public school teacher of our Home. She holds a first-class certificate and has taken up her work in a very capable and earnest manner. We have been delighted with the spirit of helpfulness she has shown and feel she will make a true missionary. Perhaps we may be forgiven if we have a little feeling of pride, for she is truly a product of our Home, having been here since she was a few months old.[58]

The women who ran the institution took great pride in Abby's success. She was truly a testament to the motherly care that she received, and, in fact, Abby's case was not unique.[59]

Although many of the women educated in the Home did not receive the type of education that Abby did, for some, especially those who spent all or most of their childhoods there, missionary work was a goal that was encouraged and celebrated. In the following account by Matron Annie Martin, we see just how deeply engrained this idea had become:

> Perhaps the most interesting addition to our family was our dear little adopted baby … who was left motherless when only one month old. Though such a little mite she pleaded strongly for herself by her very helpfulness … We hope our dear baby may grow up to be a joy to all who are interested in her. We call her our "little missionary."[60]

This child stayed in the Home from 1920 until 1939, and existing records do not indicate the circumstances of her leaving. When she was only months old, this little's girl's future was already charted by the matron and staff; however, not all "family members" received the same education or opportunities.

Domesticity and the Domicile

Although there were certainly a number of "success stories," with young women graduating into gendered professions and working as nurses, teachers, or missionaries, most of the women who passed through the Home did not follow this course. For many young women, especially those who came as adolescents or adults or who were deemed to lack the aptitude for higher education, training in service work was intended to provide them with useable life skills that would both enable them to generate an income and make them more attractive as marriage prospects. For them, the threshold between the private and the public realms would be much more difficult to cross. Even work skills would guarantee that they would remain confined to the private realm as they would perform service work in other women's homes. Cultivating such skills became one of the Home's central mandates. These work skills included the performance of domestic duties and so provided free labour within the Home, allowing it to "partly sustain itself." As one early administrator suggested, if the girls were "clever at fancy work or were a knitting machine secured, there would be money in knitting."[61] Putting the women and girls to work was always framed as voluntary helpfulness or, in some cases, as a way for them to fill their leisure hours.

Sarah Bowes was matron of the Home from 1895 to 1898. Before becoming matron, she was president of the Victoria branch of the WMS. In her 1895–96 WMS report, she explains: "In winter the girls spend their leisure filling orders for knitting, children's underclothing, etc. In summer they mend and help make articles for the Home."[62] Gendered expectations were literally built into the spatial organization of the houses in the form of kitchens, parlours, and sewing rooms. The adage "a woman's work is never done" was doubly so in the Home. The work that the women and girls were expected to perform arose out of two imperatives: first, given that the Home was envisioned not as an institution or even as a boarding house but, rather, as a domestic space, the women and girls, as family members, were expected to contribute to its cleaning and maintenance; second, work such as sewing and knitting was regarded as useful training.

Even during holidays, when the residents were away from the confines of the house, work remained a central component of their daily lives.

In 1916–17, for instance, Maggie Smith reported that the girls' training continued during their summer camping trip. "We are not idle," she explains, "for besides the ordinary work, there are always improvements to make, sewing (we bring a machine), Red Cross knitting, and this year, the girls have already earned over $20 picking fruit. We feel our summer at camp fits us for our year's work, and keeps us strong and well."[63] There is no mention of whether the "girls" were allowed to keep their earnings, but what *is* clear is that work was an important component of their transformation. The bodies of Chinese and Japanese women and girls were transformed through their docility, but in very gendered ways.[64] Transformations were not viewed as instantaneous but, rather, as ongoing projects that required constant work – both on the part of the transforming Chinese and Japanese women and on the part of white women.

The women in the Home were trained in a number of innovative ways that contributed to the financial upkeep of the institution. Weddings, for instance, became an important source of revenue. Indeed, the Home had long been a site for many Japanese and Chinese weddings; but, in 1911, it began hosting receptions as well. According to Matron Smith, in 1911 they "had three Japanese wedding receptions in the Home; they furnish everything, we lay the tables, and our girls serve."[65] Here, the expertise of white women in "laying the tables" was supplemented by the labour of the Home's residents. The following year, three large receptions were held. Although some of the weddings that took place were for residents of the Home, most were for Japanese or Chinese brides and grooms from the larger Victoria community. The labour of Japanese and Chinese women helped to sustain the institution financially, although it was usually framed as part of their ongoing training.

The privileging of Western practices was apparent in the training that Japanese and Chinese women received. Dressing them in "English clothes" became not only an important assimilation tactic but also a training exercise targeted at skills such as sewing.[66] In 1899, Ida Snyder refers in her report to the women in the residence as workers and identifies her own role as that of superintending. She explains that she quickly "began to realize the real difficulties a matron has to contend with in superintending work, when the workers do not know what to do or how to do it, and added to that, do not understand one word of what is said to them."[67] In other words, the instruction of these transformative domestic skills was often impeded by a lack of English-language skills. And the language barrier was not the only barrier. The matron explains: "[It] is a very practical piece of work even teaching them to make fires. One of my Japanese girls was two weeks learning that simple process, for Oriental-like, she persisted in putting in the coal first."[68] The work of unlearning would function to dissociate a girl from her "Orientalness." The physical space of the house became a training ground for the cultural and racial "whitening" that was to take place. The geographical and historical context within which the house was situated assumed that Western ways of approaching both gender and work would and should be adopted. Further, the very process of transformation further buttressed these assumptions: it was necessary to utilize the Western, or English, way of approaching work not only to legitimate the mandates of transformation but also to facilitate the successful transition of the young women to the outside world (especially if they would be serving in other English homes).

The Home mimicked the Victorian home both through its structure and through its production of discourses and practices. Creating a family was not merely discursive: much physical and emotional labour went into creating the Home and the family within it. Despite the familial discourse within the Home and the Westernizing of its residents, the young women who left the institution were never seen as fully Western or fully white. Their transition to the outside world was tied to the realities of race, gender, and class that existed outside the Home. This is not to say that these realities did not exist within the Home; however, they were buffered by the Home's familial discourses. Such discourses were riddled with ambivalence: despite being included as part of the Christian family, these girls/women would never become part of the white family. The protection of the Home could only extend so far. Moreover, the training that took place inside it was meant to prepare the girls and women for very specific roles outside it.

In 1899, Matron Snyder reported: "most of the Japanese women who were with us have taken positions as servants when leaving the Home."[69] One young woman, "Belle," entered the mission after having been rescued from a brothel at the age of nineteen. She stayed for two years and was then "hired out" as a servant, and it was reported that she was "giving satisfaction" in the home in which she worked. She eventually left the Home to work for a Mrs. Snyder in the east, and she eventually married.[70] Other women who were hired out to do domestic or service work were also described as "proving [to be] most efficient help"[71] or "giving good satisfaction,"[72] although some were "a great disappointment."[73] Records show that, in many cases, the matrons negotiated servant positions for those residents for whom suitable marriage partners could not be found. Training women to be servants was not, however, only the prerogative of those who ran the institution. Many Japanese women, for instance, were placed in the Home by husbands or fathers to learn service skills or, as one report puts it, "English and English ways,"[74] so that they could work with their husbands or fathers in English homes. Despite the classed and racialized assumptions that underpinned the mandates of the institution, Japanese and Chinese men and women used its services as a way to improve their own economic and social positions. The Home also offered white women ways of following their own aspirations. Completing Lefebvre's triad (conceived space, perceived space, and lived space), in the next section I examine how the women who resided within the Home lived and interpreted this space in ways that both embraced and challenged gendered, racialized, and spatialized norms.

BEYOND THE THRESHOLD: ASPIRATIONS IN THE LIVED SPACES OF THE CHINESE RESCUE HOME

FIGURE 8   Woman's Missionary Society.
Source: Image E-01216 courtesy of the Royal BC Museum, BC Archives

The women pictured in the above photo (Figure 8) are delegates to the Woman's Missionary Society conference of 1912. Far from being confined to their homes, these women were involved not only in running missions such as the Chinese Rescue Home but also in other forms of charitable work. Certainly for those who were involved in administering the Home, the house itself conjured up expectations regarding the roles that white women were to play – surrogate mother, nurse, and teacher. However, the house also offered spaces from which to resist gender imperatives of the time and to aspire to new heights. Despite its size, the house was not fundamentally different from the private spaces in which many women lived and worked. It was precisely this home-like atmosphere that allowed the women working within it to further their aspirations without disrupting common expectations regarding a woman's place in the social and economic hierarchies. At times the women of the Home used "social skills" that had been developed in the private realm to further their objectives in the public one.

In order to maintain their power and prestige, the WMS women who oversaw and ran the Home participated in an active campaign to establish the importance of their work both internally (at the level of the Methodist Missionary Society) through the recording and reporting of "success stories" and externally, through the publication of their work. Every success in the institution resulted in prestige for the women who ran it. These white women were quick to promote their successes, and they used creative strategies to earn them the recognition they desired. For instance, Sarah Bowes submitted a marriage announcement to a local newspaper describing the dress of the bride and groom as well as particulars about those in attendance. The second half of the wedding announcement, however, said less of the marriage and more about the Home and its mandate:

> Mr. and Mrs. Sam are the eighteenth couple married from the Home, all of whom are comfortably settled and in the enjoyment of the blessings of Christian citizenship. This speaks well for the work of the Home and affords a strong claim for the continued support and sympathy on the part of the Christian people of this city and province at large. Every one of the 18 women thus settled in peaceful and reputable homes of their own, have been won from a state of slavery to which death itself would have been infinitely preferable.[75]

Framed as a wedding announcement, this article is about far more than the marriage of Mr. and Mrs. Sam. The announcement strategically applauds the work of the WMS while, at the same time, attempting to garner support from the "Christian people" of Victoria and British Columbia. This evangelistic project depended on white women's ability, through equating Christianity with citizenship, to juxtapose these newly transformed Chinese and Japanese women with the foreign Others that they once were. The record book also includes other such clippings of events held at the Home. Although the WMS women probably did not have much influence in the (typically male-dominated) realm of print journalism, this strategic form of advertising drew on and promoted skills that women, as social planners, had acquired through a lifetime of domesticity. By using avenues that were typically the domain of women, such as wedding announcements and other social events, the WMS was able to publicize its work, subverting, but not entirely disrupting, gender boundaries. This publicity was important for two reasons. First, funding for the institution, although primarily obtained through the Methodist Missionary Society, was also obtained through local donations and support. The Home needed local community support as it was into this community that many of their charges went as domestic servants. Second, publicity fed the aspirations of the white women for whom the institution offered independence and prestige in a community in which they often lacked both.

Interest in the work that the WMS did in Victoria earned it prestige not only in its local community but also nationally. The Mission Board in Ontario, for instance, sent a letter to the advisory committee inquiring into the work being done in Victoria. At another meeting, letters were read from women in Plainfield and Claremont, Ontario, expressing interest in the work being done in the west. These letters garnered much attention from the advisory committee, and this interest in the WMS's work sparked an additional plan, the discussion of which occupied the board for five months. The board proposed that it "get some photos of the girls as well as the Home and [offer] ... them for sale to the Mission Boards and auxiliaries in the east as a possible means of bringing the Home and its work more prominently before the friends, at the same time affording a source of income to the society."[76] The women also suggested that they advertise the sale of these photos in the "Guardian and Outlook."[77] The inclusion of the "girls" in the photos would likely have made this home mission much more marketable by introducing a "foreign" element, especially in a context within which racial hierarchies underpinned the logic that sustained such work. The success of mission work offered the WMS women both recognition and respect in their communities. And so, not surprisingly, publicizing their work often occupied their time. The question now is: How did they measure their success?

While the public narration of "success stories" was a prominent feature in the work of the WMS in both Vancouver and Victoria, it is also interesting to look at how success was conceived and measured. Indeed, it was often measured in creative ways that reflected the motivation of the WMS women as well as their assimilationist assumptions. Success stories were prominent throughout the various reports and the Home registers, and many of them also quantified the number of women that were visited in local communities and the number of houses entered. The following is an excerpt from Matron Morgan's report of June 1897:

> During [Morgan's] ... recent visit to the mainland she found 10 Chinese women in Vancouver, and entered 3 new homes. She also found 7 Japanese women and arranged with Mrs. [illegible] to meet with them once a month. In Westminster she visited 5 homes. At Steveston she met 13 Japanese women with whom she held a meeting. She also visited 2 Japanese women in Moodyville.[78]

In January of the following year, her report took on a similar tone, indicating that she had "made two trips to the Mainland and Nanaimo during the [quarter] and entered 6 new homes in Victoria following to circumstances over which she had no control she only visited 42 families altogether. Total number of visits made 366."[79] Here, the use of numbers tells a story of the expansiveness of outreach while, in significant contrast, the responses of the women visited are rarely mentioned. This tendency to quantify success through identifying the number of home visits erases the potential subject of conversion and, in fact, objectifies her: the success here is that of the white woman missionary, not of the outreach work itself.

In addition to outreach work, the running of the Home, its financial undertakings, and the maintenance of working relationships with local auxiliaries and boards (as well as the general board in the east) occupied much of the WSM women's time. The matrons also worked closely with teachers and evangelists within the institution as well as with its residents and community members. In addition, matrons and advisory committee members dealt with tradespeople during the construction of the new Home. The influence of the various matrons and other Home workers often extended outside the spaces of the "home" as they were often called upon to work closely with lawyers when taking up court cases in attempts to retain guardianship over some of the residents. Although the Home was not a government-funded institution, its administrators worked closely with many government agents, interacting regularly with police and immigration officials. And, as mentioned in the previous chapter, one representative was called to testify in front of the Royal Commission on Chinese Immigration. These relationships were important not only for the success of the work – for instance, many of the women in the

Home were placed there by government agents – but also for adding to the work's legitimacy and prestige. Rescue work was not always purely altruistic: many of the women involved in reform or rescue work were often already influential in their communities, and many saw this type of work as a way to gain or increase status and influence.[80]

The work that white women performed cultivated whiteness as authority and power, despite the fact that white women were subjected to many limits. While the power exerted by women who oversaw the running of the institution was certainly limited, their moral authority was not. Although women may have had little or no power in political and economic realms, in the moral realm women's authority usually went unchallenged. This moral authority found its roots in the domestic roles that women played. According to Hunt,

> The association of women and morality was readily linked back to the more prosaic domesticity when women were ordained to have responsibility for the moral training of the young. Yet this distinctive moral identity of women also offered a form of intervention in the public realm on condition that the public dimension be conceptualized in religious or moral terms.[81]

White women, thus, benefited economically and socially from their mission work. However, they were not able to escape gendered expectations completely.

In January 1908, when the Methodist Church of Canada Missionary Society donated a parcel of land for the purpose of expanding the Home, the WMS women felt it necessary to appoint two new "associate members" – both men – to the executive. When in April of the same year a special meeting was called to accept tenders for this project, the men took control, including opening the meeting with a prayer, a task routinely undertaken by the chair of the committee. Likewise, in May 1911, when it came time to discuss the selling of land, "a committee of gentlemen were named to consult" with the advisory committee.[82] In November of the same year, another special meeting was called regarding the sale of the lots, with all members present. Also in attendance was "a committee of gentlemen composed of Mesrs. [sic] Spencer, Burkholder, Adams and Pendray, the opinion of the gentlemen being needed regarding the sale of two fifty feet [sic] lots," and the gentlemen were further "empowered to communicate with different agents."[83] These men acted as bridges between the domestic/private realm and the market/public realm. Despite the fact that the women felt inclined or compelled to consult with and "empower" men with regard to financial matters, they continued to wield a great deal of power even here. When, in the following year, their real estate agent approached the committee, he stated that "he found it difficult to find a buyer on account of the deal being such a large one and advised the committee to allow it to be divided into two lots in order to make the sale an easier matter."[84] The committee gave him the authority to do this without any of the previously named gentlemen being present.

Although the WMS women might bow to the authority of men in some regards, such public deferral was not always quite what it seemed. When the advisory committee brought men into the meeting to discuss financial matters, their advice was sometimes sought on other issues but was not always taken. In June 1907, when the committee discussed the "necessity for larger and more improved premises," it brought in a "Dr. Sutherland, Revs. Dean Thomson, Turner and Adams, also J.W. Hooper the architect" to advise it on the matter.[85] While still in the meeting, a discussion took place regarding admitting a "Hindu woman" into the Home. During the discussion, "Dr. Sutherland" offered the women a "word of caution" on this matter, after which they decided to turn the matter over to the executive board to make a decision.[86] Given that these women routinely made these types of decisions on their own, their decision to turn the matter over to the executive board may have been a tactic to placate Dr. Sutherland as the decision to admit this woman had already been made at an earlier meeting, and she was subsequently invited into the Home (an invitation she eventually declined).

Sometimes the relationships forged within the Home or in relation to the work undertaken there afforded women opportunities to work outside it. In 1898, for instance, the institution lost a valuable member of its staff when Matron Bowes took a position in Vancouver as "police matron and City Missionary."[87] White women were also able to extend their power by challenging Chinese and Japanese men's legal rights as slave owners, guardians, and parents and/or their matrimonial rights as husbands.[88] The domesticity of the Home thus provided legitimacy to white women's sometimes very public roles. But its walls also provided spaces that supported the aspirations of Japanese and Chinese women.

While the Home offered many white women an escape from the private realm, it also offered Japanese and Chinese women escape from negotiating multiple gender systems. According to Lee Mong Kow, who testified before the Royal Commission on Chinese and Japanese Immigration, what the Home called "slavery" was in fact an accepted practice among the Chinese.[89]

According to Lee Mong Kow, Chinese men would sponsor the immigration of some women by paying their passage money and head tax. In exchange, the women would agree to work as prostitutes to repay the debt.[90] In addition, as Peggy Pascoe describes, Chinese women were subject to strict gender expectations, which included subservience not only to men but also to mothers-in-law. Further, wives who did not produce male heirs "might find their husbands taking concubine … Wives who did not behave according to custom might be divorced and sent back to their own families in disgrace."[91] In Canada, these oppressive systems were often magnified by the fact that immigration laws had significantly stemmed the immigration of women to Canada, resulting in the increased risk of sexual exploitation for those who did come. These oppressions were also further exacerbated by class distinctions in Canada, as Denise Chong's *The Concubine's Children* illustrates.[92]

Thus, for many of its early residents, crossing the threshold of the Home often meant freedom from oppressive circumstances, whether slavery or prostitution. Once in the institution, these women were certainly subjected to other relations of power as white women sought to evangelize and train them in Victorian morals and Christian values. For many, however, these interventions, while not always welcome, were regarded as preferable to prostitution, slavery, domestic abuse, or unhappy marriages. One woman, Margaret Chan, recounts her journey to the Home as following:

> My aunty was not good to me – always beat me, made me do all the work. My uncle was good. My aunty's so cruel … Finally, they were going back to China, and they going to sell me to some people with a lot of children – so I run away to the Oriental Home. I was thirteen and a half, maybe fourteen.[93]

Chan travelled alone from Vancouver to Victoria and was admitted to the Home in 1917. She recounts that she was required to attend church three times a day. Chan remained in the residence until she graduated from high school in 1923. While Chan does not disclose how she came to hear about the institution while in Vancouver, once there she used the opportunity to obtain an education, eventually going on to "normal school" to obtain her teaching certificate. She was even able to borrow fifty dollars from the Home's teacher so that she could return to Hong Kong to get a teaching job.[94] In this case, life in the Home offered Chan opportunities that she would not otherwise have had.

For many Japanese women, the Home may have offered a chance to gain autonomy. In her book *Hiroshima Immigrants in Canada, 1891–1941*,

Michiko Midge Ayukawa explicates some of the reasons that Japanese women from Hiroshima came to Canada.[95] While a variety of factors contributed to the influx of Japanese women, for many, becoming a picture bride was a way of fulfilling dreams of adventure. For some, at least, the men who met them at the docks were not what motivated them to travel to Canada: marriage was simply the only way most Japanese women could travel to the West. Ayukawa recounts the story of Ishikawa Yasu:

> Until the age of twenty – which was old by the standards of the day – Ishikawa Yasu, whose siblings teased her about her homeliness, had not had any marriage proposals. She made up her mind to go overseas to practise midwifery, to earn a lot of money, and to prove her worth. However ... she learned that she could go only as a bride ... She recalled: "I had no idea what kind of person I had married, and what kind of life he was leading. Anyway, I had my heart set on coming here, and that was all I could think of. That was my dream, and I thought things would turn out all right. I was just a child, you see."[96]

Most who travelled to Canada as picture brides had never seen the men who were to become their husbands, knowing of them only through letters or recommendations from family members and friends. While most were not surprised by the men who met them, some were. Some of these men were older, others were "feeble-minded," still others were abusive or neglectful. What surprised many of these women was the isolation and the back-breaking work that was expected from them. It was these conditions that sometimes led them to seek shelter in the Home, for not only did the institution offer escape from abusive relationships, it also offered sociality and a break from physical toil. It is important to note that, while many Japanese women came to Canada to escape strict Japanese gender systems, they would have to negotiate new gender systems once they went to the Home.

While some women voluntarily sought shelter in order to escape unhappy lives, others came to further their own aspirations within a white dominated nation. Some of these women left the Home soon after they entered it. This dual-crossing of thresholds is an indication that, for some, the Home was a stopgap measure, allowing Chinese and Japanese women a space of refuge while they planned other modes of escape. Once freed from their lives outside the institution, some wives, prostitutes, and "slave girls" used the space as a temporary shelter from which they would soon escape, some to other men, others to Japan or China, and still others to cities like San Francisco (which the Home workers believed to be a hotbed of prostitution). Although the Home clearly privileged marriage and Victorian moral authority, it also offered some women the opportunity to leave the confines of their domestic lives when the latter was deemed unhappy and dysfunctional. For women who found themselves without husbands, either through death, divorce, or abandonment, the mission provided an alternative approach to isolation or widowhood, broadening the very few options that were available.

Many of the residents entered for reasons that were not deemed acceptable by those who administered and managed the Home. According to the minutes of March 30, 1900: "A Japanese woman had been taken into the home, but it was found her only motive was to learn English & lead others astray. She was therefore allowed to go after a trial of ten days."[97] While it is unclear what led the advisory committee to believe that she was there to lead others astray, clearly her motives for being in the residence were not compatible with the motives of those who ran it. The matron's fear that this woman might lead others astray points to real worries concerning alliances that were forged within the Home. This is borne out in the many stories of women who fled the dwelling together. It appears that the Home can be seen as a place where women forged social relations and alliances.

The advisory committee minutes tell the story of one woman whose husband brought her to the Home against her will and who then subsequently made her escape. In 1919–20, one matron reported: "A Chinese woman, a third wife, came to us in the fall, but as we had every reason to believe she wished to go with another man, who had a wife in China, we encouraged her to return to her husband after two months stay here."[98] As this example indicates, the policy of privileging marriage was not as straightforward as might be expected. On the one hand, those who ran the Home decried the practice of Chinese men having multiple wives; on the other, they encouraged this woman to leave the residence and return to just such a scenario because they feared she might be tempted into an adulterous relationship. Chinese women used the institution to empower themselves in other ways as well. Much like the women who used the Chinese Mission Home in San Francisco, Chinese women in Victoria used the Home to leverage for better treatment.[99] In at least one case a woman, while in the institution, was able to negotiate a contract with her husband and his family before she agreed to return to her own home.[100] Claiming that she was badly treated by her mother-in-law, this young woman, "Mary," who, according to the institution's records, was twenty years old, was taken by her father to the Home for shelter. Nine days later, a contract was signed by her, her husband, and her father-in-law, after which time she left. The four-page document, kept in the

Home's records within a folder marked "Miscellaneous," promised that the father-in-law would "provide a home and domestic arrangements" for his son and the young woman, including "furniture, furnishings and equipment ... as [would] be approved of by the party of the third part [Mary] as sufficient and satisfactory." Further, the document promised that a monthly stipend would be paid to the couple. Under these conditions, and upon promises that they would be free from interference and cruelty, the woman returned to her husband.[101]

Given that many in the province believed Chinese and Japanese populations to be inassimilable, the interventions by WMS women and other mission workers offered Chinese and Japanese women the promise of belonging.[102] The Home was a space of ambivalence, imposing restrictions upon Japanese and Chinese women while simultaneously affording them a space/site of community and sociality. Religious participation, as Alison Marshall indicates in her discussion of Chinese bachelor societies, often had more to do with "their desire to fit into local communities" than with their desire for religious salvation.[103] Similarly, the Home was not simply about providing services for Chinese and Japanese women: it was also about the imagining and re-imagining of the self within a *national* domestic context. It was about erasing difference as a way of asserting superiority. This was achieved by first embracing difference and then transforming it into sameness. Japanese and Chinese women could never fully be at "home" or equal within the institution without undermining the project itself. Going into the Home, they were required to mimic and to revere those who welcomed them as well as to distance themselves from what had made them "strangers" in the first place. But they could never be released from the "strangeness" upon which the mission project was founded. Thus, their transformation was less about transforming from stranger into friend than it was about defining the stranger as the "friendly stranger" – one who might be trusted but never fully known.

This promise of being accepted, even as a friendly stranger, may have been an important motivation for Japanese and Chinese participation in mission activities. However, despite what many saw as mimicry or assimilation, participation in mission programs did not necessarily mean that Japanese and Chinese communities embraced Christianity wholeheartedly or uncritically.[104] As has been shown, mimicry or adherence to the Home's rules may have been less about the values instilled in the women who resided there and more about the opportunities they were afforded in exchange for their compliance. While white women measured the success of the institution according to the number of Chinese and Japanese women they reached, the latter measured its success through their ability to avail themselves of opportunities for education and skills that often translated into respectability and financial reward.

Blunt aptly describes the home as "a material and an affective space, shaped by everyday practices, lived experiences, social relations, memories and emotions."[105] Despite its public mandate, the Chinese Rescue Home was no exception. Constructed in its material form as a Georgian manor house, the Home reflected and transmitted values associated with the British motherland and the Methodist fatherland. Offering an easily traversed threshold between the private realm and the public realm, the Home conjured up notions of family and motherhood, which were reproduced in the training of Chinese and Japanese women as wives, nurses, teachers, missionaries, and servants. However, the institution also provided shelter for both white women and their charges while they attempted to reach places that they might otherwise never have been allowed to go. Those who entered the Home were afforded certain freedoms precisely because it was situated at the threshold between the foreign and the domestic and between the public and the private.

Built as a house, the Home encouraged the WMS women to model highly gendered roles for their charges. However, it also offered all the women – white, Japanese, and Chinese – opportunities to further their own goals. The WMS women used their moral authority to both police and to protect the sexuality of Japanese and Chinese women through their confinement in the Home. Once inside, these white women had the power to make important decisions regarding not only the behaviours of the resident women but also their futures. Decisions regarding when the residents would be "allowed" to pass back across the threshold to enter into service were made by the Home, as were decisions regarding who they might marry. The WMS women acted as guardians (albeit not always legal guardians) and, in some cases, took on decidedly maternal roles in relation to the residents. In this way, home spaces allowed for increased power for white women. Although much of this power was limited to domestic spaces, the Home allowed women to cross the threshold from domestic relationships to institutional guardianship and moral reform. Similarly, despite their appearance of dependence, Japanese and Chinese women engaged in dual-crossings of thresholds as they used the spaces of the Home to serve their own ends. Within the Home, the domestic realm played multiple roles, limiting and empowering the women within its walls. Domesticity and moral authority were, in fact, imperative in garnering state support. The following chapter pursues these themes through a discussion of a high-profile kidnapping case that involved the Chinese Rescue Home.

4

Outside the Walls of the Home

Men, Marriage, and Morals
in the Public Arena

The space of the Chinese Rescue Home was exceptional in that it allowed for carefully managed and intimate cross-racial contact.[1] Within its walls cross-racial contact was seen as not only acceptable but as desirable and necessary to fulfilling the project of Christian conversion and transformation. Ideologies of nation coalesced with discourses of gender, whiteness, and Christianity to produce domestic spaces of moral and racial transformation. Cross-racial contact was legitimized for two reasons: first, women were viewed as moral authorities, and it was in their roles as moral regulators that they were able to intervene in the lives of Japanese and Chinese women; second, the domestic realm was viewed as the most appropriate place for such interventions. The domestic realm was crucial not only because it reinforced the private/public divide but also because it was the ideal space within which to domesticate these women as it allowed for physical training in proper womanhood/domesticity. Dealing with cross-racial relationships outside these walls was more complex and required further negotiations.

Moving outside the Home and following its relationships and representations in newspapers and other documents provides a clearer picture of how and why the institution was exceptional when it came to cross-racial contact. By examining public responses to the work done in the Home as well as the reactions of the community and the state to one man who attempted to take on a similar role, we see that the absence of women's moral authority delegitimized the latter's attempts. Three related cases, two hearings, and one high-profile "kidnapping" case, highlight how state and civil agents worked to closely police cross-racial endeavours outside the Home. The cases cover an eighteen-month period, from February 1887 to August 1888. A timeline of the events that led up to the cases discussed here is included at the end of this chapter. The first two hearings deal with accusations of police corruption. On two separate occasions, John Gardiner, one of the founders of the Home, accused police superintendent Charles Bloomfield of failing to carry out his duty.

The first case concerns Bloomfield's failure to help the Home in its rescue of two women; the second concerns Bloomfield's failure to detain or arrest Walter Menzies (once a "friend" of the Home), following his being accused of kidnapping by Gardiner; and the third case concerns Menzies. After he was finally apprehended, Menzies was charged with kidnapping two of the institution's residents and then selling them, one in the United States and one to a Chinese man in Victoria, although these charges would later be amended. An analysis of the coverage of these three cases in two newspapers, the *Victoria Daily Times* and the *British Colonist,* shows the ambivalence of the state's role in rescue work during the period when the Home was run primarily by men.[2] I then examine the public's role in policing racial and gendered boundaries when the state failed to intervene in what was seen to be unsanctioned cross-racial contact. Finally, I juxtapose the importance of marriage to the Home with the court's treatment of it in order to draw attention to the shifting meaning of "rescue work" and how it was legitimized through its association with women. These cases all highlight just how important discourses of the domestic and of domesticity were to this type of work. The relationships between the state, the public, and the Home, as the newspaper coverage reveals, were not unidirectional. While the state played an active role in defining the domestic, it is interesting to see the complex ways in which citizens attempted to discipline it (and each other) while, at the same time, being both defined and disciplined by it. It is important to emphasize that the state applied its force not only through its power to act but also through its refusal to intervene.

Within the walls of the Home, racial difference was contained, managed, and, by some accounts, transformed through the formation of familial ties. Very little intervention was necessary from outside the institution's walls unless residents left before the supposed transformation was deemed complete. In these cases, attempts were made, sometimes with the assistance of the police, to bring these women back, to keep them at "home." Once the women and girls were deemed ready to leave the institution, gendered, racial, and class boundaries were maintained through their placement in service positions or back into the Chinese and (later) Japanese communities, most often as wives of Christian Chinese or Japanese men. However, in the absence of white women's (Christian) moral authority, similar forms of cross-racial contact were treated with fear and suspicion. This required that more force be applied (and from more directions) in order to police the boundaries of race. Thus, outside the protective walls of domesticity, boundaries of race and gender were preserved, and those who crossed them were subject to moral regulatory projects in the form of both public censure and state intervention. Defining the limits of the outside "walls" of the Home also tell us much about how the inside was defined.

The State of Ambivalence

In February 1887, a police committee inquiry was launched, seven months before Reverend Starr would write to the Woman's Missionary Society asking for its assistance with running the Home. A key player in this case was John Gardiner. Gardiner, the son of missionaries,[3] was known as a deeply religious man who, in addition to being a "missionary of the Methodist Church among the Chinese,"[4] described himself as employed in the customs house. "I teach the Chinese, and was the principal person to start the home for Chinese girls," he explained.[5] Gardiner also acted as an interpreter and translator: in one instance, he translated documents for the courts that were subsequently used as evidence in a case in which he was the purported victim. In his capacity as collector of customs, Gardiner had the "power to refuse the landing of a prostitute" and thus was able to easily persuade or coerce Chinese women to enter the Home.[6] His practice of "spiriting" women away from "prostitution dens," as well as his control over their entry into the country, made him an enemy to some Chinese community members. In fact, two Chinese men were accused of conspiring to murder Gardiner for these very reasons. Eventually, the men were acquitted, largely because questions were raised regarding the validity of Gardiner's translations. In addition to attending raids on houses of prostitution, Gardiner also made use of connections at the local jail in order to interview Chinese women who had been arrested by police.

The subject of the first police inquiry is as follows. It seems that Gardiner, who had begun to "rescue" Chinese women and girls from "slavery" and/or "prostitution," upon learning that two young Chinese women had been taken into custody, went to the jail and interviewed them. What he discovered was "that they were girls who had been brought [to Victoria] a year before by a procuress and that they were kept in a house of prostitution."[7] Gardiner then communicated these facts to the police superintendent, Charles Bloomfield, explaining that it was his intention to "rescue these girls from the dens."[8] It was Bloomfield's reluctance to aid Gardiner in his quest to rescue these women that resulted in Gardiner's levying charges of corruption against him, which, in turn, resulted in this hearing. During the inquiry that was launched to deal with these accusations, Gardiner testified that, after discussing his intentions with Bloomfield, he (Gardiner) then proceeded to obtain an order of guardianship from the Supreme Court of British Columbia. But, as Gardiner explained, despite his requests that Bloomfield sign an affidavit, the superintendent failed to show up for the meeting. Subsequently, when the young women did not appear in court, Bloomfield led Gardiner to believe that they had been released on bail. Only after Gardiner sent his lawyer to ask Bloomfield to forfeit the bail bonds did Bloomfield explain that the bonds had never been signed and were thus of little use. Gardiner requested that warrants be issued for the women's arrest, but at the time of the committee inquiry, the women had yet to be found.[9]

Gardiner pled his case to the Police Committee, stating: "these girls were of great value; I had a bill of sale showing their value; it is my intention to break up this system of slavery and asked Mr. Bloomfield to help me: but what assistance do I get?"[10] His lawyer, Thornton Fell,[11] went on to explain that, after preparing the papers requesting guardianship, "amongst which was an affidavit of Mr. Bloomfield in support of the order,"[12] he had sent a draft of the affidavit to Bloomfield. His clerk returned, explaining that Bloomfield would be at the "office in five minutes to swear it."[13] Despite efforts to locate Bloomfield, it was not until the following day that the document was sworn, after Gardiner's lawyer's clerk had been tracked him down at the police court. When called to testify before the inquiry, Bloomfield explained that the women had been released by mistake and that, despite many attempts to find them, he had been unable to do so.

The inquiry continued a week later. Counsellor Higgins, who chaired the inquiry, concluded that "the charge of corruption had fallen to the ground. There had been great carelessness – he would not say culpable carelessness. The superintendent admitted that he had made an error in liberating the girls and, in absence of any evidence that he had been bribed to do so, the committee was bound to clear him of the charge of corruption."[14] Although Gardiner believed that Bloomfield was purposefully subverting his work with Chinese women, the inquiry found that Bloomfield's actions were attributable to carelessness, not maliciousness. Very little concern was raised in the hearing about Gardiner's claims that Bloomfield was undermining the work of the Home. The committee's decision instead focused on whether Bloomfield was guilty of corruption in his dealings with the Chinese. The committee did not seem to find Bloomfield's reluctance to aid Gardiner's work the least bit disturbing – an indication that, in its early stages, neither the police nor the committee that governed them viewed the Home favourably. This perception would change once the WMS took over, with police actively assisting in the return of run-away girls as well as themselves placing many women within the Home's walls.

The charges that Bloomfield failed to support Gardiner's work (1) through his unwillingness to sign affidavits and (2) through his inaccessibility were dismissed. The only question that remained was whether or not Bloomfield's reluctance to support Gardiner in his attempts to save the two women could be attributed to his having been bribed by Chinese community members. Once it was clear that there was no evidence of bribery, the case was dismissed. Despite clearing the superintendent of the charges, however, the committee did not close its meeting immediately. Instead, Commissioner David Higgins, chair of the committee, commended Gardiner for his fearlessness in coming forward. Here, Higgins made three important points, all of which are worth exploring.

First, Higgins decried the practice of the "sale of female children for immoral purposes" and called upon not only police officers but also the public to do what they could to stop it.[15] Thus, he brought to the fore the importance of civil policing in addition to formal policing in the moral regulation of (racial) problems. In reporting the commissioner's comments, the newspaper called citizens to action.[16] Here, the police, as an arm of the state, in commenting on a matter that was not directly related to the trafficking of Chinese women and children, not only underscored their own authority but also deputized the public to end this human trade. Although unwilling to chastise Bloomfield for not supporting this work, Commissioner Higgins applauded those who helped stop "this trade" and publicly shamed those who participated in it.

Second, Higgins held that, for "those who aided and abetted ... [the sale of female children for immoral purposes], hanging was too good."[17] He not only denounced the sale of these women but also went on to juxtapose the actions of those who did so with the actions of those moral citizens who tried to stop it. Those who "contributed ever so little to stop it, deserved the public thanks,"[18] Higgins explained, but for those who aided it in any way, even death was too lenient. Higgins used this inquiry into the accusations of police corruption to send a warning to those who abetted the so-called morally inferior Chinese and who perpetuated the traffic in girls and women. Although corruption was not proven in Bloomfield's case, Higgins's warning implied that police corruption in Victoria remained a possibility, and he encouraged people to report their suspicions regarding officials.[19] Although there is no evidence of other formal complaints of police corruption during this period, Higgins's warning implies that it was not far-fetched to think that acts of bribery and corruption might be occurring.

Finally, Higgins emphasized the public's duty to prevent corruption. Not only were the Chinese to be policed aggressively by private citizens but so, too, were the police themselves. Higgins, and subsequently the press, encouraged the example that Gardiner had set, emphasizing that, if all of Victoria's citizens would "come forward and publicly state their suspicions against officials, instead of slander and back-biting to damage character, the moral tone of the community would be much improved."[20] The implication was clear. In Higgins's perception at least, Victoria was a community in which moral problems extended beyond the conventional accounts of Chinese depravity. The problem was much wider: slander and back-biting threatened the integrity of the white community. If this police inquiry was any indication, the best way to end the divisions in the white community was to publicly discredit the charges of police corruption. Outright denial of corruption was not necessary. Nor was the condemnation of John Gardiner, the man who instigated the investigation. Far from this, Higgins applauded Gardiner and, by doing so, championed the success of the investigation.

As the above and the next cases show, although the Police Committee took Gardiner's complaint seriously, it paid very little attention to the fate of the Chinese girls and women. This was something that would change dramatically once the WMS took over the running of the Home. Court cases and public attention became much more focused on protecting the domestic realm and cementing the place of Japanese and Chinese women within its walls. However, men and their public responsibilities became central once more as Bloomfield and Gardiner faced off at a second inquiry. Bloomfield was once more accused of a failure to act, but this time the accusations were concerned with his failure to arrest Walter R. Menzies.

Walter Menzies, by all accounts, appeared to be a well-respected member of Victoria's community. Usually addressed as "Professor Menzies," the man represented himself as a magnetic healer. Although the term "magnetic healer" might easily suggest Menzies was a charlatan, prior to this case his trade seemed to be well respected. For instance, one article published in May 1886 states that, although the many marvelous cures cited by Menzies may have seemed impossible, "the facts remain unchallenged, and the persons whose statements have been made public have fully verified every case presented; many of the people are well-known residents, and their testimony cannot be denied."[21] Menzies was also active in the church community and was an avid supporter of the Home. In fact, his mother-in-law was one of its early matrons, prior to the WMS era. Given that Menzies was an early supporter of the institution, the relationship between Gardiner and Menzies most likely began as a positive one. What caused the rift between the two men is difficult to determine, but what transpired in May and June 1888 made it clear that any friendship that once existed was over.

Gardiner, with the support of two clergymen, evoked his role as "concerned citizen" to publicly accuse Menzies of kidnapping and selling two Chinese girls who resided in the Home. It was alleged that Menzies had sold one of the girls across the border in the United States and the other as a wife to a Chinese man in Victoria. These accusations were directed at Menzies in the form of a *Daily Times* article entitled "Trafficking in Girls," which appeared on May 30, 1888.[22] Although this initial exposé did not name its sources, in the inquiry that followed it became evident that this story had been brought forward by Gardiner, Reverend Starr, and Reverend Fraser. Initially, this newspaper report did not result in any formal state actions. The police did not move to arrest Menzies, nor did they prevent him from leaving the city. In fact, the first state actions took the form of an investigation and inquiry into the dual failures of (1) those concerned citizens who targeted Menzies in the press and (2) the police, who failed to act on their accusations.

The *Times* article, which initially exposed Menzies, was followed the next day by an article in the rival newspaper, the *British Colonist*. This article explained that the chief of police had written a communication questioning why the information in the *Times* had not been reported to the police before being leaked to the newspaper. The following day, June 1, 1888, the *Colonist* reported that it seemed "strange that the police

were not informed of the matter; or that the gentlemen having knowledge of the affair should not have sworn out an information against the
offender."[23]

The *Times* responded to the *Colonist*'s accusation that the matter should
have been laid before the police:

> The *Colonist*, which awoke this morning to the realization of the impor-
> tance of the subject, expresses surprise that the facts were not laid before
> the police. The *Times* laid the matter very fully before the police on
> Wednesday evening, and Menzies was still in the city at midnight – six
> hours after Chief Bloomfield asked the Council to hold an investigation.
> An "investigation" of the steamer between 12:30 and the time she sailed
> would have resulted in the capture, if such were desired, of the culprit.[24]

The implications here are that the police might have been more concerned with clearing their own names than with apprehending Menzies.
This was a theme that was quickly picked up in the *Colonist*. And it was
not only their writers who followed this line of thinking: so did John
Gardiner. In a letter to the editor, Gardiner asked: "What did the police
do when they *were* communicated with?" He then answers his own question, arguing that the police had plenty of time to detain Menzies "and
failed to do so. How is that for the efficiency of the police? Strange, is it,
that the police were not informed of this matter? The wonder is that after
such an act of gross negligence in the performance of his duties, public
opinion has not compelled the Chief of Police to join Menzies in his
meanderings."[25]

Letters to the editor must be understood not only as responding to
reports but also as shaping future reports.[26] Understanding the newspaper
as an active text that is in dialogue with the social body and that is a
form of action and re-action, of production and re-production, points
to the rhizomatic qualities of moral regulation and the role of the newspaper in creating and shaping reality.[27] On the same page, the *Colonist*
formed a reply. Although not mentioning Gardiner's accusations directly,
it included a short, twelve-line column that bore the same heading
as Gardiner's letter. Entitled "The 'Menzies Affair,'" the column begins
as follows:

> It is trusted that action will be taken by the Police Committee and that
> a searching inquiry will be instituted into the charges proffered against
> Prof. Menzies of kidnapping and selling a Chinese girl for base purposes.

It is true Menzies has departed, but as the Chief of Police is charged with being derelict in his duty in not detaining Menzies, the whole matter should be thoroughly sifted and the evidence of all concerned in the matter obtained.[28]

Here, the newspaper makes clear its faith in the state to deal with its official's failure to act. That a man should be detained based entirely on the merits of a newspaper account is not questioned here, an indication that the press held a great deal of power and leverage in the community. Instead, a formal investigation took place to probe "the alleged failure of the police to do their duty."[29] While the *Colonist* framed this as an inquiry into police misconduct, the initial request for an investigation came from Superintendent Bloomfield himself, who asked that the three men behind this exposé "be communicated with as to whether they reported the facts [regarding their initial accusations against Menzies] to the police or called their assistance ... [and] their reasons for not doing so."[30]Although Bloomfield had called for the initial investigation into the failure of citizens to act, very quickly the focus began to shift to his own failures.

In the investigation, the three men explained why they chose to expose Menzies in the press. According to Gardiner: "The reason was because we have lost confidence in the Chief and for reasons that we can substantiate." Gardiner then went on to explain: "This very case proves it, as there was time to detain Menzies after the *Times* appeared with the exposure."[31] Both the newspaper and Gardiner claimed that the police knew of Menzies's situation, did not act, and purposefully refused to intervene even as Menzies left the city. The police's failure to act was an indication that, while they did not actively support the work of the Home in these early stages, neither were they willing to become involved with adjudicating the right of the institution or of Menzies to detain Chinese or Japanese women – something the courts would later become involved with in various habeas corpus cases.[32] However, the Police Committee did take such public accusations seriously. Present at the meeting to investigate the alleged failures of the police were Mayor Grant, Aldermen S.T. Styles, Charles Penwill, John Coughlan, Superintendent Bloomfield, and unnamed members of the police committee. Also in attendance were Reverend D. Fraser, and Reverend J.E. Starr, and Gardiner.

Fraser, Starr, and Gardiner expressed concerns that the investigation was directed at finding that they had been engaged in wrongdoing. In fact, Gardiner initially refused to testify unless formal charges were brought against him; however, once reassured that the investigation was to be focused on the police, he replied, "if that is the lines you are going on, we are here at your service."[33] Gardiner then went on to openly accuse the police chief of knowing "perfectly well that Menzies was in town."[34] He continued, explaining that they could "prove that the chief knew Menzies was in town the night of the exposure, and that the police knew an hour and a half before the Yosemite started that Menzies was on board of her."[35] Whether or not the superintendent was aware of the matter forged the basis of the discussion to follow. The matter was left unresolved, but two days later, when the board met again, discussion resumed, this time in the absence of those who had testified. It was resolved and subsequently reported in the *Colonist* that, given that Menzies had yet to be convicted, and "not having been brought to trial, the police were not much to blame as if Menzies had been tried and convicted."[36] The investigation was considered to be closed as the police could not be seen to be guilty of letting a criminal escape their jurisdiction unless it could be proven that Menzies was in fact a criminal.

The resolution of this case is interesting both because it did not seem to consider the past investigation, despite the fact that many similarities existed, and because of the logic according to which it was resolved. Gardiner was called to testify in this investigation, and yet the previous investigation, which he initiated, was not referenced in his testimony. Gardiner did, however, comment that he had lost all confidence in Bloomfield, something that was no doubt affected by the previous case. This investigation, like the previous one, also dealt with Chinese women who were at one time accused of being prostitutes and who had had contact with Gardiner. This contact occurred while he was in an official capacity as an administrator of the Home. As in the previous case, the committee did not seem to be concerned with the protection of Chinese women. Nor did it address Bloomfield's alleged disregard for their protection. By focusing only on Menzies, the committee deemed that Bloomfield was not at fault. The investigation's dismissal was premised not on whether or not Bloomfield knew enough to act but, rather, on whether or not Menzies was guilty – something only knowable subsequent to a court case. The irony is that this case had to be dropped because Bloomfield had allegedly allowed Menzies to leave the jurisdiction. Thus, the reason for his being investigated in the first place became the reason the investigation was dismissed. This circular logic allowed Bloomfield to escape investigation once more. Although Menzies was eventually found guilty, the investigation into Bloomfield's actions was never reopened.

The press, while instrumental in exposing Menzies, could not bring him to trial. Despite the fact that Gardiner and his colleagues acted in concert with the newspaper in order to publicly expose Menzies in such a way that the police would have no choice but to act, the latter still refused to intervene, forcing Gardiner and the *Times* to then expose them. The state was then forced into acting, if not in support of the Home, then certainly in clearing the police of wrongdoing. It is also likely that it was the subsequent, almost unrelenting attention that the press paid to this case that was instrumental in convincing Menzies that he had no recourse but to return to face the charges. There was little chance that he could return unnoticed to resume his life in Victoria. Thus, the "moral geography" of Victoria was mapped in such a way that the city was closed off to Menzies unless he was able to prove himself innocent of these charges.[37]

TRANSFORMATION OR TRAFFICKING: THE SEARCH FOR (MALE) MORAL AUTHORITY

The *Daily Times* exposed Menzies and his alleged crimes with sensational headlines: "Trafficking in Girls" appeared as the bold headline, followed by two sub-headlines that were even more sensational. "A Trafficker in Human Flesh – A Magnetic Healer Turned Slave Dealer" reads one, while the other reads "An Unprecedented Case of Villainy – Details of the Plot Laid Bare."[38] Throughout the story, the newspaper sensationalized the case, portraying Menzies as an opportunistic magnetic healer who, driven by greed, kidnapped and then sold Chinese girls, upon whom his "magnetism was being exerted with more than usual vigor."[39] This description of him not only called into question the legitimacy of his profession but also hinted at the possibility that he might be involved in sexual relationships with these girls. While these suggestions were never substantiated, they exacerbated existing anxieties surrounding sexuality and racial mixing.

Although Menzies's actions were not substantially different from those routinely practised within the walls of the Home, Menzies lacked the moral authority necessary to "transform" the young women and, therefore, was accused of trafficking them. The scandal that followed was premised on the distinction between transformation and trafficking. This distinction is important as the line between the two would be instrumental in defining the limits and possibilities of the Home. The newspapers used various tactics to draw their readers into the scandal of this particular case.

Throughout one article, the author uses "call outs" to emphasize words such as "slavery" and "shame" in order to draw the reader in, again hinting at the case's never-to-be-corroborated sexual aspects.[40] By calling attention to the "slavery and shame" from which Gardiner rescued the two Chinese women, the author legitimated the existence of the Chinese Rescue Home. Although cross-racial contact was also evident between Gardiner and these women, here, the contact was authorized by his role in administrating the Home and, thus, through the domestic spaces that would house the women. Domesticity, Christian purity, and benevolence inoculated Gardiner and were juxtaposed with Menzies's characterization as a sexualized "magnetic healer." Further, Gardiner's contact with the women he rescued was short-term and always buffered by the matron of the Home.

In addition, in using the following phrases, this article juxtaposes Gardiner's work with Menzies's actions: "MARRY THE CHINAMAN," "HAVE THE GIRL FOR $150," and "SMUGGLING LOI HO."[41] It accused Menzies of *selling* the Chinese girl, Ah Lin, to the "Chinaman" for $150. Further, it indicated that it was Reverend Starr, another founder of the Home, who had uncovered this plot to sell the Chinese girl under the guise of marriage. According to this account, Starr "refused to perform the ceremony, unless Mr. Gardiner or some trustworthy interpreter could be present, giving as his reason that the majority of Chinese marriages in this country had been farcical in the extreme."[42] However, given that the young woman, Ah Lin, had claimed abuse at the hands of the matron of the Home, avoiding contact with Gardiner was likely an important consideration. The Chinese man, Ah Chee, and the two women, Loi Ho and Ah Lin, were framed as victims of Menzies, but the greater problem seemed to be the propensity of the Chinese (and Menzies) to disregard or, worse yet, to misuse the sanctity of Christian marriage. Menzies's crime, then, was that he facilitated an already inherent Chinese depravity. The sensational nature of this article rests on its ability to create the problem as a foreign, dangerous, and exotic one. One objective of such sensationalism was to inform and protect Victoria's white readership.

The *Times* began its story of the Menzies case by explaining that it was its "painful duty to publish the detailed account of certain operations, the like of which is not in the memory of the oldest resident of this province, and for vileness of purpose, for the audacity of the operator, and the utterly revolting nature of the crime, has never been surpassed."[43] Although there had been many crimes whose severity far exceeded the ones of which Menzies was accused – his crimes entailed neither loss of life nor physical assault – the *Times* categorized this particular crime as having never been surpassed in terms of "vileness of purpose." Moreover, Menzies was accused of crimes no greater than those that were frequently attributed to the Chinese population in Victoria. His accusers claimed that he kidnapped and sold young Chinese women into the slave trade in one case and into a false marriage in another. Certainly these were crimes that were routinely attributed to Chinese men as the Home was, in fact, built on these assumptions. Thus, one must ask why Menzies's crimes were seen as unsurpassed in the province. The answer lies not in the nature of the crimes but, rather, in the fact that they were allegedly committed by someone who had previously been viewed as a respectable white citizen and by virtue of their supposed effect on the white population. Menzies had violated not only racial boundaries but also sexual and gendered ones.

This violation took place not through *contact* with Chinese women (for, as others in this case were quick to point out, within the walls of the Home the WMS also facilitated marriages and held Chinese women, sometimes against their will) but, rather, through the *unsanctioned* contact with Chinese women and the facilitation and perversion of white rites of marriage. Menzies's contact with the women was not part of the Home's transformative project but, instead, a *relationship* between a white man and Chinese women. Further, this was a relationship that was seen to pervert the Christian institution of marriage – a point that the judge would emphasize in his ruling once the case went to trial.

Gender and gender boundaries were central to this case. Although the alleged victims were Chinese, the newspaper repeatedly emphasized that they were women, thus pointing to their vulnerability as females. The "Chinese girls" were first described as "two young girls of this city" and only belatedly as *Chinese* girls. In fact, the *Times* account references the Chineseness of these girls in an almost apologetic way, explaining that they were "Chinese girls, to be sure, but girls nonetheless."[44] The newspapers, by emphasizing the gendered nature of the crime, implied that the risk was not isolated to the Chinese community. Yet their readers were not likely to fall victim to Menzies's alleged trafficking scheme, both because his victims were Chinese and because Menzies himself had left town. White readers, the *Times* implied, were at risk in other ways. First, their trust in Menzies was misdirected: even his "legitimate art of healing" had to be questioned so that they would not be duped by him. Second, the *Times's* readers were at risk from the Chinese population as well, the crimes' being framed as having their origin in the Chinese community.

The white audience needed to be educated regarding the threat posed by this purportedly deviant population. The *Times,* therefore, was quick to point out not only Chinese attitudes towards marriage but also the rebellious nature of the Chinese girls themselves as being at the root of this crime. It explained that, after Gardiner had rescued the Chinese girls from their lives of shame, "these two, disliking the rules and discipline of all well regulated institutions of a like reformatory nature, preferred leaving the 'Home' and hiring themselves to two European families in this city." Thus, it was at least partly their greed and rebellion that caused them to be "taken advantage of by the 'Professor.'"[45]

Although framed as ingratitude, the motivations for the young women's departure from the Home can also be understood as strategic. Once freed from their former lives as "prostitutes" or "slave girls," these young women were not likely to be content to be subjected to new forms of domination. Their freedom won, these young women were determined to make the most of it, even if it meant leaving the security of the Home. However, as they would quickly learn, outside the institution their chances for success were far from certain. Their contact with whites outside the Home put not only themselves at risk but also Victoria's white populace. Menzies's crimes were considered so great that they were to be understood as "a terrible outrage upon society, an infamous wrong upon humanity, and a scandal and disgrace to the community in which, in the broad glare of day and under the very noses of the guardians and enforcers of the law, it has so brazenly been enacted."[46] Here, the *Times* underscores the outrageousness not only of the crime but also of the scandal and disgrace that it caused the white population. White society was at risk not only from exposure to the vile crimes of Menzies but also from the contamination that was brought into the white community through the intermixing of Chinese and European populations.

Lending Legitimacy: The Women Weigh In

The newspapers that reported on the Walter Menzies case became sites where competing truth claims were negotiated in a public forum. These struggles over truth unfolded in the publication of editorials, letters, and affidavits of those involved in the case. To this end, women actively participated in the discussions, using their moral authority to lend legitimacy to each side. Once Menzies had left the country, the state, through the courts, could not act. For this reason the case would be "tried," at least initially, in the press. One of the first people to weigh in on this case was Jennie Menzies, the wife of Walter Menzies. In her letter, Jennie Menzies not only championed her husband's innocence but also levelled some accusations of her own against Gardiner and the Chinese Rescue Home. That it was Jennie Menzies who wrote the letter to the newspaper and not her husband suggests two things. First, white women's moral authority was used not only inside but also outside the institution's walls as Menzies condemned the behaviour of both Gardiner and the Home's matron. Second, her "testimony" was meant to bring the cross-racial contact back into the more legitimate domestic realm.

On July 4, 1888, an explanatory article accompanied Menzies's letter in the *British Colonist*. The article explained that the *Times*' reporting had been one-sided and that it was only right that the other side of the story be told: thus the newspaper was publishing Jennie Menzies's letter. The article did not stop there. While it did not defend Walter Menzies's actions directly, it did point out that they were, according to "some people who claim to be well-informed on the matter," not substantially different from those of John Gardiner, his accuser. According to the article: "Mr. Gardner has been in the habit of demanding and receiving from Chinese who married girls out of the house monies on account of board, etc."[47] Jennie Menzies's letter continued in this vein.

Dated June 26, 1888, Menzies's letter was sent from Oakland, California. She laid out her account of the events that culminated in the accusations levelled at Walter Menzies. In her version of events, she carefully documented her role in aiding her husband's "rescue" of one of the Chinese girls around whom this case revolved. Writing almost a month after her husband had been accused of skipping town in order to dodge investigation, Menzies claimed to be "much surprised to see ... an account of the inveigling – so-called – of two girls from the 'Chinese Home' by Professor Menzies."[48] She quickly followed this by stating: "[There] are many people in Victoria who know how untruthful that statement is, none better than Mr. Gardiner himself."[49] Immediately placing herself in opposition to Gardiner, Menzies calls into question not only the facts as they had been laid out in previous accounts but also Gardiner's integrity. Given his involvement in the matters of the Home, Menzies was also calling into question the integrity of the institution. As a woman, Jennie Menzies drew on her authority to morally assess the work of the Home.

Jennie Menzies was not content to blacken the reputation of the Home by inference and innuendo alone. Her version of events begins with the following account:

On the 14th of January last the two girls in question ran away from the Home to Mrs. L.M. Fowler's house. They complained of having been terribly beaten and nothing would induce them to return to the Home. That was Saturday. Mrs. Fowler waited all afternoon and up to midnight, expecting someone to come to see if they were there. She had been their matron. No one came or made any inquiry whatever about them.[50]

Here, Menzies not only implicates the matron in charges of physical abuse but also implies that she and Gardiner were unconcerned about the absence of these two girls. According to Menzies, she and her husband had spoken to Gardiner after the incident and had informed him that they would take one of the girls and find someone else to take the other. Here she implies not only that she is associated with the Home but also that she has its consent.

By accusing the Home of misconduct and neglect, Jennie Menzies simultaneously reinforced her own moral authority and placed both herself and her husband in the role of rescuers. Penned by Jennie Menzies and not her husband, the letter was able to avoid allegations of sexual depravity by framing their *own* home as a substitute rescue home. The domestic space of the home helped to legitimize the Menzies's interventions. Given the legitimacy offered by women's moral authority, it was imperative that a woman intervene on behalf of these young girls. Yet, despite the motherly care that Jennie Menzies could offer, no religious transformation is suggested in her account. Therefore, the newspapers continued to view the relationships forged between the Menzies and their charges as suspicious. Despite her confessed involvement in this case, Jennie Menzies was never charged. From the safety of California, she was able to defend herself and her husband and also to cast a shadow over Gardiner and the Home. This case, in fact, was "tried" for a full month in the newspapers before any formal charges were laid. Jennie Menzies and other women and men used the press to do what the courts were unable to do: address (or level) charges and offer testimony before the court of public opinion.

Despite the fact that the "Professor" and his wife were not in Victoria to defend themselves, the letter made it clear that neither had anything to hide. Jennie Menzies plainly stated that she and her husband "made no secret of it, and the only reason Prof. Menzies would have had for making evasive replies would be to *shield Mr. Gardner and the 'Home.'*"[51] She went on to state that, "except for the matron of the Home, there was no one the girls were more afraid of than Mr. Gardner."[52] Here, any secretiveness was framed not as linked to the Menzies's guilt but, rather, as a protective strategy. Why Jennie Menzies would feel the desire to protect the institution was unclear and highlights an interesting contradiction. Although she claimed that her husband was only secretive in an attempt to spare Gardiner and the Home, she simultaneously implicated the Home and Gardiner in behaviour that should have been reported, not hidden. One must ask: What fuelled the desire to protect Gardiner and the Home? Further, why did Jennie Menzies overcome this desire to protect and why did she do so in such a public fashion?

The initial desire to protect the Home may have been attributed to racial loyalties. To accuse Gardiner and the Home based on the stories of two Chinese girls would have upset the racial logics of this period – logics that would become obvious in the court case that followed. The testimony, formal or informal, of the Chinese girls could not be privileged over and above the reputation of the white men and women who ran the institution. However, as the case became less about the accusations of the two Chinese girls and instead shifted to accusations levelled by one white man against another, the Menzies's need to protect the Home was overcome by the need to defend themselves against such an attack. The accusations against Gardiner and the Home were not about the protection of the Chinese girls but, rather, about the preservation of Walter and Jennie Menzies. In her letter, therefore, Jennie Menzies directs numerous charges against the Home in general and against Gardiner in particular. Among these is the aforementioned abuse as well as claims that the young girls were turned away from both Gardiner's home and from the Chinese Rescue Home even though they were barefoot in the snow. She also charged Gardiner with *pretending* to rescue a young woman from Chinatown, subsequently charging the woman's husband for her board and clothing, and then having them remarried according to Western traditions before allowing her to be released. In Jennie Menzies's eyes, this was evidence that Gardiner was marrying Chinese women to Chinese men who were willing to pay. If her moral condemnation was ironic, given that she was defending similar actions on the part of her husband, it was also evidence of the power of women to morally intervene in such matters.

Jennie Menzies's letter and the accompanying column were the first attempts to defend Walter Menzies. It must be noted that the letter appeared in the *British Colonist,* the rival of the *Daily Times,* even though it was in response to an article in the *Times.* If Menzies also sent a letter to the *Times,* it was not published. The drama continued to play out as the two newspapers each took sides in this public "trial." After Menzies's letter was published, the *Times* responded with a front-page article, which, according to the *Colonist,* was "inspired by Mr. Vrooman, [and] casts certain doubts as to the authenticity of Mrs. Menzies's letter ... and also contains several absurd insinuations in regard to *The Colonist's* position in the matter."[53]

The *Times's* immediate response to Menzies's accusations provides evidence of the weight of women's moral authority. It was quick to discredit Menzies's letter on a few fronts. In the first sentence of its article, the *Times* describes the letter as "*alleged* to have been written by Mrs. Menzies,"[54] immediately pointing out its suspicion that perhaps the letter was not even authentic in its authorship. If it was written by Walter Menzies and passed off as a letter from his wife, its moral authority and domestic legitimacy could easily be brushed aside. In addition, the *Times* also discredited the *Colonist's* publication of the letter. By entitling the article "The Colonist's Gardnerphobia" [*sic*], the *Times* calls into question the *Colonist's* motivations for publishing both Menzies's letter and an additional article on the subject. Chalking its reporting up to an irrational fear of Gardiner leads one to ask what exactly the *Times* was suggesting that the *Colonist* feared. Given that the *Colonist* did not seem to take issue with Menzies's contact with the two Chinese girls, it was likely not fear of cross-racial contact that was the issue: instead, it may have been the *relationships* that were being forged within the Home and the alleged transformations. This indicates that, while white superiority was central to transformative discourses, not everyone who was white supported the work of the Home.

Despite the fact that cross-racial contact was usually contained within the walls of the Home, anxieties around the work done there may have been due, at least in part, to the types of relationships that were forged within it. Walter Menzies, while he was accused of adopting immoral tactics, had returned the "Chinese problem" to the Chinese community, reinscribing racial boundaries in the process. Further, the *Times* explicitly accused the *Colonist* of "plotting" and implicitly accused it of poor journalism as it quickly showed that its own investigation had proven some of Jennie Menzies's claims to be false. While Menzies had claimed that

Gardiner sold a Chinese girl in marriage for a sum of money, the *Times* found evidence that the parties in question were, in fact, already married before they had come into contact with Gardiner. This article exposed Menzies's accusations as "basely false and therefore malicious"[55] and, at the same time, discredited the *Colonist,* which supported and printed her accusations.

On July 6, 1888, the *Colonist* responded to the *Times* by turning to another woman. This time it offered a copy of an affidavit written by Jessie Fowler, which corroborated Jennie Menzies's letter. The publication of this affidavit had both legal authority and female moral authority. The *Colonist* did not go as far as to deny Menzies's guilt but, instead, began to cast equal or greater suspicion onto Gardiner and his conduct. At first content to counter the *Times*'s article with the letter from Menzies, the *Colonist,* when the *Times* attempted to discredit this letter, turned to court records to build its case. That the courts were seen as a space where truth was both a goal and a necessity was clear in the *Colonist*'s use of court records as evidence. An affidavit was made to stand for truth in ways that a letter to the editor could not. Although contradictory affidavits often appeared in court cases, this particular affidavit was given the weight of truth because: (1) it corroborated the facts as they appeared in Jennie Menzies's letter; (2) it was written by a party who was not directly implicated in this case; and (3) as the *Colonist* made clear, there were other available "affidavits on file there and in possession of officials in the city touching on this same Chinese trafficking."[56] Thus, Fowler's affidavit was used as a strong rebuttal of Gardiner's accusations.

The affidavit in question was one that was used in a related habeas corpus case filed by Ah Chee. Subsequent to Walter Menzies's "selling" Ah Lin to him as his wife, Ah Chee learned that they were not, in fact, legally married. Gardiner agreed to have them legally married on the condition that Ah Lin return to the Home. After her return, Ah Chee claimed that he was not allowed to visit and was told that Ah Lin no longer wished to marry him. Ah Chee then applied, through a writ of habeas corpus, to have Ah Lin returned to him and removed from "the influence of Vrooman" (aka Gardiner).[57] The affidavit given by Jessie Fowler was the first of three affidavits that were to be published in this case. In her affidavit, Fowler supported Jennie Menzies's claims regarding the Home and Gardiner's treatment of Ah Lin as well as her claims that she had tried to find homes for the two girls. Although the *Colonist* asserted that there were other supporting documents on file, the fact that they chose Fowler's affidavit to support Jennie Menzies's claims speaks to the moral authority held by women.

The *Times* fired back quickly, attempting to discredit the *Colonist*. In a front-page article aptly entitled "The Menzies Apologist," the *Times* accused the *Colonist* of what it called "a mendacious attempt to prejudice the public mind against Mr. Gardner" and ended the article with a demand that this "Menzies apologist should call off his bloodhounds."[58] The *Times* accused the *Colonist* of publishing Fowler's affidavit "without a statement of all the facts and the final result of the application."[59] The ultimate result was that the case against the Home was dismissed; therefore, the *Times* suggested, the affidavit should not be given as much credibility as the *Colonist* seemed to lend it. The *Times* did not include any reference to what the affidavit said, only attacking the *Colonist* for its "one-sided version of the case," and it promised, in good time, to lay before the public the "facts of the case."[60] It fulfilled this promise five days later, but not before the *Colonist* published twice more on the matter. The first article was in response to the *Times*'s accusations and the second was a letter to the editor, which actually challenged some of Jennie Menzies's claims.

The *Colonist* began its July 7, 1888, article by linking it to Fowler's previously published affidavit, providing some context for the letter to the editor – no doubt a response to the *Times*'s accusations. This time the *Colonist* did not withhold the full context of the case, instead providing excerpts from many of the affidavits offered to the courts. All of these were indictments of Gardiner and the Home. The first headline simply read "The Chinese Matter,"[61] while the second read "Traffic in Chinese: Affidavit of Ah Chee and Statement of Ah Lin – Serious Charges."[62] Neither headline referenced Menzies or the kidnapping charges of which he had been accused. Although the second headline did hint at the trafficking of Chinese women, Menzies was not the accused in this case. While the *Colonist* did not directly refer to Menzies, it was clear that the affidavits and testimony of Ah Chee and Ah Lin were only of interest to it because of their connection to Menzies and Gardiner. The case from which the affidavits were drawn had received no attention prior to the publication of Gardiner's accusations against Menzies, notwithstanding that it had been the focus of the court a full three weeks prior to the *Colonist*'s publication of the affidavits.

While the *Colonist* used these affidavits to discredit Gardiner as Menzies's accuser and to shift suspicion away from Menzies and onto Gardiner, soon other Victoria citizens contributed to the debate by submitting letters to the editor. The letter from Jennie Menzies paved the way for others, with letters from Cecilia Spofford, Reverend Starr, and Annie Leake (then matron of the Home) subsequently appearing in the *Colonist*, the first on 8 July, 1888, and the latter two on 13 July, 1888. Spofford's letter pointed out some inconsistencies in Menzies's letter. Jennie Menzies had claimed that no one would take responsibility for Ah Lin; however, Spofford claimed that she had offered the girl a home. Her letter did not seem to take either side, neither defending Gardiner nor offering any new accusations with regard to Walter Menzies. The only goal of this letter, it seemed, was to set the record straight. As a member of the Women's Christian Temperance Union and a supporter of provincial suffrage campaigns, Spofford was an avid moral reformer who lent her moral authority to what was quickly becoming a very public debate.[63] Spofford ended her letter as follows: "I have no desire whatever in this matter but to see 'right' prevail, and when I read Mrs. Menzies's letter felt it was my *duty* to contradict statements which I knew to be incorrect."[64] While refusing to take sides, Spofford saw the press as an ideal venue for fulfilling her civic duty to ensure that the "truth" was fully told.

This focus on truth-telling was not only evident in the letters that were written to the newspaper but also in the newspaper's commentary. Of the four letters to the editor in this case, three were accompanied by "Editorial Comments." The only letter that did not have such commentary was that from Spofford. In the column that accompanied the letters of Starr and Leake, the *Colonist* began by evaluating and then weighing in on the veracity of their "testimony," much as it did with Menzies's letter. In both cases, the *Colonist* spoke to what it believed to be the truthfulness of the letters, despite the fact that the testimonies offered differed substantially. In the case of Menzies's letter, the *Colonist* posited that her statement "had the ring of truth";[65] in the case of Leake, it suggested that her story bore "the impress of truthfulness";[66] and of Starr and Leake it stressed its belief that they were "honest in what they said and sincere in their endeavour to do good work among the Chinese."[67] Although the *Colonist* did not go as far as to say that it had been deceived by previous correspondence or affidavits, it concluded that the latter were "worthy of further investigation."

The *Colonist*, however, did not shoulder the blame for believing these affidavits to be true, nor did it place the blame on those who may have misled them. Instead, with regard to the affidavits, it claimed: "if false, they are replete with perjury of a vicious type, and the individual against whom they are directed, should at least have taken the trouble to reply to them or proceeded in some manner that would have established his innocence."[68] Here, it was Gardiner's failure to publicly defend himself through his own truth-telling that was to blame for any misconceptions. The *Colonist* defended its own actions and its intentions, claiming that its position "was not assumed through malice, or a desire to wantonly besmirch Mr. Gardiner's character, or to injure anyone acting with him."[69] Furthermore, the paper continued, the "evidence submitted pointed to certain facts, and these facts, except by assertion, have not been disputed."[70] Again, it was Gardiner's unwillingness to defend himself or to supply evidence to support his innocence that was to blame for the *Colonist's* misconceptions. If it was the newspapers' duty to expose wrongdoing and to seek out the truth, it was also the duty of those accused and those who could verify or contradict "evidence" to do so.

Matron Leake, for her part, did offer a defence. She opened her letter with the words "in justice not only to Mr. Gardner, but also to 'The Chinese Home,' permit me the use of your columns to make public the following facts."[71] Leake answered charges that had been laid against her in Menzies's letter and in the affidavits that had been published in the newspaper. Although her testimony took the form of a "Letter to the Editor" and not an actual affidavit, the structure of the letter is noteworthy. The "facts" laid out in it are numbered from one to seven and are significant in that their order and logic mimic those of the affidavits of Fowler and Ah Chee, which the *Colonist* had previously published. Here, it is clear that Leake was familiar with and deeply influenced by the state's records, shaping her own testimony to mimic them.

The affidavits of Jessie Fowler and of Ah Chee, whose formal name was "Lum Tsze," both contained exactly seven points that were numbered in the same manner as were the points in Leake's letter. Also, all three of these "testimonies" begin by identifying their authors in relation to the case: Fowler by explaining her relationship to the Home, Ah Chee by stating both his formal name and the name he was often called, and Leake by identifying her relationship to both the WMS and the Home. As Leake continued on with points two to seven, she continued to mimic the format and tone of the two affidavits, carefully and logically citing dates, places, and people; leaving out any emotion; and including only the facts that could be verified by other sources. One clear difference between Leake's letter and the affidavits offered by Fowler and Ah Chee is that the latter were concluded with sworn declarations that were witnessed by either a justice of the peace or by a "Commissioner for taking affidavits in the Supreme Court of British Columbia."[72] This seal of legitimacy was not included in Leake's letter. However, Leake's own work as a moral reformer gave her moral authority, as did the accompanying letter from Reverend Starr.

Starr's letter had two goals. It should be kept in mind that Starr acted as a notary of sorts, giving legitimacy to Leake's "testimony." As the pastor of the Pandora Street Methodist Church, Starr's reputation was viewed as beyond reproach. In fact, in the "Editorial Comment" the editor described Starr as an "honorable and upright man and honest in what he says and sincere in his endeavors."[73] Starr, thus established as trustworthy – perhaps even more so than a justice of the peace – opens his letter with his first goal, that of presenting to the editor the letter written by Annie Leake. He begins: "The matron of 'The Chinese Home' has forwarded to me the enclosed letter with the request that, if I approve, I will hand it to you for publication."[74] Thus, by submitting the letter, Starr gives his stamp of approval to Leake's testimony, verifying not only its truthfulness but its authenticity. His first goal achieved, Starr quickly moves on to his second.

In beginning with "I should also myself like to say a word on behalf of Mr. Gardner,"[75] Starr calls into question the integrity of the evidence by acting as a character witness. Although he does not introduce new evidence in his letter, he attacks the *Colonist* for journalistic misconduct, rebuking it as follows: "when giving publicity to your belief, the part of a true journalist, I submit would have been to publish all the facts which *you knew were at your disposal*."[76] Here, Starr questions the *Colonist*'s motives, insisting that it did not have the public's interest at heart, was not concerned with justice, and did not disclose the full evidence that was at its disposal. He faults the newspaper not for what it did print but for what it did not. That his friend, Gardiner, was being used to divert attention away from the accused is not the subject of his critique; rather, his focus is on the *Colonist*'s failure to present the public with all of the information necessary to make an informed judgment.

Starr's desire for balanced reporting is evident in his own testimony on Gardiner's character. Unlike the *Colonist*, which he critiques, Starr does not provide either a condemnation of Gardiner or a glowing endorsement; instead, he begins by framing Gardiner as "not infallible. Like other men he has his faults."[77] However, Starr is quick to counter these faults by speaking to Gardiner's generosity, his reputation, and his self-sacrifice. In the face of all of the accusations, and knowing Gardiner's faults, Starr concludes: "Knowing as I do the *real truth*, I deem it an honor to say I could trust him with my life."[78] Here, Starr offers what he contends that the *Colonist* had not: the "real truth," knowable only through acknowledgment of both the good and the bad (i.e., the "real truth" as the whole truth and nothing but the truth). Following the publication of these letters, the *Colonist* vowed that it would not report on the case again unless there were further developments. This avowal seemed to mark the beginning of a ceasefire in this very public case as the *Times* followed suit.

The press' publication of competing claims to truth highlighted the existence of competing claims to morality. The alleged sale of Chinese women as well as the abuses that they were alleged to have suffered at the hands of the Home's matron stood as cautions against cross-racial intimacies. Further, publication of inquiries into the police's failure to act drew attention to the fissures in the moral landscape. These fissures marked points of disagreement about how best to deal with Chinese populations. Concerns were raised not only about whether or not Menzies was selling Chinese women but also about whether Gardiner was doing the same, an indication that not all believed in the redemptive power of the Home. It must be noted, however, that, subsequent to this case, Gardiner's name was rarely mentioned and that no similar accusations were levelled at the WMS women who ran the Home, despite their common practice of finding husbands for the residents and receiving money for the women's care. It was likely the institutional nature of the Home that made the receipt of these funds acceptable. Yet the work of saving and domesticating women was legitimated precisely because it took place within the domestic realm, the domain of women. The men who interfered in these "private" matters, especially as they concerned marriage, were quickly brought to task, both by the public and by the state.

THE STATE OF MARRIAGE

Upon Walter Menzies's return to Victoria on July 26, 1888, he was quickly arrested and charged with "feloniously causing Loi Ho, under the age of sixteen, to be secretly confined and taken out of Canada against her will,"[79] although this was quickly amended to "kidnapping with intent."[80] On August 3, 1888, a second charge of "obtaining $150 from Ah Chee under false pretences" was added to the original charges, with the kidnapping charges being dropped the following day.[81] On August 21st of the same year, Menzies was arraigned in the Supreme Court of British Columbia on the charge of "procuring a girl under 21 years of age to have carnal dealings with a Chinaman named Ah Chee."[82] This was an important distinction, as it rested entirely on how the state was to define what constituted marriage. If Ah Chee and Ah Lin were to be considered married, the charges would fall. Thus, marriage would become a central point of discussion in this case. In order to provide some context for this discussion of marriage, I now provide a brief discussion of the Chinese Rescue Home's role in marriages.

Marriage was, in fact, an important facet of the institution. While many of the residents stayed only a short while, for those who remained in residence for longer periods, leaving respectably usually meant going out into service work or being married, preferably to a Christian Chinese or Christian Japanese man. Although the records did not always provide reasons for why women left, it was clear that many were married before leaving. The Home was often used as a wedding site for residents as well as for Chinese and Japanese community members who desired a Western marriage. For many years the Home was also a transitional space for Japanese women who entered the country as wives of Japanese men. Although legally married under Japanese law, many of these marriages were not initially recognized by Canadian law. Thus, so-called picture brides and others were often directed to the Home by immigration officials until their husbands could be found and new marriages performed. Here, the state's investment in not only policing immigration but also in the private relationships of new immigrants was clear. The Home also provided each of these brides with a Bible as a memento of her "special day." When new laws were passed recognizing the marriages of picture brides, the advisory committee was keenly disappointed at this lost opportunity. However, other marriage opportunities still existed as the house provided the ideal space within which to train residents for their future roles as wives and mothers.

Cooking, cleaning, sewing, and mending were necessary not only to the running and maintenance of the domicile but also to training a woman for the role of wife. As discussed in the previous chapter, as a house, the Home provided the ideal space for training women to be wives and mothers. It had all the amenities necessary to teach the women how to cook, clean, sew, tend to young children, or build a fire. Marriage was a dominant concern among those who were involved in the running of the institution. Finding suitable partners for their "girls" was one of the many concerns of the matron and the Home's advisory committee. Elizabeth,[83] for instance, entered the Home at age seventeen, staying for four years. The date she left was also the date that she was married in the Home to a baker from Ladysmith, BC, a town over eighty kilometres north of Victoria. Given the isolation that these young women often experienced and the distance between this particular town and Victoria, it is probable that this marriage was arranged by the women who ran the Home. On at least two other occasions, the advisory committee minutes show instances in which Chinese men had come to the Home in search of a wife. Screening these men was imperative as not all those who applied for wives were to be trusted. Testifying at the Royal Commission on Chinese and Japanese Immigration (1902), F. Kate Morgan, a teacher and evangelist with the Home, discussed the suspicion with which these applications were viewed: "A Chinaman will profess to become a Christian to get a wife."[84] Here, it is clear that a profession of faith was not enough: Christianity had to be evident in the behaviour and lifestyle of the would-be husband.

In January 1901, the board met to discuss the future of one particularly disruptive girl named "Bev."[85] Although a "Chinaman had applied to the home for a wife," he was not deemed suitable for her.[86] Three months later it was reported that "a suitable husband had been found for Bev and [that] she had been married from the home to a professedly Christian Chinese merchant of Nanaimo." This was a relief to all involved as "the conduct of the girls ... very much improved since Bev left."[87] Marriage became not only a respectable way of leaving the Home but also an important means of removing disruptive or uncooperative women such as Bev in a way that would not result in their returning to their "immoral" lives. Despite the fact that Chinese men far outnumbered Chinese women in Victoria, not all of the young women found husbands while resident in the Home. This suggests that the women who ran the Home were very particular about picking men for "their girls" to marry. The preoccupation with marriage was certainly tied to white women's roles as moral reformers. However, as the Menzies case makes clear, this did not stop men from attempting, with varying degrees of success, to take on these same roles outside the walls of the Home.

On Wednesday, August 21, 1888, the trial began in the case of *Regina v. Menzies*. The state's interest in the case became clear as it shifted away from crimes against the Chinese and towards a crime that was more concerned with policing the bounds of intimacy and morality. The *Times* presented an account of the trial that evening, with the *Colonist* publishing its account the following morning. The former published a story only thirty-three lines in length, while the latter devoted almost 250 lines to the case. The *Colonist* included much of the court transcripts, including portions of the testimonies of Ah Chee, of a doctor who was brought in to testify with respect to Ah Lin's age, as well as of Ah Lin and Mrs. Hopkins. It also included the comments of the presiding judge.

The *Times* took a distinctly different approach, listing the charges and then reporting on counsel for each side. This was followed by a very brief discussion of the testimony of the first witness. The *Times* went to press when the court proceedings were still in progress, hence the incompleteness of its story. Although the first witness, Ah Chee, was reported to have been examined and then cross-examined, the newspaper did not include any of this testimony in its report. Instead, the *Times* chose to focus exclusively on the judge's comments. This focus on the judge as authority might partially explain why the newspaper chose not to include the full testimony of Ah Chee. According to the *Times,* "His Lordship during the time the evidence was in progress said the testimony given by the Chinese was a mockery of justice. The papers before the court were the most important evidence."[88] The *Times* seems to have taken this charge quite seriously as it chose to include only very small amounts of either Ah Chee's or Ah Lin's testimonies, around which this case was built.[89] Instead, it focused its reporting almost entirely on the testimony of Jessie Fowler, who recalled the story of Ah Chee and Ah Lin, once more underscoring white women's authority. White witnesses were regarded as the only voices of reason. That these voices were to stand in for the unintelligible Chinese was further evidence of the privileging of whiteness and the reinscription of the "Chinese problem." The *Times* also included the remarks of counsel (both sides) and of the judge. Only at the end of the article did it mention that Ah Chee had been recalled and re-examined, devoting only eight lines to his testimony, three of which had no apparent bearing on the case. This decision would seem to underscore the judge's belief that the testimony of a Chinese witness could not be trusted.

The *Colonist*, however, provided a much fuller account of the trial. Over the course of the two-day trial, it seemed to be reporting on a much different case than that discussed in the *Times*. On the first day, the *Colonist* provided a list of five witnesses, and it included the judge's commentary throughout. On the second day, it reported on an additional three witnesses, pointing to the diversity of voices and to the contested nature of the "facts."

Justice John Gray made no secret of his attitude towards the Chinese and, especially, towards their presence in the courtroom. Despite the fact that, as a commissioner for the Royal Commission on Chinese Immigration (1885), Gray defended Chinese immigration, he argued in his report that there should be joint tribunals "for the purpose of creating confidence in the administration of justice, and ascertaining truth when the Chinese are concerned."[90] His belief that Chinese were unreliable witnesses was not questioned by either the *Times* or the *Colonist,* which suggests that his attitude was commonplace and was acceptable in a person of his authority. In its report, the *Colonist* opened with the testimony of Ah Chee. Justice Gray interrupted Ah Chee's testimony several times. The first time, early in Ah Chee's testimony, Gray interjected: "The court for the trial of Chinese cases is, it seems to me, the greatest burlesque in the country."[91] Gray's comments are significant for a few reasons. First, his reference to this case as a "Chinese case" is suggestive as the person being tried was a white man. Based on this comment, it would appear that the judge viewed race as a central component of this case. Second, his reference to "burlesque" likened the courtroom and the trial to the theatre and to performance. In fact, Gray's own "performance" within the courtroom was a clear indication that his role was not only to preside over and to pass judgment but also to narrate an elaborate performance. Consider, for instance, the following exchange between the prosecutor, the defence attorney, and Gray regarding Ah Chee's testimony:

Mr. Irving –He answered that question.

Mr. Drake –I want to get that answer from the witness myself.

His Lordship –You will accomplish a great feat if you do so.[92]

Here, Gray comments not as an impartial judge but as one of the players in what he sees as a theatrical performance. He openly derides the testimony of Ah Chee. Later in the case, he would go even further in discrediting this witness in particular and Chinese witnesses in general.

Gray's reference to burlesque is troublesome for a third reason. In his indictment of Chinese testimony, he contends not only that it is tantamount to burlesque but also that it is the *greatest* burlesque in the country. His focus is not only on deriding Chinese performances but also on suggesting that they be enjoyed as a type of amusement. This objectification of Chinese as "performers" for white audiences is a clear indication that not only were Chinese not to be taken seriously but also that their only conceivable role was to serve the needs of the white population. Finally, given that burlesque is associated with parody and exaggeration, Gray's comments say something about race. The *Merriam-Webster* dictionary defines burlesque as "a literary or dramatic work that seeks to ridicule by means of grotesque exaggeration or comic imitation" and as "mockery usually by caricature."[93] Chinese witnesses were seen not only as mimicking whiteness but also as being comic in their mimicry, their performances amounting to mockeries of white tradition.[94] This is certainly evident in Gray's response not only to Chinese testimony but also to other Chinese performances of whiteness, such as marriage.

Upon hearing one witness testify as to how Menzies and Gardiner each tried to arrange the marriage of Ah Chee and Ah Lin, Gray interrupted, exclaiming: "It is a perfect mockery of justice. How can we believe these people? A marriage certificate should never be issued to such persons. The act never contemplated any such thing."[95] To this, defence counsel Drake replied: "I wish to know the marriage ceremonies of the Chinese law." His Lordship was quick to reply: "They sell them."[96] Here, the judge emphasized not only the untrustworthiness of Chinese witnesses but also their inherent immorality. In fact, although the courtroom was framed as a place where the facts were to be evaluated and questioned, morality was a central concern for Gray in this case, especially as it was to be applied to marriage.

When Reverend Fraser was called to testify that he had refused to marry the two victims without an interpreter, Gray again interjected his own moral judgment. Although not directly relevant, as Ah Chee and Ah Lin were not married in either a civic or a religious ceremony, Gray commented: "It has struck me as abnormally wrong that these people who have not the slightest conception of the solemn rights of matrimony and Christianity should be married by a Christian Clergyman." Gray did not see Christian marriages for Chinese as simply wrong but, rather, as *abnormally* wrong. While the sanctity of Christian marriage might be violated by whites, for Chinese such violation was linked to their "abnormality." When the witness replied, "It has not struck me that way. I look upon the heathen as God's children," Gray again weighed in on the matter: "I think it would be better if they should go before the civic authorities rather than to a clergyman."[97] His comments had no bearing on the case, serving only to once more discredit Chinese people as being unable to understand or to perform Christian morality. The state was clear in its condemnation of those who might tarnish the Christian institution of marriage.

Regardless of how the court might have felt about Chinese marriage, the defence claimed that the marriage between Ah Chee and Ah Lin was, in fact, legal and that, therefore, no "illicit intercourse" had taken place. The prosecution, however, claimed that the marriage could not be recognized because of Ah Lin's age. In order to support its claim that Ah Lin was too young to be legally married, the prosecution did not rely on Ah Lin to testify but, instead, called in an "expert witness" to determine her age. Dr. Jackson concluded that Ah Lin, based on her "general appearance and physical development,"[98] was about fourteen years old. Here, the doctor's testimony was framed as expert evidence in order to provide what the court believed Ah Lin could not: the truth.

Despite making it evident that he believed that the testimonies of Ah Lin and Ah Chee lacked credibility, on August 24, 1888, Justice Gray pronounced the defendant guilty. Again the judge was quick to point out that he "attached very little importance to the evidence of the two Chinese witnesses. The turning point of the matter was that Menzies gave a receipt and worded it as he did, which to his mind was conclusive evidence of having deceived the Chinese. The Chinese evidence was valueless, except so far as it corroborated the evidence of other witnesses."[99] Chinese evidence was only to be considered true when it corroborated the testimony brought forward by white witnesses. At the same time, however, the only way to evaluate the truth was to measure it against the truth as told by white witnesses. This logic guaranteed that, in cases where Chinese testimony was at odds with that of white witnesses, it would be deemed false and thus discredited.

Gray's disdain for Victoria's Chinese population would become even more evident in his concluding remarks, as would his investment in policing the boundaries of the domestic, of intimacy, and of morality. Throughout the case, the prosecution portrayed Ah Lin as a hapless victim, a child of fourteen who had been victimized first by the Chinese men who turned her into a prostitute and then by Menzies who allegedly sold her to Ah Chee. The defence, however, painted her as a troubled and troublesome prostitute whom Menzies had attempted to rehabilitate but who could not and should not be trusted. Gray clearly saw her in an even worse light than did the defence. His remarks were scathing. He condemned Menzies for prostituting the girl, whom he described as "a notoriously bad character, a Chinese prostitute." But what offended him even more was that, having knowledge of her bad character, Menzies had traded "her off to a man as a *wife*."[100] Gray felt that it was an insult to marriage to have proposed that it take place between such unfit parties. He continued: "I am bound to say nothing can justify you, with a full knowledge of the utter unfitness of the parties, going around to Christian ministers of the different churches in this city to ask them to perform the solemn service of their church."[101] The issue for Gray was not the deception of the two Chinese victims but something far greater – the sanctity of Christian marriage.

In the case of *Regina v. Menzies,* the state attempted to prove that Menzies had, in effect, prostituted Ah Lin by selling her to Ah Chee under false pretences, thus "promoting illicit intercourse between Ah Lin and Ah Chee."[102] The outcome of this case was dependent on two factors. First, did Menzies promote the illicit intercourse and, second, did the illicit intercourse take place? The defence argued that Menzies had not, in fact, sold Ah Lin but had only asked to be reimbursed by Ah Chee for expenses incurred while Ah Lin was in his care. The money that he received, therefore, could not be understood as promoting relations between Ah Lin and Ah Chee. However, the receipt that Menzies had given to Ah Chee was seen as damning evidence that Ah Chee had paid for his marriage to Ah Lin. Selling Ah Lin to Ah Chee in marriage, though, did not constitute the promotion of illicit intercourse. The case was contingent on whether the couple had consummated a marriage for, if they had, then "illicit intercourse" could not be understood to have taken place. Thus, the case hinged not on whether Menzies had sold Ah Lin to Ah Chee but on whether a legitimate marriage had taken place.

The court decided that no such marriage had taken place and that, therefore, when Menzies told the couple that they were married his deceit *caused* them to engage in illicit intercourse. Thus, the prisoner was found guilty as charged. For Gray, although he saw the crime itself as a "particularly offensive one, leading a young girl by false representation to prostitution,"[103] the greater crime, and the one to which he devoted most of his comments, was the disregard and disrespect paid to the sanctity of Christian marriage. During this trial, it was the contamination of white domesticity that was at stake, not the virtue of a Chinese woman. Although the case was contingent on the fact that Ah Chee and Ah Lin were *not* married, Gray did not view Christian marriage as the answer; rather, he was clear that Menzies's crime lay not in his having failed to have the couple married but in his having the audacity to have attempted to have them married in a Christian church.

Gray chastised Menzies for degrading the Christian office by simply asking Christian ministers to marry two people who "had neither knowledge of what the ceremony meant, or the language in which it was to be performed, of the mutuality of affection or contemplation of the future, in accordance with the views of any Christian church." Gray was clear that Menzies should have had the couple married according to their own customs, or "if [it was] necessary that there should be a civil marriage, let them go in a civil magistrate or the registrar." He continued: "I cannot understand the sacred service of a Christian church being so *prostituted* and dishonoured."[104] Gray used the same charges levelled against Menzies with regard to his treatment of Ah Lin to speak to what he saw as being the real victim. It was not only Ah Lin who was prostituted but also the Christian church. And, clearly, Gray viewed the latter as the greater victim. It is likely that one of the reasons that the Home had support from the community, and later the courts, while Menzies did not, is twofold. First, before marriages were arranged through the Home, a process of domestication was to take place under the apt tutelage of white women; second, as a religious institution, the Home ensured that the couples who were married were first converted to Christianity. Menzies undertook to fulfill neither of these criteria.

In his sentencing, Gray condemned Menzies for this "dirty business." Furthermore, he did so in a way that underscored the racial hierarchy that favoured whiteness. Whites, he argued, were to be held to a higher standard under the law: "It is no answer to say the Chinese buy and sell these women and do not regard marriage in the light we do." Addressing Menzies, Gray opined: "You belong to what we believe a higher scale of civilization. You are either English or American, and ought to feel that bartering children for prostitution, whether under the form of marriage or otherwise, is a disgrace as well as a crime."[105] Here, a higher moral calling is attached to whiteness, and, thus, a higher standard of conduct is demanded. It is the racial hierarchy equating whiteness with truth and morality that, in the end, is responsible for Gray's disregarding Chinese testimonies. Further, it is this same hierarchy, in particular Menzies's inability or unwillingness to live up to it, that resulted in his being so harshly punished. Menzies's punishment – in this case, eight months in jail – was meant to protect the racial hierarchy that he had violated both through his attempts to allegedly prostitute Ah Lin and through his even more abhorrent crime: the prostitution of the church.

The Home functioned in a space on the edge of the domestic, both in terms of the domestic/foreign divide and in terms of the domestic/public divide. This space was, in some ways, shaped by public discourses and state interventions that took place beyond its walls. In this chapter I move outside the Home space in order to address perceptions of the evaluative and regulatory work that took place inside the Home as well as its relationship to other institutions. Drawing on a case that had close ties to those who ran the Home as well as to those housed within it shows how moral entrepreneurs functioned in complex ways as each tried to carve out and map the contours of the moral landscape, even as it applied to the domestic realm.

The ambivalent response of the state to the Home is shown in the Menzies case as well as in the failure of the police to act in the Home's interests. Manoeuvrings and negotiations that took place outside its walls not only defined the Home's reputation but also delineated its work from that being done outside it. In the Menzies case, as in the Home, women played an important role as moral authorities and reformers. State interventions also contributed to the moral landscape by defining the boundaries not only of cross-racial contact but also of the domestic realm, particularly around marriage. The harsh penalties meted out to Menzies sent a clear message that men should not intervene in what was seen as the legitimate work of women. The exceptionality of the Home becomes clearer through this discussion of the functions and functioning of that which was outside of it. Victoria's citizens were divided on the subject of Menzies's and Gardiner's guilt or innocence, making clear that the Home was not without controversy. It was regarded with both reverence and suspicion not only by the white community but also by the Chinese community. This was also evident in habeas corpus cases, where the institution's custody was challenged by Chinese community members. The following chapter outlines the state's investment in shaping and defining the boundaries of domesticity within the Home and in deciding who might reside within its walls.

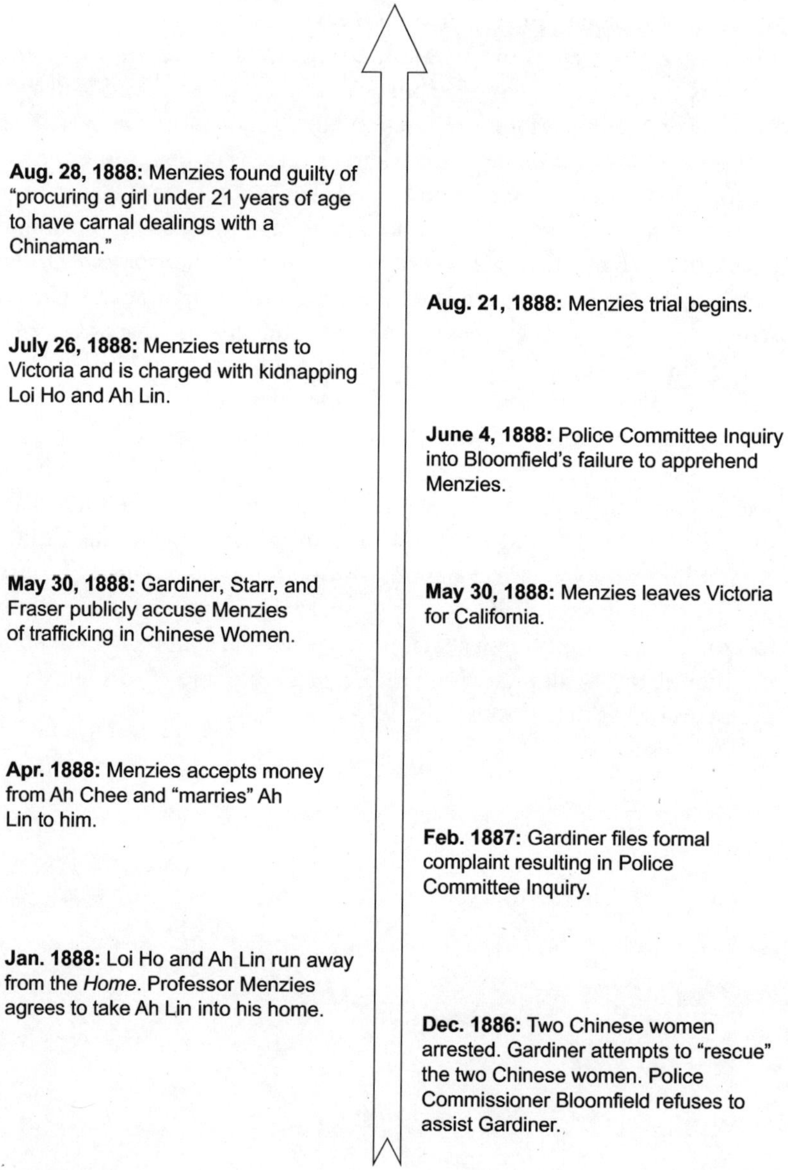

Aug. 28, 1888: Menzies found guilty of "procuring a girl under 21 years of age to have carnal dealings with a Chinaman."

Aug. 21, 1888: Menzies trial begins.

July 26, 1888: Menzies returns to Victoria and is charged with kidnapping Loi Ho and Ah Lin.

June 4, 1888: Police Committee Inquiry into Bloomfield's failure to apprehend Menzies.

May 30, 1888: Gardiner, Starr, and Fraser publicly accuse Menzies of trafficking in Chinese Women.

May 30, 1888: Menzies leaves Victoria for California.

Apr. 1888: Menzies accepts money from Ah Chee and "marries" Ah Lin to him.

Feb. 1887: Gardiner files formal complaint resulting in Police Committee Inquiry.

Jan. 1888: Loi Ho and Ah Lin run away from the *Home*. Professor Menzies agrees to take Ah Lin into his home.

Dec. 1886: Two Chinese women arrested. Gardiner attempts to "rescue" the two Chinese women. Police Commissioner Bloomfield refuses to assist Gardiner.

FIGURE 9   Timeline for Menzies/Bloomfield cases.

5
Roofs, Rafters, and Refuge

The State, Race, and Child Custody

Habeas corpus cases were one way that the state took an active role in defining the possibilities and limits of domesticity, especially as it was concerned with race. This is clear in the four habeas corpus cases discussed in this chapter. Three of these were reported in the British Columbia Law Reports. Another received extensive newspaper coverage. Given that the latter was the only case in which the Chinese Rescue Home lost, it provides an important counter-example to the other three. Habeas corpus is defined as a "command that was issued by a judge to a person having custody of another person to bring the prisoner before the court ('Let me have the body') so that the court could inquire into the validity of that person's detention."[1] Here, the focus is primarily on the detention of a prisoner and the validity of that detention. Given the importance of law in defining and regulating society, an analysis of these cases shows how common knowledge of race is tied to both ideas and spaces. I use the metaphors of roofs and rafters as a way of exploring three important and overlapping themes.

First, the Home was envisioned as a surrogate parent to Chinese women and children – literally giving them a roof over their heads. It was seen as an appropriate site of racial governance due to its ties to "proper" domesticity and to Western "family values." Second, the state provided the legal framework, or rafters, for these practices through its interpretation of habeas corpus cases as custody cases. In examining these cases I focus on the family. In particular, I explore the Home by analyzing the legal concepts of parent and guardian, especially as they related to the institution's role as surrogate parent. Although these were habeas corpus cases and not familial custody cases, the applicants in three of the four cases had to construct themselves as appropriate and legitimate guardians of the young girls over whom they wished to regain control for, if they had no legal rights as guardians, then they had no right to file writs of habeas corpus on their behalf. Their fitness and legitimacy as parents or guardians would be determined by the court. Third, I show how the Home became a space of refuge from outside threats, especially the threat of the "stranger." I juxtapose the construction of family with the stranger, seen both as the antithesis of Western ideals of family and as a threat to them. The discourse of the stranger is tied to discourses of race; however, race intersected with the law in contradictory and ambivalent ways.

The following cases each provide insights into how the law was enacted, sometimes in racially charged ways, to provide resolution between Chinese community members and the Home. My examination of these cases confirms Constance Backhouse's argument that the "fiction of 'race' is never so obvious as when one looks backward in time."[2] The first habeas corpus case in which the Home was involved was reported in the British Columbia Law Reports in 1893 and revolved around Ah Gway, who was described as being approximately fifteen years old.[3] The applicant, Chin Su, filed a habeas corpus case against the Home, claiming parental rights and that the Home was holding Ah Gway against her will. The applicant's parental rights were not acknowledged by the courts and the case was dismissed. The second case is that of Choy Wan.[4] This case involved a twelve-year-old Chinese girl who came to the Home on September 4, 1895. The applicant, Mong Kow Lee, argued that the girl was under his guardianship and that she had run away and that, this being the case, the Home had no right to keep her. In this instance, the court agreed. The third case began in 1898 and concerned a sixteen-year-old child, Quai Shing. The applicant, Sing Kow Seid, claimed to be her adopted father. Quai Shing had allegedly been removed from the applicant's home by police and placed in the Home. The applicant filed a writ of habeas corpus in an attempt to regain custody of the child. He lost the case, appealed, and lost again. The last case is that of Soy King. This case was initiated by Sam Kee in July 1900. In this instance, the applicant's guardianship of the child was affirmed by the courts, but his habeas corpus application was denied. Each of these cases offers insights into parental surrogacy as well as into discourses of custody and refuge.

A Roof over Their Heads: Parental Surrogacy and the Home

While the Woman's Missionary Society interacted with Japanese and Chinese residents of the Home in the realm of domesticity, this realm was neither entirely private nor entirely separate from state interventions or concerns. The women who ran the Home functioned as surrogate parents or guardians and, as such, their actions could be the subject of both legal and social interventions. These interventions and concerns took the form of ordering familial relationships by determining the guardianship of the very first girls to be admitted into the Home and by defining what constituted a familial relationship. Each of the cases offers interesting insights into the relationship between the state, the Home, and members of the Chinese community. They each also underscore the ways in which the Home itself was constructed as a legitimate institution both inside the courts and outside them. Although the Home was not a state institution, the fact that these legal battles revolved around habeas corpus and not kidnapping charges suggests that the Home was seen, at least by some, as a legitimate site of detention. The state's sanctioning of the institution began with some of its first rescues.

John Gardiner, an active evangelist in the Chinese Mission School in Victoria, "found that there were some Chinese girls held in houses of prostitution against their will, who would be glad of any means of escape."[5] The court agreed with Gardiner's assessment that the four girls who had been recovered "were held against their will as slaves for immoral purposes," and once the court appointed Gardiner as their guardian, he "undertook the cost himself" and rented a house for these young women.[6] Despite the fact that the Home was founded by a private citizen and was later run by a religious organization, state involvement, although not consistently applied, was routine and constant. The state intervened in more than guardianship cases: throughout the institution's history, police and immigration officials played active roles in bringing the Home's wards under its roof.

Police and immigration officials placed women in the Home and the police facilitated their return when they "escaped" from it. That the rescue home was part of a carceral network is further underscored by the type of cases that were brought against it. Although WMS records often refer to habeas corpus cases as custody cases – an indication that the women viewed themselves as surrogate parents – in all of these cases the courts ruled not on custody but, rather, on whether or not the Chinese applicant had the legal right to challenge the detention of the "prisoner" in question, rather than the Home's legal right to custody of a child. Despite its status as a private institution, the Home served a public (i.e., state) function.

Although these four cases are the only ones that were readily accessible in the legal records and newspapers, I did find references to cases that were not published. While it is impossible to know exactly how many cases were heard before the courts, it appears that there were many. The case of Quai Shing, although deemed important enough in the legal world to be published in the British Columbia Law Reports, did not seem to be a major point of discussion for the Home's advisory committee. In fact, although the first hearing concluded in October 1897, the board did not mention its victory or, indeed, allude to this case at all when it met in November and December 1897. This case would not be discussed until January 1898, when Matron Sarah Bowes presented her quarterly report. In this report, she provided the board with a history of Elsie's (Quai Shing's) case, "how she was brought to the Home from Vancouver and the lawsuit which following [sic] when her former owner claimed her and tried to regain possession of her, the judges however deciding that the child should be left in the care of the Home since no one else seemed to have any better right to her."[7] In fact, although custody was sometimes mentioned in meeting minutes and in formal reports, the discussions were very superficial, implying that, for the women who ran this institution, issues of custody were either of relative unimportance or were fairly commonplace.

The WMS women's confidence that the courts would ultimately grant them custody was evident in a number of references in the minutes of the advisory committee. As discussed in the Introduction, when Emily ran away from the Home to a convent, the board recommended that it write immediately "to the Convent demanding the return of Emily to the Home and emphasizing our authority in the matter."[8] The women's confidence in their right to custody of Emily may seem strange, given that no official custody had been granted to them in Emily's case or, indeed, in the cases of most of the residents. However, given their repeated success in the courts, the women who administered the Home had every reason to feel confident that the state would support them, even in a case against a Catholic convent. The following month, after receiving a reply from the convent, the board called a special meeting and "Mesdames Spencer and Bettes were appointed to wait on lawyer Fell to ask his advice as to what steps, if any should be taken to bring Emily back into the Home."[9]

Although their counsel advised them that they did not have legal standing to remove Emily from the convent, the girl eventually returned "home" of her own accord. In other cases, when Chinese men threatened the Home with lawsuits if girls/women were not returned to them, the WMS women did not waver. In fact, in some cases, it appears that the WMS's willingness to take legal action was enough to discourage Chinese men from formally pursuing their cases. The WMS women did not question their right to act as surrogate parents. And rarely did the courts question this right.

While the court certainly played a role in maintaining the WMS's power over Chinese men and women, how it framed the Home varied in each case. For instance, in the Quai Shing case, the Home was described as "a missionary institution in the City of Victoria, instituted for the purpose of adopting, educating and bringing up Chinese children."[10] This description is interesting as, ten years earlier, the Home had been founded not as an orphanage but as a place of rescue, primarily for Chinese prostitutes and "slave girls." In fact, it was a full thirteen years after this case that the name of the institution was changed from the "Chinese Rescue Home" to the "Oriental Home and School," a name more befitting the description offered in court. In addition, in court documents, the Home was most often referred to as the "Chinese *Refuge* Home," not the "Chinese Rescue Home," as it was called in the institution's own documents. The use of "refuge" in place of "rescue," however, opened up the possibility for broader definitions of the Home. In the minutes of the advisory committee for this period, there was no discussion of the children who resided there. Rather, the discussion revolved around Emily and her third escape (October/November); an "interesting wedding which had taken place" (January); a discussion of Japanese and Chinese women in Union Bay, BC, who "might be visited" (February); and a discussion about bringing another woman into the Home who, if left to her own devices, "might carry on her immoral practices."[11] While it is unclear why the Home took on this second identity as an orphanage or a refuge home, it is probable that this was a legal strategy to make it seem like the most suitable place for the courts to place "children" such as Choy Wan, Quai Shing, Soy King, and Ah Gway. Framing the Home as a surrogate parent legitimized it as a place of shelter, as a place providing a much needed roof over these children's heads.

In a later case, not discussed here, the Home was described somewhat differently. It was described as "a local philanthropic institution which has been established for the purpose of reclaiming and reforming fallen girls and women of the Chinese race."[12] The differences in the description can most likely be linked to the differences in the types of cases being presented. In the case of Quai Shing, the applicant claimed to be her adopted father; therefore, placement in an orphanage-type setting would seem less problematic. The later case, however, dealt with a woman seized by immigration officials who claimed she was a prostitute. What is clear, even when the definition of the Home is not, is that the court supported the institution in many of its decisions but also required that it be moulded to meet the court's demands.

The Child's Rights

When deciding custody cases, determining the best interests of the child invariably focused on free will. In all of the cases, the child in question was constructed as a consenting resident. This was not surprising as these cases were all concerned with what was claimed to be unlawful custody on the part of the Home. Given that the institution often argued that it was rescuing the girls and women precisely because, having been rendered slaves/prostitutes, their free will had been violated, it is ironic that unlawful custody and confinement were central to these custody cases – only the accusations were directed at the Home itself. The later use of barbed wire on the Home's fences and locks on its windows and doors suggests that confinement was one of the Home's imperatives, despite its claim to the contrary. However, the carceral nature of the Home was never acknowledged in court records, the focus instead being on the best interests of the child. Defining the domestic sphere was first and foremost about defining a home, and constraint was not compatible with ideological constructions of the home. In fact, given that the white women who ran the institution were concerned with training these young women in proper domesticity, their authority in these cases was never challenged. What the courts did challenge was whether the racial mixing that was required in order to achieve these ends was in the best interests of the child in particular and the family in general.

In the Ah Gway case, as well as in the cases that followed, the best interests of the child were established through the testimony of the child and the matron, although in some cases others weighed in. Deposed in the first case were Gardiner, the chaplain, and Matron Morrow, all of whom testified about Ah Gway's freedom. They contended that no force or restraint had been "placed on the movements of the infant: that she could leave the Home at any time and although Chin Su or other strangers were not allowed unlimited liberty or access, still she might see and converse with the infant at all reasonable hours, in the presence of two other China women [*sic*], residents there."[13] Likewise, in the Quai Shing case, while the applicant's affidavit painted his relationship with her as paternal in nature, and the Home's confinement of her as unlawful, Quai Shing herself told a much different story. Her story, in fact, mirrored the story of Ah Gway in a number of ways. Both girls claimed to be about sixteen years old; both claimed to be orphaned, kidnapped, and sold as slaves; and both were alleged to be living in households (at the time of their apprehension by the Home) in which there was a chance that they would be "exposed to risks"[14] or that was an "improper and immoral place of abode."[15] Both girls also testified that their choice was to remain in the Home and, in the case of Ah Gway, that physical restraint would be necessary to keep her in her previous home should she be returned there. Both cases were resolved in the Home's favour.

Despite similar tactics on the part of the Home's counsel, the case of Choy Wan was not so favourably resolved as were the others. Choy Wan's affidavit and one from Matron Sarah Bowes were used to claim that no force had been applied to keep her in the residence. Choy Wan, for her part, denied that she was Lee's servant and accused his mother of ill treating her. The child, while out on an errand, had appealed to those who ran the Home to give her shelter, stating that she had been a slave in China and had been bought by Lee's family. Bowes's affidavit explained the circumstances by which the girl had come to be a resident and stated that "she was there of her own free will and was free to leave whenever she wished."[16] Here again, the Home offered the child's consent as evidence that it was not confining her or violating her rights in any way. Further, Bowes explained that the institution was not a home "simply for fallen women, but for all Chinese girls and women requiring aid."[17] This home space, she implied, was not a space of confinement but a space of refuge. However, in this case, the court sided with Lee, the judge determining that the rights of the applicant and the sanctity of the family were of primary importance.

FROM ROOFS TO RAFTERS: STATE SUPPORT OF THE HOME

If the Chinese Rescue Home provided a protective roof over its inmates' heads, the state provided the legal supports, or rafters, that lent it legitimacy. This was not a straightforward endeavour, however. From the beginning, the lines between habeas corpus and custody were blurred. Although all four of the cases were brought before the court as habeas corpus cases, most became primarily concerned with custody as well as with the rights and responsibilities of parenthood. The state's role in deciding custody in the following cases was dependent on its understanding and interpretation of pre-existing legal definitions of parenthood and how these related to the best interests of the child. These considerations were tied to the determination of the legitimacy of guardianship claims, which, in some cases, were dependent upon the fitness or suitability of the guardian or "parent." In determining the rights of parents, the Ah Gway case was important as it was cited as a precedent in two of the three other cases discussed in this chapter. Acting as counsel for the Home was Thornton Fell.

Active in the community, especially within the Presbyterian Church, where he was an elder and member of the board and for which he also offered legal representation, Thornton Fell was the Home's counsel for many years. He was a well-known businessman from an important family in Victoria and was an important ally of the Home. The son of James Fell (a prominent businessman who served as a councillor in 1864 and 1865 and was mayor of Victoria from 1885 to 1887),[18] Thornton Fell was also politically active in the city. Like his father, he was a counsellor for Victoria, holding a seat from 1904 to 1907, and he was also a "prominent barrister in Victoria who served as Clerk of the Legislative Assembly."[19] According to the minutes of the Home's advisory committee, Fell was consulted on a number of legal matters, including the Ah Gway case.

In this important case, Chin Su contended that Ah Gway was her niece, entrusted to her and her husband while she was visiting her sister in China. Given that her sister had been recently widowed, the applicant claimed that she had agreed to take on the responsibility for Ah Gway's "nurture and education, until marriage, the infant being alleged to be betrothed to a young man in China."[20] Here, Chin Su argued that, as the aunt of Ah Gway, she was her legitimate guardian. Further, by referring to her agreement to take on the child's nurture and education, Chin Su constructed herself as a true parent to Ah Gway. Thornton Fell opposed the motion that demanded that Ah Gway be returned to Chin Su. He did so not on the basis of the Home's right to hold the child but, rather, on what he contended was Chin Su's illegitimacy as guardian and on the argument that the child was in the Home of her own free will. Here Fell made two important points: first, by arguing that Chin Su had no legal rights of guardianship, he called into question her right to apply for habeas corpus in the first place; second, given that the child was claimed to be in the Home of her own free will, no confinement could be said to have taken place. These two points were effectively made through discrediting biological familial ties and privileging emotional ones.

Fell's strongest witness in this case was the child herself. According to Ah Gway's deposition:

> she had never known her mother or any parent; her earliest recollection was of being under the care of a woman in Shanghai, who did not profess to be her mother. Some years ago this woman handed her over, she believed in consideration of a sum of money, to another woman, who carried her to Canton and who, in Canton, handed her over (again supposed for a money consideration) to Chin Su.[21]

Here, Fell uses Ah Gway's testimony to dispute not only Chin Su's legitimacy as guardian but also her suitability as a parent as any woman who would "buy" a child certainly could not be considered a fit parent. Women's roles were to fit whatever was defined as "proper" domesticity and white maternalistic standards. Constructing Ah Gway as an orphan allowed the case to be reframed around custody. Thus, the Home's role as surrogate parent was established so that the court would see the institution not as a place of detention but, instead, as a familial roof with which to shelter this orphaned child.

Parenthood and guardianship were often dependent on highly gendered understandings of who had rights to children. Although the Home positioned itself as surrogate home and mother, the court was much more concerned with the father and his rights. In the Chin Su/Ah Gway case, for instance, Justice Matthew Baillie Begbie,[22] himself a prominent judge and the province's first chief justice,[23] dismissed the writ of habeas corpus on the grounds that there seemed to be "no restraint, lawful or unlawful, of any personal liberty" and then determined that what was at issue was the matter of custody. Begbie chose to take neither side in determining which party had greater claim to custody, arguing instead that it did not "appear that any person had a valid claim to that custody."[24] This was a point that would be taken up in subsequent cases in which custody was an issue. According to Begbie: "Nobody can have a valid claim *except the father* or a duly appointed guardian; or some person as a schoolmaster, to whom the infant has by proper authority been confided or apprenticed."[25] While the Home was not deemed to be father or "duly appointed guardian," it was rarely called upon to defend its rights as surrogate parent. The courts only questioned the institution's guardianship as it pertained to questions of racial mixing (see below).

The law privileged a patriarchal understanding of the family. Although the Talfourd Act, 1839, sought to allow a mother's visitation and access rights, no rights to guardianship were to be given to the mother, the law favouring the father in most cases.[26] In *From Father's Property to Children's Rights: The History of Child Custody in the United States,* Mary Ann Mason explains these laws by referring to both patriarchal and capitalist influences on the law. Laws, she argues, were initially crafted based on the understanding that, although children were "not considered property under common law, as it has become fashionable to expound ... a child's labor was a valuable resource to parents and other custodial adults."[27] Thus, fathers, "without dispute, had almost unlimited authority of custody and control over their natural legitimate children, leaving almost no room for maternal authority, at least during the father's lifetime."[28] This was largely due to the "general legal impotence of married women. Under English common law a married women (*femme couvert*) could not own property, either real or personal."[29] It wasn't until women began to gain more legal rights (e.g., property rights) that a shift began to take place in custody laws. In British Columbia, the gaining of legal rights for women coincided with greater custody rights, but this would not occur until 1917. According to Cramer, the "Equal Guardianship Bill 'giving mothers equal right with fathers to the guardianship of their children' [was passed] two weeks before the suffrage bill."[30] Because these cases took place well before such legislation was passed, and despite the fact that Chin Su claimed to have been granted custody to Ah Gway by her mother, it was ruled that Chin Su did not have "any legal rights at all over the infant's person."[31]

Begbie was quick to acknowledge that the authority of a mother had been "greatly extended" in England. However, he did not extend that authority in this case for two reasons: first, he explained that he was "not aware that this legislation had been adopted in Canada" and, second, he indicated that he was unaware of "the state of the law in China." He also asserted that it would be difficult to ascertain "that a Chinese widow possessed similar authority, or had legally deputed it."[32] He ruled that the Chinese law on custody was not only unknowable but also, in this case, unnecessary. In two of the three cases that followed in which the applicant was a man, the court decided that he was the legitimate guardian, although only one of the two men retained custody.

In the second case and in the two cases that followed it, where the applicants were Chinese men, their legitimacy as guardians was to form the basis of their claims against the Home. However, each of the stories is slightly different, as are their outcomes. A *British Colonist* account dated September 5, 1895, and entitled "Little Choy Wan," explains that Mong Kow Lee, a "well known Chinese interpreter for the customs, applied in chambers to be made guardian of little Choy Wan, a Chinese girl twelve years old."[33] Although this story was reported in the *Colonist* five times between September 5 and September 19, the case was very quickly resolved. In fact, by September 6, the court had issued an order and had heard and ruled on an appeal. Unlike the Ah Gway case, which began with Ah Gway's admittance on February 3, 1893, and was resolved almost two months later on April 2, 1893, this case was over in three days. Lee argued that he had hired Choy Wan as a nurse for his ailing widowed mother, that she was a servant in his family, and that he was "paying the mother a certain sum for her services."[34] Lee's argument, unlike Chin Su's, was that the child was not a member of the family: instead, he portrayed the relationship as a business contract and himself as the child's employer.

In the case of Choy Wan, the court determined that Mong Kow Lee did, in fact, have guardianship over the child. The Ah Gway case was not cited in this decision, although it was referenced in the later habeas corpus cases discussed here. Given that Lee had argued that he was paying the *mother* of the child for the services of Choy Wan, the father once again did not factor into the arrangement. However, it may have been precisely the business nature of the relationship that garnered the judge's support for Lee's application. The judge in this case did not provide reasons for his assumption that Lee was the proper guardian of the child but, rather, simply affirmed that this was so. It is possible that Justice Davie did not rely on whether the applicant had the authority of the father in order to determine guardianship of the child, as cited by Begbie; rather, it is likely that he focused on the latter portion of this decision, the notion that a guardian such as "a schoolmaster, to whom the infant has by proper authority been confided or *apprenticed*,"[35] was appropriate. The judge may have determined the child, as a servant, to be a type of apprentice and that, for this reason, Lee could be seen as the appropriate guardian. It is probable that Davie also gave considerable weight to Lee's stature in the community and his work as an interpreter for the Department of Customs.[36]

In the third case, Sing Kow Seid appealed a decision by Justice M.W. Tyrwhitt Drake in October 1897. Although the case file provided very little background information on Seid, the *British Colonist,* in an article not related to this case, described the applicant as a "Chinese interpreter

for the C.P.R."[37] In another article in the *Colonist*, Seid is described as
a "well-to-do Chinaman."[38] The only other information that could be
gleaned from the case, as reported in the newspapers and the British
Columbia Law Reports, is that he lived with his wife and two young
daughters. One son had apparently died the previous year by accidental
poisoning and another son was being educated in China. Thus, Seid was
known to be a well-established family man in the community. The case
concerned Quai Shing, whom the applicant alleged was under the age
of sixteen, although the child herself claimed to be "about sixteen years
old."[39] The applicant in the case argued that Quai Shing was his adopted
daughter, that he had adopted her from Lim Fei, "who was believed to
be her uncle, and that since that time the applicant had kept the child as
a member of his own family."[40] Here, Sing Kow Seid attempts to establish the legitimacy of his right to guardianship of the child by claiming
that he had formally adopted her in China. He underscores this through
references that indicate that he had kept her as a member of his family.
Maintaining that Quai Shing was family was important, given that both
of the previous cases hinged on proving the applicant's legal right to the
child. Seid strengthens his case by arguing that, while he was away, Quai
Shing had been forcibly removed from his home by a police constable and
had been subsequently placed in the Home. This reference to the police
constable (a state official who had seized the child) marks out the Home
as a site of confinement.

In this case, the court initially determined that the applicant, Sing
Kow Seid, had no legal right to the child. However, Seid appealed this
judgment, arguing that, "having placed himself *in loco parentis*," he was
"entitled to the same rights in regard to custody of the child as a father."[41]
Council for the applicant further argued that the "policy of law is to
extend the right of guardianship beyond mere consanguinity."[42] However,
council for the respondents argued that the law of England did not recognize the rights of adoption and that unless "the applicant be the parent, he
had no more right than an absolute stranger."[43] While the final decision
dismissed the appeal, the judges were not unanimous in their decision.
Judge George Walkem and Judge Paulus Irving agreed with the original
decision, citing the case of Ah Gway and others as a precedent for denying the rights of an adoptive parent/guardian where the father's express
wishes had not been evident, but Judge Davie did not agree. In fact, in
his lengthy and strongly worded judgment, Davie not only disagreed that
the applicant had no legal claim to custody but also further implicated the
Home in a criminal matter.

In his judgment, Davie argued that the cases cited in Ah Gway, as well as the Ah Gway case itself, did not deny the legitimacy of the adoptive relationship but, rather, emphasized that the adoptive parent had no rights "as *against* the father."[44] This was the distinction that threatened the undoing of not only this case but also the Ah Gway case. If the adoptive relationship was deemed legal and had the rights associated with parental rights, except as against the rights of the father, the court could not intervene in the best interests of the child, except in a "case of gross moral turpitude."[45] Here the court made a distinction: it was not simply that the father had ultimate right over the guardianship of his child but that it was only in cases that argued *against* the rights of the father that the court could intervene. If the father was not party to the case, his rights could not be understood as being violated, and therefore his protection was not a concern of the court. However, the other judges did not agree, and the court upheld the earlier decision. Although a weakening of the state's structural support was evident, the court sided, this time, with the Home.

The privileging of the father's rights threatened to undermine the authority of those who ran the Home. Davie's efforts to elevate the rights of Chinese guardians over institutions such as the Home meant that not all were in agreement when it came to defining the boundaries of domesticity. What would become clear in the Soy King case, however, was that guardianship rights would not be enough to guarantee that the plaintiff could regain custody of the child. On June 30, 1900, Soy King, or "Dorothy," as she would soon be called, entered the Home. On July 11 of the same year, the *Colonist* reported that a habeas corpus application would be heard on the matter in the Supreme Court chambers. Sam Kee applied for a writ of habeas corpus on the grounds that he had gained custody of Soy King four years before and that, when she was found at the Home, "the authorities refused to give her up."[46] This case was distinct from the previous three because the applicant's legal right to guardianship of Soy King was seen to be much stronger. This meant that the suitability of Sam Kee would have to be determined in order for a decision to be made. Given the strength of Sam Kee's claim to guardianship, the Home was forced to move beyond its previous stance, which had been largely to undermine the applicant's legitimacy as guardian and to avow its own support of and respect for the children's free will. Although, like Lee, Sam Kee had some stature in the Chinese community, his ties to the white community in Victoria were likely not as strong for, according to Stanley, Kee did not reside in Victoria long before moving to New Westminster and then to Vancouver.[47] In this case, therefore, the Home offered the court two separate grounds for ruling in its favour. First, it argued that Soy King, as in the earlier cases, was a slave and that her father had never entrusted Sam Kee with her care. Second, it argued that, even if the court were to rule that he did stand in loco parentis, he had lost his right "on account of (a) cruelty; (b) failure to properly maintain and educate; and (c) grossly immoral conduct."[48] While the Home would ultimately retain custody of this child, as the analysis of the judgment shows, this was the only case where the court based its final decision solely on the applicant's suitability as a parent rather than on whether he had the legitimate right to file the habeas corpus.

Justice Martin viewed the Soy King habeas corpus application as "quite distinct from that which arose in the cases of *In re Ah Gway* (1893), 2 B.C. 343, and *In re Quai Shing* (1898), 6 B.C. 86."[49] Unlike the two cases cited by Martin, the Soy King case was unique as the applicant claimed to "stand in *loco parentis*" to her. In the case of Ah Gway, the applicant claimed to have been entrusted with the care of the child by her sister, who was the child's mother. Similarly, in the case of Quai Shing the applicant claimed guardianship, citing authority given to him by the child's uncle. In this case, however, Sam Kee claimed that he "was confided to his charge by her *father*, a resident of China, to be cared for, supported, and educated as his (Sam Kee's) own daughter."[50] Here, Sam Kee claimed to have the authority of the father, who in the earlier cases was deemed to be the only true parental authority (although Davie challenged this interpretation of the law, the two other justices did not agree).

In the case of Ah Gway, for instance, when Begbie stated that "nobody can have a valid claim except the father,"[51] he was challenging the mother's authority, which he saw as only valid if there was no legitimate father to dispute it, and even then her authority was limited. However, as this authority was not automatically afforded to a Chinese widow, it was left to the court to decide the fate of Ah Gway. Likewise, in the case of Quai Shing, the court agreed that the applicant had no legal right to "custody and possession of the child."[52] The case of Soy King, therefore, differed substantially as the applicant claimed to have the father's authority when seeking possession of the child. In the case of Soy King the state reaffirmed the rights of the father through the acknowledgment of the rights of the adoptive father. This acknowledgment was short-lived as the issue of fitness still remained. It was on this point that the court decided in the Home's favour. In making this assessment, the family was juxtaposed with its opposite – the stranger.

Refuge from the Outside: The Stranger
and the Best Interests of the Child

One of the most common discourses used by the courts to assess the validity of the habeas corpus cases was that of the "stranger." Drawing on Sara Ahmed's discussion of the stranger, I argue that the courts used discourses of strangeness and the stranger to mark the Chinese "body out of place," as outside proper family or domestic relations.[53] In these cases, the stranger is a figure that is delineated as the Other while acting rhetorically to reinforce and police racial and familial boundaries. Ahmed's discussion of the fetishization of the stranger, or the stranger as object, is useful in understanding how it is that the stranger can be framed as *unknown* precisely because of the invisibility of how it is that we come to *know* or recognize her/him. The construction of the stranger is about the construction of difference, but it is also about the construction of danger. Ahmed explains that "'the stranger' is produced as a figure precisely by being associated with a danger to the purified space of the community, the purified life of the good citizen, and the purified body of 'the child.'"[54] However, discourses of the stranger are not always this straightforward.

Sometimes the racial Other is framed as a stranger because of the threat posed to the child, while in other cases, it is the white stranger who poses the most danger to the "purified space of the community." Thus, it is not only the racial Other who is marked off as a stranger to whiteness: in some instances, whiteness is also framed as a stranger to Otherness. Here, the boundaries of race are policed from both sides for, if the racialized Other is defined in relation to whiteness, so, too, is whiteness defined in relation to the Other. The stranger is the subject who is out of place. While Ahmed argues that "the policing of valued spaces allows the legitimation of social exclusion by being tied to a heroic 'we' who takes shape against the figure of the unspecified stranger," in the court cases discussed here, the role of the stranger is not so clear cut.[55] Whites are not necessarily framed as strangers to socially exclude whites but, rather, to legitimate the social exclusion of Chinese. Whites are only deemed to be out of place when they challenge or threaten existing racial hierarchies. Here, the racial project of delineating and ordering race is based on essentialist representations of race and, just as important, is about locating these within existing social structures of domination.[56]

The right of the court to determine the best interests of the child was tied to who had legal rights to her or his guardianship. Thus, in cases in which the applicant was determined to have no legal standing, the court was called upon to act as guardian of the child. The rights of guardianship could not, in these cases, be equated with the right to custody. There-fore, the state weighed not only legal right but also the moral fitness of guardians. In this endeavour, the state used assessments of the applicant's fitness as a parent as well as discourses of friend and stranger to frame its decisions. While it is tempting to define the stranger in terms of who is known or not known, this approach is not sufficient here. As Ahmed explains:

> The stranger is produced as a category within knowledge rather than com-ing into being in an absence of knowledge. The implications of such a rethinking of the relationship between knowledge and strangers are far reaching: it suggests that knowledge is bound up with the formation of a community, that is, with the formation of a "we" that knows through (rather than against) "the stranger."[57]

Likewise, in the courts, the stranger was not necessarily unknown to the child but, rather, was constructed as a potential threat to both the child and the formation of community (i.e., both the white community and the mixed-race "family" that resided within the Home were threat-ened). The stranger in these cases, like Ahmed's stranger, was produced and known through the formation of community and family. Given that the stranger was defined through his/her opposition to definitions of family or community, the stranger was known and produced through existing definitions of both.

It is in the case of Ah Gway that the discourse of the stranger first arises with regard to the Home. In his ruling that the applicant had no legal right to the child, Begbie positioned her as a virtual stranger. The matron of the Home had testified that the young woman was to be supervised or chaperoned should "Chin Su or *other strangers*" come to visit.[58] The language used here serves to frame Chin Su as a stranger to Ah Gway, the reference to "other strangers" implying that she is numbered among them. The court supported the Home in this regard by deeming Chin Su to have no legal right to the child. What the court was arguing was not that Chin Su was unknown to the child but that she was, in fact, a "body out of place," the stranger who was, through her "very proximity, *already recognized as not belonging.*"[59] The court thus recognized her as out of place, allowing for "both the demarcation and enforcement of 'this place' as where 'we' dwell."[60] In this case, "place" is home and "we" is family. Chin Su was, then, determined to be a threat to the family. Thus, framing her as a stranger was not about her lack of relationship to Ah Gway but about the danger she was perceived to pose to the child, the home, and the family. Here the discourse of the stranger is racialized and marks Chin Su out as a racial outsider. However, this racialization is not straightforward as Ah Gway, despite her race, was to be included within the family. Here the only racial threat is that which opposes the values of white domesticity that were to be instilled within the child.

If the stranger had been framed as simply one who was not knowable, it would be difficult to reconcile Begbie's decision to keep the child in the Home. By denying the legitimacy of the applicant's claim to custody, Begbie also effectively denied the legitimacy of the Home's claim. If a woman claiming to be the girl's aunt had no authority, then by what authority could the Home claim the same right? However, the discourse of the stranger, as it is equated with threat to the child, meant that the Home, despite its far shorter history with the child, was not to be constructed as a stranger in relation to her. Although the Home was unfamiliar, it was considered to be safe. Thus, Begbie ensured that Ah Gway would stay beneath the Home's roof, stating: "[This is] where she desires to remain, and where, I think, her best interests are lodged."[61] The child, like the other Chinese girls who resided in the Home, belonged there and thus could not be viewed as a stranger. And so the court refused to grant the writ of habeas corpus, meaning that, in the absence of a legal guardian, the institution's informal custody would not be interfered with.

It was precisely because neither party had a legal right to claim custody of Ah Gway that she remained in the Home. The application of habeas corpus required Begbie to "remove her from one unauthorized custody ... to another custody equally unauthorized."[62] Although Begbie recognized that the custody of the Home was equally unauthorized, given that he found no grounds for the charge that Ah Gway was held against her will and that neither party had a greater right to custody, he declined to remove her. Thus, the Home was allowed to keep Ah Gway not because it had a greater right but because it posed no threat to either her or the community. Further, Ah Gway herself did not pose a threat to the family or community as she had been "domesticated" (or was in the process of being domesticated) by those who ran the institution. Thus, while Chin Su could be constructed as a stranger to the child, the Home, by virtue of its function as a rescue mission, could not be so constructed without delegitimizing it altogether.

In the case of Quai Shing, discourses of the stranger were also to be at the forefront of the discussion of guardianship. Here, the discourse of the stranger worked in other ways. When the Home's council for the respondents argued that, unless "the applicant be the parent, he has no more right than an absolute stranger," the Home itself was constructed as a stranger to the child. Here, the term "stranger" is meant to put both the religious institution and the applicant on equal footing, in this case each having no *legal* rights, thus giving the Court full discretion in determining Quai Shing's best interests. In his October 1897 judgment, Judge Drake began by outlining the case, explaining that Sing Kow Seid had applied to have "the body of a Chinese girl under the age of sixteen" brought before the court, "alleging she was in unlawful custody."[63] This charge, however, was quickly countered by Drake. Despite the fact that the applicant claimed to have adopted the child from her uncle and that he had "kept the child as a member of his own family," Drake went on to explain that the "applicant [was] no relation of the girl, and [was] not a guardian or in any way interested in her welfare otherwise than having been her employer."[64] Further, he quickly contrasted this relationship with the relationship that the young woman had with the Home, where she was described as "apparently satisfied with her position, and ... well cared for and trained for future usefulness, both morally and intellectually."[65] These references to moral and intellectual training were important as legal guardians had obligations to provide for the education of those in their care. Religious and moral training could also be undertaken, but, according to law, "the guardian must instruct the ward in the faith of the father or in accordance with the father's wishes."[66] Although this certainly was not the case with respect to the Home, Drake ignored this point of law, choosing instead to counter claims that the child was held against her will by alluding not only to her satisfaction with her "position" in the residence but also referencing the moral and intellectual nurturance that she was receiving there. In this way, although the Home could not be considered as having more *rights* than an absolute stranger, morally it was seen as having taken on the role of family. Thus, despite the fact that Quai Shing and the Home may have begun as strangers, Quai Shing, like Ah Gway, was made to belong through processes of domestication, care, and transformation. If Quai Shing was no longer a stranger in the Home, then the Home could no longer be a stranger to her.

Quai Shing's satisfaction, as well as her moral and intellectual training, erased the threat that she may otherwise have been seen to pose to the white community. Further, Drake clearly saw the Home not as a carceral institution but as a surrogate home. Rather than being strangers, those who ran the Home were seen as surrogate parents – specifically, as mothers. Drake emphasized this by referring to the children as "waifs and strays," thus positing the Home as a charitable institution where the homeless could be "homed" and strays could be domesticated. The child was, hence, not "out of place" but at "home" and, therefore, part of a family.

Defining the family was also a primary concern of the court in the case of Sam Kee and his application for custody of Soy King. Here, the court acknowledged Sam Kee's rights as standing in *loco parentis*, but Judge Archer Martin was quick to point out that this right was not absolute. In cases where a parent forfeited her/his rights "by certain sorts of misconduct" the Crown would act as *parens patriae*.[67] Literally "parent of the nation" or "parent of the country," *parens patriae* is defined as the power of the state to act as the legal guardian of those who are viewed as not competent or those without natural guardians. The doctrine of *parens patriae* was also used within the court system to justify the removal of children by social reformers who otherwise would have been deemed strangers to them. These social reformers had "little tolerance of cultural, ethnic, or class differences, particularly when it came to alcohol or what was considered immoral sexual behaviour."[68] That these young Chinese girls were viewed as unable to protect themselves from such threats was clear. Although for Ah Gway and Quai Shing the state also intervened, this intervention was based on the contention that no one else had rights to guardianship. However, in this case, the court had determined that Sam Kee had guardianship rights; therefore, he could not be framed as a stranger to the child unless it could be proven that the applicant had forfeited his rights through misconduct.

In her work on the social reform of family courts in Ontario during this period, Dorothy Chunn shows that the state adopted an "interventionist attitude toward marginal families." The Children's Protection Act, 1893, gave the Children's Aid Society the power to "apprehend any children deemed to be at risk and detain them in special shelters prior to a legal hearing."[69] Although similar legislation was not in place in British Columbia until 1902, the police and the courts routinely placed Chinese girls and women in the Home as a way to protect them from their "owners." Unlike the aid societies, the police and courts did not temper this intervention with the possibility of the reinstatement of parental rights through rehabilitation. Clearly, it was believed by some, including the courts, that Chinese populations were not redeemable. Interventions into child custody were seen as reformatory only insofar as the child could be subjected to moral reform through Christian interventions.

The gross immoral conduct with which Sam Kee was charged had to do with his "bigamous relations with two women," a charge even more damning as it was not one that the applicant denied.[70] In reaching his decision, Justice Martin considered the primary matter for the court to consider to be "the welfare of the child, and that its moral and religious welfare must be considered as well as its physical well-being."[71] Yet this claim was qualified by the following: "the immorality to extinguish the right of the parent or guardian to the custody of the child, must be of a gross nature, so that the child would be in serious danger of contamination by living with him."[72] The discourse of contamination can be tied closely to the discourse of the stranger. The stranger is *produced* precisely because of his/her threat to the purity of "the good citizen, and the body of 'the child.'"[73] The threat was not in the behaviour of the stranger but in his/her potential to contaminate the child. Therefore, in this case, it was not enough for a man to be in an adulterous relationship: he must also have exposed the child to this relationship in such a way that she/he would be contaminated by it.

In the case of Soy King, Justice Martin was satisfied "that the atmosphere of his home [was], as viewed from the standard of social life in this country, so grossly immoral that there [was] serious danger to apprehend that Soy King [would] be morally contaminated by further residence under his roof."[74] I take up the reference to "standard of social life in this country" in a later discussion of the role of race in shaping the decisions of the courts. Here, however, it is enough to point out that the social standard of this country was equated with "home" and that Sam Kee was clearly marked off as the stranger. The Home would therefore retain custody of Soy King. She was baptized there three years later and remained in this domicile for over five years. She left the Home in October 1905 when she married. Her connection with the institution, however, did not end there. Six years later, when her children were two and a half and five years old, respectively, they were both placed in the Home by their father, "as the mother was not living a good life and neglected her children."[75] They would remain there, except for a two-month period, until 1931.

Unlike in the previous three cases, in the case of Choy Wan, the court did support the applicant's request for habeas corpus. This time the court, despite the child's claims of mistreatment, did not construct the applicant as a stranger to her. Rather, the applicant's relationship with the child was framed as that of an employer; therefore, he was not seen as posing a threat to her. However, this is not to say that the Home's administrators did not strive to show that they were, in fact, the more suitable guardian for the child. A letter to the editor from Matron Sarah Bowes appeared in the *British Colonist* on September 8, 1895. This letter was in reply to a report published on September 6, following an incident at the Home. The report indicated that the order made on Wednesday (September 4) appointing Lee guardian of the little Chinese girl was signed by the chief justice but that, when Lee came to collect her the following day, Bowes asked for a delay until she could notify the institution's lawyer, its having been arranged that Choy Wan be allowed to stay at the Home until the appeal. The appeal was set for two days later (September 6), after which time the child was handed over to Lee.[76] In a letter to the editor, Bowes contested this report. She did not dispute the young girl's remaining in the residence; rather, she framed the situation not in legal but in moral terms:

> On Thursday p.m. Mr. Aikman and Mong Kow came into the home for Choy Wan. I produced the child in presence of the above named, also of Mr. Coleman, the interpreter, and Miss Wickett, the teacher of the home. The question was asked me by Mr. Aikman, "Do you give up the child?" and I replied "Yes, if she is willing to go." She was not willing to go, but shook her head and began to cry.[77]

Bowes's construction of this event is interesting for two reasons. First, although she was willing to abide by the court's decision, she indicates that the child was afraid of Lee. This positions Lee as the stranger who entered the Home with the purpose of removing the child from her *home*. For her part, the child is framed as unwilling to leave her "home." As Ahmed contends, "home is not simply about fantasies of belonging (where do I originate from?) but ... it is *sentimentalised* as a space of belonging."[78] Bowes's story, through its emotionality, portrayed the Home as a place where the child belonged and where she wanted to stay.

Second, by constructing the space of the Home as the child's own home, Bowes underscored the threat that Mong Kow Lee posed not only to the child's sense of home but also to her free will. Bowes's refusal to turn over the child highlights the institution's support of Choy Wan's own wishes. She emphasized her willingness to give up the child "if she [was] willing to go."[79] However, when the child shook her head and began to cry and three times "expressed herself as unwilling to go with Mong Kow," Bowes, along with the teacher and interpreter, "protested against her being compelled to leave contrary to her will."[80] While the general facts regarding Choy Wan's continued stay in the Home were not disputed, Bowes wrote to "place the facts truly before the public," emphasizing that it was not *her* will but the child's that was being privileged by the Home in this dispute. Here, she placed before the public the institution's support of the best interests of the child, implying that the court's ruling was not in those interests and, further, that the ultimate threat to Choy Wan's free will was Lee. However, the court would ultimately be vindicated in the press.

The next and final time that Choy Wan appeared in the newspaper was on September 19, 1895. A single short paragraph in "The City" column of the *British Colonist* provided readers with an update on "little Choy Wan's troubles."[81] The paragraph explains that, according "to the terms of the order by which she was restored to the possession of Lee," Choy Wan was required to appear before Chief Justice Theodore Davie in his chambers. Here, the court was shown to have the best interests of the child as its main concern. After interviewing Choy Wan, the order was made absolute, as the young girl "expressed herself as entirely satisfied with his [Lee's] treatment of her and anxious to remain in his care."[82] Although originally, according to the Home, the child contended that she had been bought by the applicant and was his slave, in chambers Choy Wan was said not only to have expressed her satisfaction with being returned to Lee but also to have been *anxious* to remain in his care, perhaps supporting the judge's contention that she was a child who had simply run away because of being punished and who saw the Home as a way to protest this punishment. By framing the child as now willing and, indeed, desiring to remain in the home of Lee, this article shows that, ultimately, the court had decided in her best interests, that Lee posed no threat to her and was therefore no stranger to her.

Discourses of the stranger allowed the courts to mark off certain populations as posing a threat to the community and to the child, if not always legally, then certainly practically, without explicitly referring to race. In all of these cases, the stranger was not defined as someone who was unknown to the child but as someone who posed a potential threat to the purity/well-being of the child or to the sanctity of the family. While the stranger was usually defined as a racial "outsider" to the family, the stranger discourse was also shot through with racial ambivalence as Chinese girls and women were deemed to be "at home" in the Home. This was due to their perceived willingness to be in the institution and to their domestication, in both senses of the word: the Home's inmates were to be both homed and tamed. These relationships were not determined through racial affiliation but through discourses of belonging, even though these discourses were racially imbued.

The "Race" for Custody

John McLaren argues that the "law was viewed by whites in the province as an important instrument in constructing a distinctive Chinese identity and in regulating their conduct." Although he argues that "there is little, if any, direct evidence that racial background played a role in the disposition of individual cases," because of the domestic nature of these cases (and the relations that they permitted), race was an important factor in the outcome of each.[83] While the judges in these cases often claimed that the court was blind to race, the impossibility of this impartiality is evident. Judges claimed that the laws must be applied equally to all regardless of race, yet the application of law relied on racial categories that were always already legally constructed. As Haney López points out, although the tendency is to "assume that races exist wholly independent of and outside law," critical race theory shows the extent to which, both historically and today, race has been and is "at least in part fashioned by law."[84] In addition, the cases themselves cannot be understood as separate from or uninfluenced by other laws, for instance immigration laws, which could not claim to be colour-blind, invested as they were in maintaining white dominance within the nation. Chinese women's place, both symbolically and geographically, must be understood as legally determined, even prior to the cases in question. The very categories that judges used were reflective of an already existing lack of equality under the law. Given that Chinese women could only enter Canada as wives or daughters of existing immigrants, their status in the nation was always already governed by both their race and their gender. Further, the courts' decisions were focused on regulating private, familial spaces and relationships. Obviously, eradicating race from such decisions was impossible in a context within which cross-racial contact was both feared and carefully policed.

The state acted to decide the legal merit of the applicants' cases and, in doing so, also decided what sorts of relationships were permissible. While in at least one case the courts deemed that the boundaries between Chinese and whites should be maintained and granted custody to the Chinese applicant, in other cases the applicant was conceptualized as a virtual stranger, a tactic used to distinguish the Other from the white self. While this might suggest that the law was not evenly applied, in both outcomes it was the courts' need to uphold the supremacy of whiteness that was central to these decisions. The custody cases were also spatially defined as the goal of the state was to determine which spaces were acceptable for young Chinese girls and women. To this end, judges often mobilized ideas of racial difference in their decisions. It is, thus, important to remember, as Constance Backhouse argues, that for "all the slipperiness of racial definition in law, it is apparent that dramatic, real-life consequences flowed from racial designations."[85]

By placing Chinese girls and women into the space of the Chinese Rescue Home, or by refusing to allow for their removal, the court legitimized certain types of white/Chinese relations. It was only when the court determined that these relations might threaten the white family, where the boundary between whiteness and Chineseness was deemed most critical, that it ruled in favour of the applicant.[86] In these cases the state enacted the "rule of law" and its impartiality in order to protect and police whiteness. And, in the habeas corpus cases discussed here, this was especially true with regard to preserving the sanctity and purity of the family in that most private of spaces – the home. Following from Hunt, who shows that the Societies for Reformation of Manners, as "agents of moral regulation," were "located within civil society, but had significant links with both Church and state," in this chapter I demonstrate the complex and ambivalent relationship between state and non-state actors, especially in a context in which courts, as direct agents of the state, had to act as impartially as possible.[87]

In the Quai Shing case, Justice Davie makes the claim that "the law knows no distinction of race or religion, but all stand equal before the law."[88] This is not to say, however, that race did not matter or that those who heard these cases were immune to its influences. As a survey of these four cases shows, discussion of and allusions to race are prevalent in all of them: First, assumptions around race frame how the applicants are regarded by the courts; second, racial difference enters the discussion as a way to protect white society from the racial "equality" of the law; and third, culture is used to stand in for race as a way to justify racial segregation or separation.

Although in the Ah Gway case race is never openly addressed, the issue of language and translation point to the ways in which the trial was racialized. The discussion around language and translation also highlights existing biases around the so-called Chinese "race." Although she was the applicant in this case and therefore not on trial herself, Chin Su, from the start, was treated as potentially criminal. Not unlike the Menzies case discussed in the previous chapter, the issue of language and translation was brought to the forefront not as a way to protect the applicant but as a way to protect the court from the allegedly untrustworthy Chinese. While the Menzies case shows clear instances of racist language around what the judge saw as the "mockery" of Chinese testimony, in the Ah Gway case this attitude is much more covert. When council for Chin Su "proposed to read the affidavit [of Chin Su], drawn up in English,"[89] explaining that the applicant, who did not understand English, had been read the affidavit and had had it explained to her in her own language, Begbie advised him that this was not admissible: "The affidavit should be written in Chinese and read to her or by her, and sworn so: then a sworn translation of that will be used on the application to me."[90] Here, Begbie explained that not only did the earlier method make it possible that the "deponent may be made to swear to matters she never intended" but also that "it would be very difficult to maintain an indictment for perjury in the case of false statements."[91] Thus, before the trial had even begun, the court was already considering the possibility of indicting Chin Su for perjury.

Although the courts were sometimes quick to dismiss the testimony of Chinese, in Lee's application of habeas corpus with relation to the child Choy Wan, his testimony appears to have been taken at face value. After determining that Lee had legal guardianship of the child, Davie, who was one of three judges who would also preside over the appeal of the Quai Shing case, references race, or its irrelevance, in his decision. On the one hand, Davie explains that the "Chinese were entitled to the same protection in their domestic relations as white people";[92] on the other hand, this is not to say that race did not matter. In fact, Davie highlights the importance of racial distinctions when he offers the following comparison:

> Supposing a white child in China had run away from its proper guardian and gone to a refuge conducted by Chinese. What would white people say if some Chinese tribunal gave it over to the Chinese Institution instead of delivering it to its white custodians? The proceeding would be denounced as an outrage. So in the present case, it would be a most monstrous thing that, because the child had got a whipping and had consequently run away to a refuge kept by white people, a British court should deny the Chinese custodian the possession of her. The refuge home was a most worthy institution, but it was better for the child to remain among people of her own nationality than to force her to be brought up by aliens to her people.[93]

Here, Davie highlights the equal treatment of all "races" under the law but, at the same time, clearly shows that race must be a consideration in these cases. In his decision, Davie, in fact, highlights the global concerns of law. By reversing the context whereby a white child was given over to a Chinese family, Davie decries the decision as an outrage. Here, he is not content to highlight the "monstrous" nature of a decision that would keep the Chinese girl from her Chinese guardian; rather, he uses a global context to highlight the case in a way that privileges the white family. This strategy is based on three logics.

First, by locating the white family as a central example, Davie makes it clear that his decision was based on assumptions that white families required special protections from the precedents that could be set by allowing the Chinese child to be taken from her legal guardian. The law, being blind to race, must protect the Chinese family in order to protect the white family. Second, Davie's decision to relocate the argument to the global sphere allowed him to centre the discussion on the white family and thus privilege it as the norm by which all families should be judged. It would not have been enough to say that removing the Chinese child from her guardians was monstrous as racial stereotypes (invested as they were in viewing women and children as illegitimate citizens) posited the Chinese family (especially in Canada) as exploitative at best and abusive at worst. As others have argued, Chinese women and children were often viewed as prostitutes and slaves, or at the least as potential prostitutes and slaves.[94] Third, Davie's decision favoured the logic of racial separation. Race clearly mattered in defining the boundaries of the domestic as the issue was whether a child could or should be given over to a guardian of a different race. In fact, Davie was not content with distinguishing between differing races; rather, he highlighted their incompatibility. By stating that "it was better for the child to remain among people of her own nationality than to force her to be brought up by aliens to her people,"[95] Davie presented the white race as *alien* to the Chinese race, making it clear that the races were, and should remain, strangers to one another.

In both this case and in the Quai Shing case discussed below, Davie made racial comparisons to highlight his refusal to support the continued residence of either child in the Home. While it is probable that Davie refused because of the ramifications for white foster or adoptive parents, as outlined in his judgment, another possibility lies in the prominence of the applicants in these two cases. While the Ah Gway case revolved around a female applicant who was said to be the aunt of Ah Gway, the cases of Choy Wan and Quai Shing were both filed by Chinese men who had some stature in the community. In fact, Mong Kow Lee appeared in the *Colonist* six months later, this time as the host of a Chinese military attaché who "called upon several of the leading men of the city" during his stay.[96]

In the original Quai Shing case, the references to race were not overt. Although race was not openly discussed in this case, a racial history is evident through the citing of precedents. Drake cited the Agar-Ellis case, a case where the mother was considered to have "unlawful control" over her children because she attempted to expose them to a type of religious training that was contrary to the father's wishes. Both parents were British, and most of the discussion was over whether the children should be raised as Protestant or Roman Catholic and whether the mother's refusal to abide by the father's wishes constituted unlawful control. Given that his reason for citing the case was to discuss unlawful confinement or control and who should be called to testify, this case seems only weakly related. However, Drake specifically drew attention to how the Agar-Ellis case followed the Hottentot-Venus case. His reference to this now-famous case is compelling for a number of reasons. First, however, it is necessary to provide a bit of context for the Hottentot-Venus case.

According to Qureshi, "Converted peoples were often displayed in England as evidence of missionary beneficence in spreading civilization."[97] Sara Baartman was to constitute one of these displays of beneficence.

> Sara Baartman arrived on England's shores within this traffic of animals, plants and people destined for display as objects representing colonial expansion and as a means of economic gain; she served as both an imperial success and a prized specimen of the "Hottentot." Brought over in 1810 by Alexander Dunlop, the surgeon of an African ship and exporter of museum specimens from the Cape, she sailed from the Cape to Liverpool upon the strength of a promise to help her earn her fortune.[98]

Displayed as a human curiosity, Baartman was poked, pinched, and baited by the public, and, according to one source, "it took all the authority of the keeper to subdue her resentment."[99] Abolitionists protested against her display out of humanitarian concerns, and these concerns prompted a court case, the basis of which rested on issues of free will. "Ultimately, the court found in favour of the defendant, Cezar, upon the presentation of a contract between Baartman and Dunlop."[100] Given that there were very few similarities between the Quai Shing case and the Hottentot-Venus case, one must ask why the judge chose to cite it.

Sara Baartman was twenty-one years old when brought to London and was thus an adult, while Quai Shing was alleged to be a child of sixteen at the time of her case. Although the reasons for citing this case were to determine whether the child's testimony was to be considered, in Baartman's case, no such determination was necessary. In her case, Baartman was living a highly sexualized and public life. Her show catered mainly to white Londoners (both men and women attended these shows). In the case of Quai Shing, however, the child was confined to the private sphere, where her sexuality was strictly policed. The similarity is that, in both of these cases, it was precisely the sexuality of the woman/child that needed to be controlled or protected. In the case of Quai Shing, the threat from her Chinese guardian was a threat to her sexual morality as Chinese women were often framed as naturally promiscuous, something that could only be stemmed through the intervention and transformative promise of the Home.

The more obvious similarity between the two cases is the focus on racial difference. In both cases, the "detainees" are non-white, while those accused of controlling/detaining them are white. In both cases there are accusations of slavery and/or prostitution, although in the Hottentot-Venus case it was Baartman's white manager who was accused of holding her against her will, while in the Quai Shing case, it was the applicant who faced accusations of slavery, despite the fact that it was the Home that was being accused of unlawfully detaining the child. Citing the Hottentot-Venus case, given that it had very different concerns than the Quai Shing case, implies that race is an important issue. It is important to note that although Baartman was an adult at the time of her case it was not she who was the applicant but the abolitionists. Thus, in neither case was the writ of habeas corpus instigated directly by the girl or woman who was allegedly being held against her will. In fact, in both cases, it was determined that both "victims" did not wish to be released.

In both cases the applicants were unsuccessful in gaining the release of the girl/woman, but the reasons for the refusal of the courts to intervene are very different. In the case of Sara Baartman, the court determined that, because there was a contract between Baartman and her manager, there was no infringement of her free will. However, in the case of Quai Shing, although free will was certainly an issue, the case was decided largely on what the court saw to be the best interests of the child. As in the case of Ah Gway, so in the case of Quai Shing the court determined that neither the Home nor the applicant had legal rights to custody and that, consequently, it was the state's obligation to consider what was best for her. Thus, while Baartman was ultimately given autonomy in the case (although some argue that the contract was, in fact, likely forged), Quai Shing was at the mercy of the courts. Soon after the courts decided in favour of the Home, Sing Kow Seid appealed the Quai Shing case.

As mentioned earlier, the three justices did not agree on the appeal of this case. While two of the justices upheld the appeal, one, Justice Davie, did not. In this case, as in his involvement in the original Quai Shing case, Davie was quick to affirm the legitimacy of the guardian's claim. Having established the legitimacy of Sing Kow Seid's claim, Davie quickly went on to assert:

> We are now dealing with the case of an unmarried female, under the age of sixteen years, regarding whom the Criminal Code distinctly enacts, by section 283, that every one is guilty of an indictable offense and liable to five years imprisonment, who unlawfully takes, or causes to be taken, any unmarried girl being under the age of sixteen years, out of the possession and against the will of her father or mother, or of any other person having the lawful care or charge of her.[101]

Here, Davie not only affirms the legitimacy of Seid's guardianship claims but also suggests that the Home might be guilty of an indictable offence in keeping her from her guardian.

By framing the applicant as a guardian rather than as a stranger, as did Justice Drake, Davie positions only the Home as a stranger in this case. He argues that previous cited cases dismissed the rights of the guardian or foster parent only insofar as they were against the biological parent. He further contends that the cases would have resulted in much different rulings should they have been put forward by a stranger who tried to take custody of a child from the foster parent. Not only is the Home positioned as "the stranger" who swept in and took custody of the child but, further, as a *criminal* stranger, as "benevolence and good intention are no defense in law to an indictment under the statute."[102]

In order to strengthen his argument even further, Davie quickly moved beyond the case at hand to discuss the ramifications of disallowing the rights of the adoptive parent by asking:

> How many thousands of homes might be plunged into mourning, more bitter than that of death, if the law stood idly by and permitted the orphan and adopted child, received into the family circle, reared as the rest of the children, knowing and being reminded not that it is of different blood from them, and perhaps not so, to be ruthlessly torn from the fireside, by a mere stranger who (benevolent although his intentions might be) conceives the idea that he can look after the child better than its own foster-parents.[103]

Two points need to be made here. First, although Davie does not explicitly mention race, his reference to differences of "blood" is compelling. While he marks off the child as not related by blood to his or her new "family," the child in this instance does not need to know or be reminded of this different blood precisely because he or she can pass as family. However, the "stranger" here is marked off as the benevolent white stranger, who, despite good intentions, must always be a stranger to the child as there can be no (racial) passing in this family.

Second, Davie conjures up both hearth and home to show how, despite the applicant's Chineseness, the ramifications might be felt much more widely in the white community. Without any direct reference to race, Davie shifts away from this singular case and its Chinese applicant (1) through reference to "many thousands of homes" and (2) by painting a picture of the classic Victorian home, with the family gathered around the fireplace. Here, although race is an absent discourse it is nonetheless prevalent. The judge erased race as a strategy not to argue for equal treatment of Chinese populations but, rather, to show the consequences for white populations of the precedent that might be set in such cases.

Davie references race in a more direct way early in his judgment when he explains that the rights of the foster parent could be lost if the court deemed it was in the best interests of the child, citing a case where a child was removed from the care of a foster parent and given over to a stranger because "it was right that the child should be reared in one faith, and the foster-parents were going to bring it up in another."[104] The judge, however, is not arguing that the court had a right to remove the child from the foster parent because of religious differences; rather, he is arguing that the institution was denying the child the right to be "brought up according to instincts, customs and religion of her own people."[105] He argues that Quai Shing was "made the subject of an attempt to proselytize her to the customs, habits and creed of an alien race." By appealing to race in general, and by referring to the "white race" as an "alien race," Davie again hints at the wider ramifications of such a practice. Although he references race, he is adamant that "the law knows no distinction of race or religion but all stand equal before the law."[106] However, he is not only arguing that, as a Chinese man, Sing Kow Seid should be treated equally but also that the force of the law that was applied to Seid could be equally applied to white citizens. And it is for this reason that it held the threat of setting a dangerous precedent. On this, Davie is unequivocal: "If we were in China, and the tribunals were to uphold the right of benevolent Chinese societies to take our children from us and raise them as Chinamen, we should denounce it as an outrage, but is it not precisely the same kind of outrage upon the Chinese which is asked recognition in this case?"[107]

Thus, Davie recommended that the case be remitted to Judge Drake, "with the opinion that the applicant has a legal claim to the custody of the child ... but that he may be deprived of that custody, if upon investigation the learned Judge finds gross moral turpitude in the applicant's household, or other misconduct sufficient in the Judge's opinion to deprive him of the custody of the child."[108] However, Davie went on record not only to state that the child should be placed in a Chinese home but also to further implicate the institution in what he suspected was the perjured testimony of Quai Shing. Although Davie declined to rule for the applicant in this case, and the two other judges ruled against him, the record shows that the court was divided on not only the legitimacy of foster parents generally but also on the role of benevolent societies such as the Home.

Two days following this case, the *British Colonist* reported that Sarah Bowes, then the matron of the Home, had been appointed as Quai Shing's guardian for a period of two years. In this article, Sing Kow Seid was said to be planning an appeal to the Supreme Court of Canada. Searching the judgments of the Supreme Court, however, did not uncover any such appeal.[109] While it is impossible to determine the "truth" of the applicant's case against the claims of the Home, by examining newspaper accounts of this case certain suppositions can be made. First, it is unlikely that Seid could have held his position as an interpreter for the Canadian Pacific Railway, and his class position, had he been involved in illegal activities such as prostitution, an accusation not made explicit in the original case but one that was implied when Quai Shing indicated that the "applicant's household was an improper and immoral place of abode."[110] Second, an early newspaper account mentioned a "report that the girl [Quai Shing] had disappeared from the Home on Friday night, but it turns out that she is still there, safe and sound."[111] While it is possible that the applicant in this case reported her missing in order to strengthen his case, runaways were not uncommon in the Home. If she did run from the Home, Seid's claims that she was being held against her will may have indeed been true. Third, at the end of his judgment, Davie brought up a number of points that suggest that Quai Shing may have been coached when making her statements.

First, the issue of language was raised, the affidavit of Quai Shing having been taken through an interpreter as she evidently spoke no English. Given that the court was dependent on one interpreter, Davie argued that it should "hear from the child herself ... to be assured that *the words of the affidavit have not been put into her mouth.*"[112] Second, and related to the first point, Davie argued that the issue of age was suspect as the affidavit claimed her to be sixteen, whereas a "personal interview" with her "might tend to confirm either this statement, or that of her father that she is not yet fourteen."[113] Here, it is clear that Davie at least suspected that the child was coached as, in such cases, the law allowed the court to consider the wishes of a child over the age of sixteen. At the time, legal guardians had the right to actual physical custody of their wards, "although not against the wishes of a male child over the age of fourteen years or a female child over the age of sixteen years."[114] Given that the testimony of all of the young women in these cases had very similar themes and language, coaching may indeed have taken place. Last, and perhaps most damning, is Davie's observation that the affidavit in question claimed that Quai Shing had been sold for three hundred and fifty dollars and that she had seen the money: "[It] might be interesting to enquire how this child became acquainted with the decimal currency of the country, and as to her knowledge and understanding of it. It would also certainly be to the point to ascertain that the extraordinary story of the affidavit is altogether the child's own."[115] Quai Shing would remain in the Home against Davie's wishes.

In the final case, race comes up only peripherally. As mentioned previously, in assessing Sam Kee's fitness as a father, his living arrangements were measured by what Justice Martin identified as "national standards of social life." These standards were measured through white cultural and social practices, especially as they had to do with marriage. Had Sam Kee kept a mistress outside his home, the court could not have found gross immorality because in *Ball v. Ball* it had been held that the court "has nothing to do with the fact of the father's adultery, unless the father brings the child into contact with the woman."[116] Thus the practice of keeping multiple wives, while often overlooked by immigration and police officials, was, in this case, found to violate the "standard of social life" in Canada. Not only did it violate this standard but it also had the potential to morally contaminate Soy King through her exposure to it. It was on understandings of white social standards that this case was decided. Although race was not cited directly, its presence was felt as the racial hierarchy, which designated whiteness as moral and Chineseness as immoral, was evident in these discourses of "national standards of social life."

The four court cases that form the basis of my analysis in this chapter provide insight into how the state received and conceived of Chinese populations, but they tell us less about how the court viewed the Chinese Rescue Home. However, the court's unwillingness to evaluate the institution's fitness implies that it sanctioned it and that, therefore, no evaluation was necessary. The court mobilized racial hierarchies in each of these cases, despite the divergent ways in which judges approached them. These racial delineations led to the court's creation of spatial designations. The Home was to act as surrogate parent to at-risk children, offering a roof over their heads. The state, for its part, provided the rafters (support) for this roof. That the Home was allowed, in most cases, to retain these young women even when the court was unwilling to grant it official custody underscores the fact that the Home was a space of exceptionality. The court's tendency to view Chinese as deviant and untrustworthy indicates a legal desire for racial separation. However, it is precisely this supposed deviance that necessitated white interventions, such as those initiated by the Home. Failure to live up to white moral standards had to be met with legal sanctions, in the cases under discussion by removing the "child" from the Chinese "guardian." Yet privileging whiteness did not always mean that the Home would prevail. In some cases, the precedent set was more dangerous than the threat that the Chinese were thought to pose.

Although in habeas corpus cases the applicant's claim is based upon accusations that a person or institution is unlawfully holding or confining another person, the court seemed more concerned with establishing the legitimacy of the applicant than with determining if the Home was unlawfully confining the girls/women in question. In cases where the legitimacy of the claim to guardianship was dismissed, the Home retained guardianship by default. In fact, the testimony of those representing the Home most often revolved around the free will of the child, not around whether the institution had a legitimate right to the child or, indeed, whether it was a fit or suitable guardian.

For Chinese, guardianship was shown to be dependent on both the legitimacy of the claim and upon the fitness of the parent or guardian. Further, the state was invested in maintaining racial separation while at the same time negotiating the impact of its decisions on individual cases as well as the implications of its decisions for the broader society. Questions of religious freedom or guardianship and custody became questions of race not because the court was invested in race but because it was determined not to be. The discourse of the law as colour blind meant that race *had* to be acknowledged precisely because, although the law was understood to be colour blind, those within the system were not. So, while some would adjudicate claims based on commonplace racial understandings and assumptions, others were careful to consider what the ramifications would be for the larger (i.e., white) population. Therefore, although judges were quick to point out that the law must be applied evenly, regardless of race, they often referenced their reasons as having to do with the protection of white society rather than with any sense of fairness to racialized populations. If the law was to define the boundaries of family or of the domestic realm more generally, it had to do so according to definitions that were in keeping with the values of white society. Sometimes it was enough to reference the racialized Other as dangerous or incompatible with the ideals of home and family (e.g., as the "stranger"); other times Chinese men and women were ultimately seen as threats to white families not because they were strangers but because of the dangerous precedents that might be set by ruling against them (e.g., allowing a child to be taken from her/his legal guardian).

Race, Gender, and National Imaginings

The door to the Canadian nation was heavy and cumbersome. Admittance was not easy for Chinese and Japanese women who came during the late nineteenth and early twentieth centuries. In fact, many travelled far from home only to be turned away without ever having been allowed to step inside. Some made it through those heavy doors only to find themselves confronted with hardship, racism, and (sometimes) exploitation. Combining a structural and poststructural approach to the Chinese Rescue Home (and the "home"), I examine how the door to the nation was policed and who held the keys. I tie together the material spaces that housed Japanese and Chinese women and the discourses that informed their regulation. Imagining the Home as a domestic space reflects a desire to view it both as material and as a social construction, as embedded in the construction of an "imagined community."[1] For this reason, I chose the spatial metaphors of hearth and home to solidify discourses that have shaped the material and social landscape in particular ways. I also use sources that lend themselves to a material analysis. Examining photographs and architectural drawings of the Home allowed for an examination of both how spaces were constructed (literally) and the ideological discourses that underpinned material practices. *From Slave Girls to Salvation* is itself an attempt to inhabit and to emerge from the margins between two theoretical spaces – the spaces between poststructuralist understandings and materialist understandings. It also inhabits a space between the historical past and the historical present.[2] In this concluding chapter, I continue to pursue the three themes that I emphasize throughout this book by looking at the theoretical and methodological implications of each. I conclude with a discussion of the limitations and contemporary significance of this historical research.

A Door into the Past: Reimagining Religion, Nation, Whiteness, and Gender

From Slave Girls to Salvation attempts to reconstruct a history of the Chinese Rescue Home by examining the complex and often contradictory logic that underpinned its founding, its ideologies, and its practices. Sometimes framed as conducting "radical" or exceptional work, this rescue mission has been regarded as iconic in BC history. Despite its iconic status, however, to date it has not been subjected to any sustained, systematic, and/or critical exploration. Perhaps the Home has been understudied because of the marginal space it has inhabited, with historians often viewing it as an aberration of sorts or as part of a broader set of exclusionary practices. Some histories of race relations in Canada focus almost exclusively on the privileging of whiteness in the formation of the nation. Similarly, studies of white women's roles as missionaries tend to focus on the privileging of whiteness in both global and national contexts. The history of the Home that I offer emphasizes the co-existence, and indeed the co-dependence, of inclusionary and exclusionary practices in global, national, and local contexts.

While much work has been done to augment white women's histories and to discuss their roles in moral regulation, focus has largely been on white women's moral reform work in national contexts as it was directed at Aboriginal women or at other white women, primarily those of working-class backgrounds. Alternatively, others have discussed the imperial nature of women's reform movements as they moved outside the nation. The importance of such approaches to understanding the global hierarchies of racial knowledge and power should not be discounted. I build on these approaches in an attempt to broaden our understanding of the moral reform projects of white women and to enrich our understanding of the relationships among and between religion, nationhood, whiteness, and gender.

Linking the Home to the national context in which it functioned uncovers some of the competing discourses around the seemingly immutable character of race and the global nature of this problem. Although Japanese and Chinese immigrants were certainly of national concern, it is clear that these "racial problems" were also seen to be part of a larger global concern. What is not so clear is how it was that the Home could both embrace and mediate these global discourses through a project that was, in many ways, contradictory to common-sense understandings of racial problems. As the discussion of the Royal Commissions shows, the relationship between religion, whiteness, and nationhood was a complex one. On the one hand, there was the perceived domestic incompatibility between the Chinese/Japanese and the nation; on the other hand, the superiority of whiteness and Christianity determined that the borders must remain open to the Chinese and Japanese not only so that they might be evangelized within the nation but, more important, so that white men and women might enter China and Japan and evangelize there. Thus, religious discourses were not always straightforward when it came to discussions of race. While many saw religious conversion as a solution to racial problems, the degree to which these "problem" groups might then be included within the nation was hotly debated. For many, admittance into Canada was to be granted only reluctantly – a price that must be paid in order to further the global dominance of Christianity. It was this ambivalence that became the basis for the founding of the Chinese Rescue Home.

Ideas of national and racial superiority legitimated the interventions of white men and (later) white women into the lives of Chinese and Japanese women. These ideas were solidified through disciplinary techniques, such as the seizure of Japanese and Chinese women under the auspices of religious benevolence. But they also materialized in the buildings that were chosen or constructed for the Home. These reflected national ties to Victorian England as well as the roots of Methodism. The Home itself existed in the spaces between the domestic and the foreign. Although located within the nation, it was marked off by the foreign bodies that it housed. It was, thus, a space of transition and transformation – a space in which racial mixing was not only allowed but encouraged. Here, Japanese and Chinese women were to be recreated in the image of white women so that they might carve out and domesticate national spaces as their own. In the Home, would-be immigrants were made ready to enter the nation's door, although, upon evaluation, some were not allowed entry. Immigration officials who placed Japanese women within its walls, for instance, relied on the matron to ensure that they were either "properly" married before leaving or were returned to Japan if husbands could not be found or if they were determined to be "bad women." Women left these spaces in various ways – some "escaped" out of windows, others were escorted by husbands, police, or immigration officials – but only those who were evaluated and deemed success stories were free to leave of their own accord. Only once the women were domesticated could they be trusted to take their place *within* the nation.

What I show in this book is how domesticity functioned and how it contributed to the construction of the Chinese Rescue Home as an active site of (re)production of the existing discourses of nationalism and whiteness. It was the coalescence of these discourses with religious and gendered ones that opened up possibilities for additional technologies of racial governance within the nation. Approaches to history that understand racial projects as merely exclusionary can result in the relegation of more inclusionary projects, such as the Home, to the margins of history. I attempt to highlight the insufficiency not only of a focus on exclusion but also of a focus on binaries such as inclusion/exclusion, global/local, and private/public. What is needed, instead, is an approach to history that is more fluid and that takes into account the multiple aims, scales, and trajectories of projects such as the Chinese Rescue Home. The use of multiple methods can aid in uncovering the multiplicity of goals and trajectories associated with such institutions.

HEARTH AND HOME: DOMESTICITY AS A KEY TO INCLUSION

An exploration of the spaces and practices of the Chinese Rescue Home shows that Christian home missions, while certainly building on understandings of a racial hierarchy, also interrupted racial discourses by constructing Asians as redeemable and, to some extent, assimilable. A history of this religious institution shows how racial projects functioned not only as practices of subordination but also as limited spaces of transformation. The ideological processes that made Japanese and Chinese women targets of moral regulation and reform were the same processes that allowed for their inclusion in the "family of God." Domesticity was integral to this regulation and reform.

The theme of domesticity threads itself through this book in ways that highlight the complexity of this concept. In focusing on the Home I attempt to highlight the vast potential that a focus on domesticity has for expanding our understanding of how institutions function. This analysis of how domesticity functions requires a consideration of the spatial, ideological, and disciplinary implications of domestic discourses. These discourses are evident locally, nationally, and globally and, thus, are key to understanding how competing gender systems were affected by the legal cases pertaining to Japanese and Chinese women associated with the Home. It is evident that spatial transformations were a necessary part of the transformation of Japanese and Chinese women. Moving Japanese and Chinese women out of their communities and into a domestic space such as the Home allowed for disciplinary practices that would, in turn, shape how Japanese and Chinese homes within their communities were organized. Thus, the "success stories" that came out of the Home were often linked to the Westernization of domestic spaces. Yet domesticity was not only about space: it relied on discourses that framed Western domesticity as superior and other forms of domesticity as both foreign and inferior. The transformation of Japanese and Chinese women from "foreign" subjects into "domestic" subjects relied on practices that challenged Japanese and Chinese gender systems and that attempted to replace or realign them with Western ones.

It was no accident that the Chinese Rescue Home was housed in domestic spaces. Housing women's bodies meant "homing" them at the same time. The houses that were homes to the matrons and the Japanese and Chinese women they oversaw contributed to the types of training that were possible. Further, they helped shape the limits not only of womanhood but also of citizenship. Moulding Chinese and Japanese women into proper citizens was one of the goals of the Home, and it was accomplished through the "domestication" of their bodies. This domestication was a gendered as well as a classed process. Once taught domestic skills, Japanese and Chinese women were meant to enter Canadian society not only as Christian wives but also as domestic servants.[3] In this way, Japanese and Chinese women were disciplined and welcomed into God's family. The metaphor of "family" was sustained through the domestic placement of these women. While Chinese men might be welcomed into the family of God in churches (the "House of God"), they were expected to leave the church and enter the public realm, albeit in limited ways. Women, however, were expected to remain confined within the domestic realm: first, as residents of the Home; second, as Christian wives and mothers; and last, as domestic servants. Although inclusion was a goal of this institution, it was a goal informed by pre-existing gendered discourses that confined not only Japanese and Chinese women to the domestic realm but also white women.

Clearly, domesticity was a crucial element of inclusion. Those who were outside the Home were not rewarded for similar racial interventions. This is particularly evident in the examination of the Menzies case.

Although the arranging of marriages was a routine practice of those who ran the Home, when Walter Menzies attempted to arrange the marriage of one of the institution's "runaways," he was soon at the centre of a city scandal. He was criminally charged, convicted, and sentenced to eight months in jail for his efforts. The state took an active interest in dictating the parameters of cross-racial endeavours: in fact, the relationship between the state and the domestic realm was constant and powerful. It was the state that often supplied women to the Home, and it was the state that determined who was to be considered a stranger in the nation and who would be considered a friend. Although it was certainly the case that the state legitimized the Chinese Rescue Home outside the courts by enabling police and immigration officials to place women there, it was inside the courts that racial delineations were made, precedents set, and spatial designations formalized. Thus, the habeas corpus cases I discuss offer insight into the state's treatment of and control not only over Chinese populations but also over domesticity itself. What I show is how the construction and production of space was decentralized through the coalescing of state and non-state agencies.

Despite the fact that the state seemed to sanction white women's forays into domestic evangelistic work, women's work with the Chinese was certainly not accepted in all situations. For instance, on July 8, 1909, the *British Colonist* reported that police commissioners in Vancouver were trying to "prohibit religious work by women, particularly young women, among the Orientals."[4] Following the alleged murder of Elsie Sigel in the United States by a Chinese man, the commissioners as well as the mayor met to discuss what could be done to persuade young women of the "evils" of such work. Although the conclusions were that no law gave the commissioners the authority to forbid this type of work, Mayor Prescott went on record as calling the association of young women with Chinese men "a piece of great stupidity" and argued that "we should not allow it."[5] Here, it is clear that, while white women could engage in missions to other women, their work with Chinese men was deemed to be dangerous; women were "encouraged" to engage only in work that kept them safe at "home."

The implications of this focus on domesticity are threefold. First, it interrupts the private/public binary. Although the domestic is often imagined only in relation to the private realm, a discussion of how domestic discourses were used in the public realm (e.g., in the Royal Commissions) and of how they were utilized to further the public aspirations of white women helps to uncover the spaces within which the public and the private overlapped and coalesced. Second, a focus on domesticity helps to highlight the ways in which discourses of home operated on local, national, and global scales. Third, methodologically, the focus on the domestic allows for a reading of architectural forms and photographic material in ways that take into account both space and scale.

Throwing Open the Door: The Production of Women's Aspirations and Authority

While women may have been encouraged to remain in the domestic realm, I point to the complex ways that domestic spaces allowed for a particular interplay of race and religion that contributed to the production of white women's moral authority. White women drew on discourses of cultural and religious inferiority to justify their work with Japanese and Chinese women. Discourses of religious benevolence aligned with those of racial inferiority to open up spaces for women to reassert their moral authority. However, it was only within the domestic realm that these cross-racial relationships were allowed to develop.

Histories of white women focus primarily on their contributions to the private realm and secondarily on their work as moral entrepreneurs. However, these studies rarely look at the ways in which the private realm impinges on the public lives of both men and women. I examine women's contributions as moral entrepreneurs and how this role intersected in meaningful ways with their roles as wives, mothers, or daughters. But I move beyond the private realm to examine how white women furthered their public aspirations by using domestic skills, discourses, and spaces. It was the Chinese Rescue Home's spatial parameters, its construction as a home space, and its location between the private and the public that allowed white women to use their marginality to reinforce their movement away from the margins.

While the interplay of racial and religious discourses imbued white women with moral authority, it was the location of the Home between the private and the public realms that allowed for the interruption of the private/public binary. Although it was constructed, both materially and metonymically, as a "home," the institutional nature of the Chinese Rescue Home allowed both white women and their Asian charges the opportunities to pursue aspirations that might not otherwise have been afforded them in the domestic realm. The Home was a space that simultaneously reinscribed racial/gender norms and challenged them. White women were able to extend their power beyond their own homes as they interacted with state officials, contractors, and "foreign" populations. Further, domestic spaces of the Home not only opened up new avenues for white women but also opened up new possibilities for Japanese and Chinese women.

Japanese and Chinese women were able to utilize the Home as a way to escape oppressive home lives, whether these entailed prostitution, slavery, or jealous/abusive husbands. Although founded on racist logics, the Home offered a space from which to challenge discourses that equated whiteness with citizenship, replacing these with discourses of Christian citizenship. Religious evangelism, although premised on racial hierarchies, opened the door to more inclusionary practices. Although opportunities for Japanese and Chinese women were often limited to domestic roles, residence in the Home afforded many with increased educational and work opportunities.

Understanding white women's moral authority as arising out of both racial discourses of inferiority and material spaces of domesticity enables us to understand how discursive and spatial practices informed one another in the production of power. This, of course, has implications for how we might understand the production of power itself. While power certainly produced discourses of inferiority and spaces of racial regulation, we must also understand that this same power was in many ways dependent upon and reproduced through already existing discourses and through the types of spaces that were produced and chosen. Further, these discourses and spaces must be understood as existing outside binaries such as public/private and inclusion/exclusion. Such binaries are insufficient to explain (or contain) the functioning of power, space, and discourse.

Locks without Keys: Empirical and Methodological Limitations

One of the limitations of my research on the Chinese Rescue Home is its sustained focus on whiteness and domesticity. While this focus allowed me to uncover how power operated on multiple scales, it meant that I could only superficially examine other themes. Domesticity was not the only reason that Japanese and Chinese women came to the Chinese Rescue Home: language training was something else that drew them. While learning English was certainly part of a larger project meant to train Japanese and Chinese in domestic service, language functioned in other ways as well: it was used as a tool of recruitment, evangelism, and assimilation. I was not able to fully examine language in this book, but doing so is an important avenue for future research.

Also missing from this book are the voices of the Japanese and Chinese women who lived in the Home. The archive speaks very little to the experiences of Japanese and Chinese women who walked through the doors of the Chinese Rescue Home/Oriental Home and School. Although I utilize a plethora of sources, including transcripts and reports of Royal Commissions, court cases, newspaper reports, missionary reports, photographs, and Home records, it was impossible to uncover the voices and experiences of the Japanese and Chinese women who lived there. While some speculation has been offered on some of their motives, dreams, and aspirations, I often found myself caught between a desire to give voice to the silent and an unshakable conviction that to attempt to build their stories from conjecture, guesses, and speculation was unrealistic at best and unethical at worst. While I have tried to include insights from biography, literature, and other studies, I am left with the knowledge that I have fallen far short of my initial desire to provide Japanese and Chinese women with a voice. Their stories remain largely untold.

Although most early residents of the Home are now dead, subsequent studies could include interviews with later wards of the Home. In addition, with research assistance, Chinese and Japanese language sources, including interviews that are housed in the British Columbia Archives, women's letters, diaries, and personal papers, could be mined as additional sources that could provide a voice to Chinese and Japanese women who settled in the area. While my initial desire was to tell the story from start to finish in as full a way as possible, the lack of sufficient time, the mountains of "data," and the space constraints meant that a smaller, more focused study emerged. Although this book ends in 1923, the Home continued to run for almost another twenty years. Over this time, a preliminary search of records shows a distinct shift in both the residents and the goals of the Home. Future work could productively explore some of the institution's new trajectories, including its growing focus on education and its shift to a younger "clientele." The focus on education and the shift away from familial relationships to more institutionalized ones is reflective not only of national factors (such as changing immigration laws) but also of more local ones (such as the changing roles of women in society). Although the Home closed its doors in 1942, this was not due to a lack of residents; rather, the War Measures Act dictated that the young charges, all Japanese children, be sent out of the "protected area." These children were sent to a residential school in Assiniboia, Saskatchewan. What happened to them after their transfer is not known and remains an important question for future research.

Using a case study approach to my analysis of the Chinese Rescue Home allowed me to present an in-depth view of the inner workings not only of the institution but also of relationships with those outside it. Historical research is necessarily limited, both temporally and spatially, by the case study approach, but it can provide insights into how racial, gendered, and nationalist relationships functioned within these admittedly narrow parameters. However, generalizing beyond these parameters is difficult to do with any accuracy. The following discussion of contemporary implications is, therefore, tentative at best. Still, it should be remembered that, through the case study, the researcher is able to "capture various nuances, patterns, and more latent elements that other research approaches might overlook."[6] Examining the present for evidence of these same patterns and nuances shows that such work is not only historical but also contemporary.

Doors, Locks, and Keys Revisited: The Radical Reinterpreted

The importance of *From Slave Girls to Salvation* lies beyond the historical reconstruction of the Chinese Rescue Home. A critical examination of the intersections of race, gender, sexuality, and nation brings to the foreground the privileging of whiteness and Christianity. While it is easy to consign these incidents to a racist past, as "relics" that have long since been remedied or forgotten, our history continues to inform the "historical present." Understanding the historical present, according to Weeks, "involves understanding the fundamental connections of history and politics, to grasp the ways in which the past has a hold on, organizes and defines the contemporary memory."[7] In this way, the history that I have presented can provide insight into the "contemporary memory."

While the door to the nation may be open to a much more diverse population now than it was in the past, we need to reconsider this door through a lens that includes the functioning of domesticity. It is easy to point to the more inclusionary mandates of Canadian immigration policy. But, as I have shown, the binary of exclusion/inclusion leaves gaps in our understanding. We need to rethink contemporary debates and spaces in light of the history outlined in this book. Domesticity still retains an important logic in immigration matters, as is seen in recent discussions around marriage and debates around the Live-in Caregiver Program, and in more local concerns such as the important place that settlement houses continue to hold in Canadian society. These contemporary concerns centre on the home and the domestic. While they cannot be traced directly back to the Home, our knowledge of how power operated within this space demands that we reconsider how it might be operating in similar ways today. An examination of these contemporary spaces shows a continued connection between racialization, domesticity, and custodial power.

I argue that the role of the state in shaping the domestic is also crucial in shaping understandings of (racialized) citizenship. We need to reconsider how domesticity continues to function as a doorway to the nation, how marriage continues to operate as a site of moral and racial regulation and as a site of border control. My research on the Home shows how fears around white slavery and Chinese prostitution implicated Chinese marriage customs, with Vancouver and Victoria newspapers frequently reporting on Chinese marriage customs as forms of sexual slavery.[8] Japanese brides were subjected to increased scrutiny as they entered Canada, their marriages often not recognized until formalized by the Canadian state. These are not only historical problems. On September 27, 2010, Citizenship, Immigration and Multiculturalism Minister Jason Kenney announced similar concerns and invited Canadians "to participate in an online consultation on the issue of marriage fraud, also known as 'marriages of convenience.'"[9]

Marriages of convenience had actually been identified as a concern by Citizenship and Immigration Canada in 2007. A news article written by David McKie states: "In February 2007, officials with Citizenship and Immigration Canada (CIC) requested an investigation into 'the high number of potential fraud cases related to possible marriages of convenience' in the Punjab region in India." McKie continues: "[the] investigation produced shocking revelations about the number and nature of the marriages, including ties to the sex trade, narcotics trafficking, embezzlement and human smuggling."[10] When polled about this national concern, 77 percent of the 2,342 respondents reported that fraudulent marriage was "a *very serious* or *serious* threat" to Canada's immigration system.[11]

Recent news stories about jilted or "abandoned" brides have highlighted claims that foreign customs such as "arranged marriages" and stigmatization around divorce in countries such as Pakistan have contributed to the victimization of women. In two CBC articles, Pakistan, India, and the

"South Asian community" in Toronto are all identified as vulnerable or problem areas. One suggestion for dealing with marriage fraud involves adopting a system like the ones found in "Australia and England, where the sponsored person isn't given full permanent resident status until he or she has lived with a spouse for three years." Withholding citizenship from those who cannot sustain a "proper" marriage for three years is an indication not only of the state's investment in "proper" marriage but also of its uneven application of citizenship rights. That this unevenness is, at least in part, constructed as a "racial problem" is evidence that racial projects are still alive and well. That marriage provides a doorway into the nation for some immigrants indicates that it continues to be a site of state intervention and evaluation.[12]

The Live-in Caregiver Program (LCP) is further evidence that relationships with new or would-be immigrants continue to be formed and regulated within the domestic realm. An obvious example is the domestication of Filipina nannies. As Geraldine Pratt argues, Filipina nannies have sometimes been "constructed as a family member, who is loved and cherished as such" as they have taken their places within the domestic realm. However, this domestication also coincides with the deskilling and "ghettoization" of Filipinas as well as their marginalization and vulnerability (confined, as they are, to the private realm).[13] Thus, Filipinas become an invisible part of the moral landscape as they perform domestic labour so that white women can be free to pursue their own aspirations. As with the Chinese Rescue Home, what is of interest here is not only how racialized groups become subject to white domestication but also how this is framed as inclusionary.

Abigail B. Bakan and Daiva Stasiulis examine the Canadian Foreign Domestic Worker Policy to uncover how it both recruits and regulates foreign workers, especially Filipina domestic workers in the LCP. They argue that both "exclusion and inclusion [are] at work within both the state and civil society in constructing the social boundaries of citizenship."[14] On the one hand, the LCP offers women a chance to immigrate to Canada; on the other hand, the conditions that are imposed on them include a two-year mandatory live-in requirement. These workers are confined to the domestic realm, where they are often overworked and sometimes exploited by their employers. The blurring of the line between the domestic realm and the workplace is problematic not only because of the potential for exploitation but also because the confinement of women to the private sphere is linked – through state policy – to their training as potential citizens.[15] Much like the women in the Home, women who participated in the earlier stages of the LCP were required to show evidence of their suitability for resident status in Canada, including their ability to "socially adapt."[16]

White women have often held the keys to settlement through their investment in domesticity and domestic training. Investigating the types of relationships that were forged within the Home provides insights into how the mundane became a site of radical transformation, a site where racial mixing was not only allowed but encouraged. What is equally intriguing is how these once exceptional projects have now become mundane. The institutionalization of the domestic has now become normalized. The relations between white women and Others through the (re)production of domesticity is everywhere. White women's goal of offering empowerment to other women continues to be common in both professional social work and in non-state-funded enterprises such as neighbourhood houses or community centres. Within these fields, many of the relationships are forged, whether formally or informally, across boundaries of class, race, and (sometimes) citizenship.

Settlement houses have a long history that highlights the interconnections between state and non-state agencies in the settlement of recent immigrants. Today's settlement houses have, according to Yan and Lauer, inherited the values of early institutions such as the Hull Houses.[17] Like the Chinese Rescue Home, the Hull House was a mixture of both benevolence and empowerment. According to Knight, although Jane Addams, one of the founders of Hull House, "has often been judged as a practitioner of benevolence, she regularly sought to promote the empowerment of those outside the circles of power."[18] Meant to ensure the social integration of new immigrants, today's settlement houses continue to build on these same values of inclusivity and benevolence. That these sites are used primarily by women, many of whom have children and are unemployed, points to the continued role that the management of domesticity plays in the settlement of new immigrants.[19] Re-examining such projects in light of what we know about the important role of domesticity in racial projects such as the Chinese Rescue Home can offer insights into how these newer projects might also challenge binaries of public/private and inclusion/exclusion.

The analysis of the Home workers and their relationship to the state aids in our understanding of how the state, non-state agencies, and civil society overlap and coalesce in their attempts to mediate and transgress class and racial boundaries. In the past, white women's part in this process was largely invisible. Now, these women are not only visible but what was once viewed as radical work has become normalized and expected. White women's role as moral authority has a long history, the conclusion of which has yet to be written. I hope that this book succeeds not only in building on recovering this historical past but also in adding to our understanding of the historical present.

Sources and Methodology

R ecords and reports of the Chinese Rescue Home in Victoria, British
Columbia, are located in the British Columbia Archives in Victoria
as well as in the Bob Stewart Archives in Vancouver. Missionary reports
and publications such as the *Missionary Outlook* are combined with
records from the Methodist Woman's Missionary Society, which include
reports and minutes of the advisory committee, intake books, journals,
newspaper clippings, and some photographs. Most of these records deal
specifically with missions to Chinese and Japanese populations, including
the Chinese Rescue Home. In British Columbia, the University of British
Columbia's Rare Books and Special Collections, the British Columbia
Archives, and the Bob Stewart Archives together provide a rich source of
primary documents. The Bob Stewart Archives has many documents
related to various home missions and evangelical work that took place
on Canadian soil. The Methodist Woman's Missionary Society, British
Columbia Conference Branch Fonds, 1904 to 1923, contains minutes
related to various Chinese and Japanese missions, including the set-up
of the Chinese Rescue Home, which later became the Oriental Home
and School. The Bob Stewart Archives also houses the Oriental Home and
School Fonds, which includes records, reports, and scrapbooks relating
to the Oriental Home and School in Victoria. Also of relevance are the
records of the Superintendent of Home Missions of the United Church
of Canada, the minutes of the Methodist Missionary Society, and the
Methodist Recorder, a monthly publication of the Methodist Church in
British Columbia. Newspapers from this time period offer community

perspectives on the Home, transcripts of two Royal Commissions provide a national perspective, and court transcripts offer insights into the role of the state in supporting and challenging the Home's authority and jurisdiction.

DISCOURSE ANALYSIS

One strategy for reading these documents "against the grain" involves employing discourse analysis as a means of investigating how constructions of race and gender are produced through religious discourse and discourses of national belonging. Joy Parr explains that "experiences are not made by discourses, but discourses are the medium through which experiences are comprehensible."[1] In *Discourses of Domination: Racial Bias in the Canadian English-Language Press*, Henry and Tator contend that discourse is

> the way in which language is used socially to convey broad historical meanings. It is the language identified by the social conditions of its use, by who is using it and under what conditions ... [and] it can never be totally free from the sociocultural influences and economic interests in which it was produced and disseminated.[2]

Thus, the archives, as well as the documents held there, are the products of sociocultural influences that are social, political, economic, and moral. I draw from a number of sources to uncover how religious discourse intersected with racial and gendered discourses to produce specific understandings of Chinese and Japanese women as foreign and as potentially transformable through practices of moral regulation.

Jorgenson and Phillips offer some key premises of discourse analysis. According to them, discourse analysis is a "critical approach to taken-for-granted knowledge"; this approach takes into account the "historical and cultural specificity" (5) of discourse; there is a "link between knowledge and social process"; and there is also a "link between knowledge and social action." Critical discourse analysis approaches discourse as forming a dialectical relationship with the social world. Discourse is viewed as "just one among many aspects of any social practice."[3] Critical discourse analysis, therefore, strives to understand the relationship between both the concrete material world and the abstract discursive world. Throughout my work, discourse analysis was extremely useful in enabling me to understand, for instance, how the physical (material) structure of the Chinese Rescue Home was embedded in – indeed constructed through – gendered, racial, and colonial discourses and how its material structure fed into and reproduced these same discourses within the Home.

First, discourse contributes to the construction of social identities, social relations, and "systems of knowledge and meaning."[4] In addition to my focus on systems of knowledge and meaning, I am committed to highlighting the many and diverse ways in which the discursive affects white, Japanese, and Chinese women's lives in material ways. Therefore, I pay particular attention to the social practices that informed and were informed by these discourses for, as Fairclough contends, "social science should include theories and analyses of both structure and action, and of their interconnection."[5] Discourse and ideology are neither neutral nor static. Ideology is embedded in social and cultural practices and, given that these practices change and (d)evolve over time, so, too, does the knowledge that they produce. These discourses, therefore, shape the everyday lives of individuals by shaping both social identity and social relations. Finally, the archival sources that I use must be understood as both material evidence of discursive practices and as the discursive practices themselves. Jorgenson and Phillips contend that "discourse is both constitutive and constituted."[6] In other words, not only does discourse shape social meaning and identities, it is also shaped by the social world. The texts that I have chosen to analyze are not separate from the historical and social specificities that informed them, nor are they distinct from the policies and practices that resulted from them. Further, religious discourses cannot be understood as singular or cohesive but must be understood as developing out of and in response to counter-discourses.

Notes

INTRODUCTION

1 "Emily" is a pseudonym. Throughout this book, names not associated with public records have been changed to ensure anonymity.

2 Patrick A. Dunae, "Making the 1891 Census in British Columbia," *Histoire sociale/Social History*, 31, 62 (1998), 223–39; David Chuenyan Lai, *The Forbidden City within Victoria* (Victoria: Orca, 1991).

3 John McLaren, "Race and the Criminal Justice System in British Columbia, 1892–1920: Constructing Chinese Crimes," in *Essays in the History of Canadian Law: In Honour of R.C.B. Risk*, ed. G. Blaine Baker and Jim Phillips (Toronto: University of Toronto Press, 1999), 407.

4 Minutes of the Oriental Home and School Advisory Committee, April 1897, Oriental Home and School Fonds, 1896–1914, MS-2439, British Columbia Archives (hereafter BCA).

5 Ibid., March 1897.

6 "Emily," in Victoria Oriental Home Register and Biography, 1888–1908 (hereafter Oriental Home Register), Oriental Home and School Fonds, United Church BC Conference Archives (hereafter Bob Stewart Archives).

7 Minutes of the Oriental Home and School Advisory Committee, November 1897, Oriental Home and School Fonds, 1896–1914, MS-2439, BCA.

8 "Emily."

9 Minutes of the Oriental Home and School Advisory Committee, November 1897, Oriental Home and School Fonds, 1896–1914, MS-2439, BCA.

10 Minutes of the Oriental Home and School Advisory Committee, special meeting, November 1897, Oriental Home and School Fonds, 1896–1914, MS-2439, BCA.

11 Ibid.

12 Minutes of the Oriental Home and School Advisory Committee, December 1897, Oriental Home and School Fonds, 1896–1914, MS-2439, BCA.

13 Ibid., special meeting, July 1898.

14 "Bad Women, 1910," Oriental Home and School Fonds, Bob Stewart Archives.

15 Oriental Home Register, Oriental Home and School Fonds, Bob Stewart Archives.

16 See, for instance, Derek Chang, "'Marked in Body, Mind, and Spirit': Home Missionaries and the Remaking of Race and Nation." In *Race, Nation, and Religion in the Americas,* ed. Henry Goldschmidt and Elizabeth McAlister, 133–56 (New York: Oxford University Press, 2004); Renisa Mawani, *Colonial Proximities: Cross Racial Encounters and Juridical Truths in British Columbia, 1871–1921* (Vancouver: UBC Press, 2009); and Mariana Valverde, *The Age of Light, Soap, and Water: Moral Reform in English Canada, 1885–1925* (Toronto: McClelland and Stewart, 1991).

17 I am indebted here to Gregory for his discussion of imaginative geographies. See Derek Gregory, "Imaginative Geographies," *Progress in Human Geography* 19, 4 (1995): 447–85.

18 Joan Sangster, *Regulating Girls and Women: Sexuality, Family, and the Law in Ontario, 1920–1960* (Don Mills: Oxford University Press, 2001), 3, emphasis in original. On the moral regulation of girls, see also Tamara Myers, *Montreal's Modern Girls and the Law, 1869–1945* (Toronto: University of Toronto Press, 2006).

19 Mona Domosh, "Geography and Gender: Home, Again?" *Progress in Human Geography* 22, 2 (1998): 276.

20 James S. Duncan and David Lambert "Landscapes of Home," In *A Companion to Cultural Geography*, ed. James S. Duncan, Nuala C. Johnson, and Richard H. Schein (Malden: Blackwell, 2004), 383.

21 Ibid.

22 Stephen Legg, Georgina Gowans, and Alison Blunt, for instance, all examine how women in India used home spaces as political spaces of anti-colonial resistance, which helped to define not only the domestic but also the national and imperial. See Stephen Legg, "Gendered Politics and Nationalised Homes: Women and the Anticolonial Struggle in Delhi, 1930–47," *Gender, Place and Culture* 10, 1 (2003): 7–28; Georgina Gowans, "Imperial Geographies of Home: Memsahibs and Miss-Sahibs in India and Britain, 1915–1947," *Cultural Geographies* 10, 4 (2003): 424–41; and Alison Blunt, "Imperial Geographies of Home: British Domesticity in India, 1886–1925," *Transactions of the Institute of British Geographers* 24, 4 (1999): 421–40.

23 This in-between space might be likened to a borderland. Anzaldua offers a deeper discussion of borderlands. See Gloria Anzaldua, *Borderlands/La Frontera: The New Mestiza* (San Francisco: Aunt Lute Books, 1987)

24 For a deeper discussion of moral regulation and social control, see Dorothy Chunn, *From Punishment to Doing Good: Family Courts and Socialized Justice in Ontario, 1880–1940* (Toronto: University of Toronto Press, 1992); Joan Sangster, *Regulating Girls and Women: Sexuality, Family, and the Law in Ontario, 1920–1960* (Don Mills: Oxford University Press, 2001); Valverde, *Age of Light, Soap, and Water;* and Peggy Pascoe, *Relations of Rescue: The Search for Female Moral Authority in the American West, 1874–1939* (New York: Oxford University Press, 1990).

25 For a more complete discussion of the method of analysis, please see the Appendix.

26 Gardiner is also known as "Gardner" and "Vrooman" in many of the documents. Unless quoting from other sources I use the spelling "Gardiner" here and throughout.

27 Franca Iacovetta and Wendy Mitchinson, "Social History and Case Files Research," in *On the Case: Explorations in Social History*, ed. Franca Iacovetta (Toronto: University of Toronto Press, 1998), 6.

28 Bruce L. Berg, *Qualitative Research Methods for the Social Sciences* (Boston: Pearson Education, 2009), 318.

29 Alison Blunt, *Domicile and Diaspora: Anglo-Indian Women and the Spatial Politics of Home* (Malden: Blackwell, 2005), 4.

30 David Wishart, "The Selectivity of Historical Representation," *Journal of Historical Geography* 23, 2 (1997): 112, 113.

31 Michel Foucault, "Nietzsche, Genealogy, History," in *The Essential Foucault*, ed. Paul Rabinow and Nikolas Rose, 351–69 (New York: The New Press, 2003), 360.

32 Jennifer Terry, "Theorizing Deviant Historiography," *differences* 3, 2 (1991): 56.

33 Foucault, "Nietzsche, Genealogy, History," 360.

34 Terry, "Theorizing Deviant Historiography," 58.

35 Ann Laura Stoler, "Colonial Archives and the Arts of Governance," *Archival Science* 2 (2002): 100 (emphasis in original).

36 Stoler, "Colonial Archives."

37 Ibid.

38 Chang, "Marked in Body, Mind, and Spirit"; Mawani, *Colonial Proximities.*

39 Phillips and Jorgenson offer some key premises of discourse analysis: (1) it is a "critical approach to taken-for-granted knowledge"; (2) it takes into account the "historical and cultural specificity" of discourse; (3) there is a "link between knowledge and social process"; and (4) there is also a "link between knowledge and social action." See L. Phillips and M. Jorgenson, *Discourse Analysis as Theory and Method* (London: Sage, 2002), 5, 6.

40 Phillips and Jorgenson, *Discourse Analysis*: 61.

41 For a deeper discussion of racialization, see Robert Miles, *Racism* (London: Routledge, 1989), 76.

42 Michael Omi and Howard Winant, *Racial Formation in the United States from the 1960s to the 1990s* (New York: Routledge, 1994), 55–56, emphasis in original.

43 Ibid., 68.

44 For a compelling discussion of the relationship between race and states, see David Theo Goldberg, *The Racial State* (Maiden: Blackwell, 2002).

45 Constance Backhouse's chapter on labour laws and the Chinese is a compelling example of how the state builds upon and produces racial knowledge through the enactment of law. See Constance Backhouse, *Colour-Coded: A Legal History of Racism in Canada, 1900–1950* (Toronto: University of Toronto Press, 1999).

46 Henry Lefebvre, *The Production of Space* (Oxford: Blackwell, 1991); Kay Anderson, *Vancouver's Chinatown: Racial Discourse in Canada, 1875–1980* (Montreal and Kingston: McGill-Queen's University Press, 1991); Sherene Razack, "When Place Becomes Race," in *Race, Space, and the Law*, ed. Sherene Razack, 1–20 (Toronto: Between the Lines, 2002); Mawani, *Colonial Proximities.*

47 Anderson, *Vancouver's Chinatown.*

48 Fanon's discussion of relationality is useful here. See Frantz Fanon, *Black Skin, White Masks* (New York: Grove Press, 1967).

49 M. Steyn and D. Conway, "Introduction: Intersecting Whiteness, Interdisciplinary Debates," *Ethnicities* 10, 3 (2010): 284–85.

50 Fanon, *Black Skin, White Masks.*

51 France Winddance Twine and Charles Gallagher, "Introduction: The Future of Whiteness – A Map of the 'Third Wave.'" *Ethnic and Racial Studies* 31, 1 (2008): 5.

52 For more on racial discourses as transnational, see Laura Briggs, Gladys McCormick, and J.T. Way, "Transnationalism: A Category of Analysis," *American Quarterly* 60, 3 (2008): 625–48.

53 Timothy Stanley, *Contesting White Supremacy: School Segregation, Anti-Racism, and the Making of Chinese Canadians* (Vancouver: UBC Press, 2011), 47–48.

54 Ibid., 53.

55 Ibid., 54.

56 Ibid.

57 See, for instance, Antoinette Burton, *Burdens of History: British Feminists, Indian Women, and Imperial Culture, 1865–1915* (Chapel Hill: University of North Carolina Press, 1994); Maina Chawla Singh, *Gender, Religion, and "Heathen Lands": American Missionary Women in South Asia, 1860s–1940s* (New York: Garland, 2000); Rhonda Ann Semple, *Missionary Women: Gender, Professionalism and the Victorian Idea of Christian Mission* (Woodbridge: Boydell Press, 2003); and Rosemary Gagan, *A Sensitive Independence* (Montreal and Kingston: McGill-Queen's University Press, 1992).

58 Pascoe, *Relations of Rescue*.

59 Ibid., 42.

60 Anzaldua, *Borderlands/La Frontera*.

61 Mawani, *Colonial Proximities*; Ann Laura Stoler, *Race and the Education of Desire: Foucault's History of Sexuality and the Colonial Order of Things* (Durham: Duke University Press, 1995).

62 Stoler, "Colonial Archives," 90.

63 Pascoe, *Relations of Rescue*; Burton, *Burdens of History*.

64 John Price, "'Orienting' the Empire: Mackenzie King and the Aftermath of the 1907 Race Riots," *BC Studies* 156 (2007/08): 53–81. For a discussion of these historical discourses of racial exclusion, see Peter Ward, *White Canada Forever: Popular Attitudes and Public Policy Toward Orientals in British Columbia* (Montreal and Kingston: McGill-Queen's University Press, 1990); Patricia Roy, *The Oriental Question: Consolidating a White Man's Province, 1914–41* (Vancouver: UBC Press, 2003); and Patricia Roy, *A White Man's Province: British Columbia Politicians and Chinese and Japanese Immigrants, 1858–1914* (Vancouver: UBC Press, 1989).

65 See Price, "'Orienting' the Empire"; Lisa Rose Mar, *Brokering Belonging: Chinese in Canada's Exclusion Era, 1885–1945* (New York: Oxford University Press, 2010); Timothy Stanley, *Contesting White Supremacy: School Segregation, Anti-Racism, and the Making of Chinese Canadians* (Vancouver: UBC Press, 2001); and Wing Chung Ng, *The Chinese in Vancouver, 1945–80: The Pursuit of Identity and Power* (Toronto: University of Toronto Press, 1999). For a discussion of Chinese exclusion and resistance in Manitoba, see Alison Marshall, *The Way of the Bachelor: Early Chinese Settlement in Manitoba* (Vancouver: UBC Press, 2011). For a compelling discussion of Japanese exclusion and resistance, see Andrea Geiger, *Subverting Exclusion: Transpacific Encounters with Race, Caste, and Borders, 1885–1928* (New Haven: Yale University Press, 2011).

66 Backhouse, *Colour-Coded*.

67 Rhonda Ann Semple, *The Lord's Dominion: The History of Canadian Methodism* (Montreal and Kingston: McGill-Queen's University Press, 1996).

68 Mawani, *Colonial Proximities*.

69 Nayan Shah, *Contagious Divides: Epidemics and Race in San Francisco's Chinatown* (Berkeley: University of California Press, 2001).

70 Marshall, *Way of the Bachelor*.

71 Mawani, *Colonial Proximities*.

72 Shah, *Contagious Divides*.

73 In her discussion of British women's place in the nation, Antoinette Burton points out that national identification was not only about the right to vote but also about women's moral authority. She argues that it was partly their perceived inferiority in relation to men that led women to pursue their imperial duty with such fervour. See Burton, *Burdens of History*. Mariana Valverde also documents the work of various moral reformers in sustaining the dominance of white Protestants, arguing that citizenship was constructed along very narrow parameters, often centring on whiteness and Christianity. See Valverde, *Age of Light, Soap, and Water*. Other scholars have written on the moral regulation of racialized populations by missionary women, but, again, these writers have largely examined these processes as imperial projects, as interventions that took place outside the West. See Semple, *Missionary Women;* Maina Chawla Singh, *Gender, Religion, and "Heathen Lands."*

74 Pascoe, *Relations of Rescue,* xvi.

75 Chang, "Marked in Body, Mind, and Spirit," 137.

76 Alan Hunt, *Governing Morals: A Social History of Moral Regulation* (Cambridge: Cambridge University Press, 1999), 1.

77 Shah, *Contagious Divide,* 111.

78 Hunt, *Governing Morals,* 7.

79 Michel Foucault, *Discipline and Punish: The Birth of the Prison* (New York: Random House, 1995), 136.

80 For a broader discussion of social hygiene, see Valverde, *Age of Light, Soap, and Water;* Billie Melman, *Women's Orients: English Women and the Middle East, 1718–1918* (London: Macmillan Academic and Professional, 1992); and Singh, *Gender, Religion, and "Heathen Lands."*

81 Although Japanese women entered the Home as early as 1895, it continued to call itself the Chinese Rescue Home until 1910. While Chinese and Japanese populations were not always constructed in the same way, similar assumptions were made about Japanese women, especially with regard to their propensity to prostitution and sexual lasciviousness.

Chapter 1: Foundations of Stone

1 See, for instance, Renisa Mawani, *Colonial Proximities: Cross Racial Encounters and Juridical Truths in British Columbia, 1871–1921* (Vancouver: UBC Press, 2009); Patricia Roy, *A White Man's Province: British Columbia Politicians and Chinese and Japanese Immigrants, 1858–1914* (Vancouver: UBC Press, 1989); and *The Oriental Question: Consolidating a White Man's Province, 1914–41* (Vancouver: UBC Press, 2003); Peter Ward, *White Canada Forever: Popular Attitudes and Public Policy Toward Orientals in British Columbia* (Montreal and Kingston: McGill-Queen's University Press, 1990).

2 Adele Perry, "'Fair Ones of a Purer Caste': White Women and Colonialism in Nineteenth-Century British Columbia," *Feminist Studies* 23, 3 (1997): 501.

3 Adele Perry, "Metropolitan Knowledge, Colonial Practice, and Indigenous Womanhood: Missions in Nineteenth-Century British Columbia," in *Contact Zones: Aboriginal and Settler Women in Canada's Colonial Past,* ed. Katie Pickles and Myra Rutherdale (Vancouver: UBC Press, 2005), 110.

4 Perry, "Metropolitan Knowledge," 113.

5 Roy, *White Man's Province,* x-xi.

6 For more on this history, see Ken Adachi, *The Enemy That Never Was: A History of Japanese Canadians* (Toronto: McClelland and Stewart, 1991); Roy Miki, *Redress: Inside the Japanese*

Canadian Call for Justice (Vancouver: Raincoast Books, 2004); and Michiko Midge Ayukawa, *Hiroshima Immigrants in Canada 1891–1941* (Vancouver: UBC Press, 2008).

7 David Chuenyan Lai, *Chinese Community Leadership: Case Study of Victoria in Canada*
(Toh Tuck Link: World Scientific Publishing, 2010), 16.

8 See, for instance, Adachi, *Enemy That Never Was*; Midge Ayukawa, "Good Wives and
Mothers: Japanese Picture Brides in Early Twentieth-Century British Columbia," *BC
Studies*, 105/106 (1995): 107; Roy, *White Man's Province*; Ward, *White Canada Forever*.

9 Women's Book Committee Chinese Canadian National Council, *Jin Guo: Voices of Chinese Canadian Women* (Toronto: Women's Press, 1992), 17.

10 Ayukawa, "Good Wives and Mothers."

11 According to the municipal census of 1871, there were only twenty-nine Chinese women
listed in Victoria (Victoria Municipal Census of 1871, viHistory.ca).

12 Tamara Adilman, "A Preliminary Sketch of Chinese Women and Work in British Columbia, 1858–1950," in *British Columbia Reconsidered: Essays on Women*, ed. Gillian Creese and
Veronica Strong-Boag (Vancouver: Press Gang, 1992), 314.

13 Women's Book Committee Chinese Canadian National Council, *Jin Guo*, 18.

14 Ayukawa, *Hiroshima Immigrants in Canada*, 35.

15 Ibid., 46.

16 Adele Perry, *On the Edge of Empire: Gender, Race, and the Making of British Columbia,
1849–1871* (Toronto: University of Toronto Press, 2001).

17 Ibid., 14.

18 Derek Pethick, *Summer of Promise: Victoria, 1864–1914* (Victoria: Sono Nis, 1980).

19 Sharon Meen, "Colonial Society and Economy," in *The Pacific Province: A History of British Columbia*, ed. Hugh J.M. Johnston (Vancouver: Douglas and McIntyre, 1996), 111.

20 Valerie Green, *Upstarts and Outcasts: Victoria's Not-So-Proper Past* (Victoria: Horsdal and
Schubart, 2000), 8.

21 Pethick, *Summer of Promise*, 91.

22 Ibid., 92.

23 Green, *Upstarts and Outcast*; Perry, "Fair Ones of a Purer Caste"; Perry, *Edge of Empire*.

24 Michael H. Cramer, "Public and Political: Documents of the Woman's Suffrage Campaign in
British Columbia, 1871–1917: The View from Victoria," in *British Columbia Reconsidered: Essays
on Women*, ed. Gillian Creese and Veronica Strong-Boag (Vancouver: Press Gang, 1992), 59.

25 For a Canadian context, see Norman Knowles, "Religious Affiliation, Demographic
Change and Family Formation among British Columbia's Chinese and Japanese Com-
munities: A Case Study of Church of England Missions, 1861–1942." *Canadian Ethnic
Studies* 27, 2 (1995): 59–80. For a more general discussion of the North American context,
see Rosemary Gagan, *A Sensitive Independence* (Montreal and Kingston: McGill-Queen's
University Press, 1992); Peggy Pascoe, *Relations of Rescue: The Search for Female Moral
Authority in the American West, 1874–1939* (New York: Oxford University Press, 1990);
and Myra Rutherdale, *Women and the White Man's God: Gender and Race in the Canadian
Mission Field* (Vancouver: UBC Press, 2003).

26 Pascoe, *Relations of Rescue*, 13.

27 For more on this point, see Rutherdale, *Women and the White Man's God*.

28 Victoria Fire Insurance map, Image VFP 1891, p. 10, courtesy of Royal BC Museum,
BCA.

29 Ibid.

30 BC GenWeb, *1901 Census of Victoria Statistics*, 10 06, 2009, http://www.rootsweb.ancestry.
com/~canbc/1901vic_cen/stats.htm.

31 Danda Humphreys, "The Pendray House," *Focus Online: Victoria's Magazine of People, Ideas and Culture,* September2010, http://www.focusonline.ca/?q=node/84.

32 "A Palatial Home: Mr. W.J. Pendray's Stately New Residence and Some of the Features of Its Decoration," *British Colonist,* March 14, 1897, 5.

33 Harry Gregson, *A History of Victoria, 1842–1970* (Victoria: Morriss Printing, 1970), 55.

34 City of Victoria, *FAQ,* 2012, http://www.victoria.ca/EN/main/departments/legislative -services/archives/faqs.html.

35 Gagan, *Sensitive Independence,* 170.

36 Ibid., 171.

37 Marilyn Färdig Whiteley, *The Life and Letters of Annie Leake Tuttle: Working for the Best* (Waterloo: Wilfrid Laurier University Press, 1999), 68.

38 Gagan, *Sensitive Independence;* Whiteley, *Life and Letters of Annie Leake Tuttle.*

39 See my discussion of the Menzies case in Chapter 5.

40 Whiteley, *Life and Letters of Annie Leake Tuttle,* 69.

41 For instance, various reports in the *British Colonist* during 1894 describe her work in Victoria, Vancouver, and Nanaimo.

42 Woman's Missionary Society, Annual Report of the Woman's Missionary Society of the Methodist Church of Canada, 1898–1899 (Toronto: Ryerson Press, 1899), lxxxviii.

43 *Report of the Royal Commission on Chinese and Japanese Immigration* (sessional paper no. 54, session 1902) (Ottawa: S.E. Dawson, 1902), 38.

44 Ibid.

45 Ibid.

46 The following were listed in the advisory committee minutes as "Matron" or had filed matron reports that were published in the annual reports of the WMS: Annie Leake 1888– 93, Miss Morrow, 1892–95, Miss Bowes, 1895–98, Miss Ferguson, 1899 (January–June), Miss F. Kate Morgan, 1898–1901, Mrs. Ida Snyder, 1902–10, Maggie Smith, 1911–19, and Annie Martin 1920–23. Note: Names appear here as written in the original documents.

47 Gagan, *Sensitive Independence.*

48 Minutes of the Oriental Home and School Advisory Committee, March 1901, Oriental Home and School Fonds, 1896–1914, MS-2439, British Columbia Archives (hereafter BCA).

49 For more on the relational nature of race, see Herbert Blummer, "Race Prejudice as a Sense of Group Position," *Pacific Sociological Review* 1, 1 (1958): 4; and Frantz Fanon, *Black Skin, White Masks* (New York: Grove Press, 1967).

50 Victoria Oriental Home Register and Biography, 1888–1908 (hereafter Oriental Home Register), Oriental Home and School Fonds, United Church BC Conference Archives (hereafter Bob Stewart Archives).

51 Minutes from the Advisory Committee of Japanese (Oriental) Missions, July 1919, Methodist Church BC Conference Fonds, 1908–23, Bob Stewart Archives.

52 For a deeper discussion of total institutions, see Michel Foucault, *Discipline and Punish: The Birth of the Prison* (New York: Random House, 1995), 231–56.

53 Michel Foucault, "Truth and Power," in *The Essential Foucault,* ed. Paul Rabinow and Nikolas Rose, 300–18 (New York: The New Press, 2003), 308.

54 "Emily" is a pseudonym.

55 "Record 40," Oriental Home Register, Oriental Home and School Fonds, Bob Stewart Archives, 16.

56 "Record 204," Oriental Home Register, Oriental Home and School Fonds, Bob Stewart Archives.

57 "Anna Lim" is a pseudonym.

58 "Record 145," Oriental Home Register, Oriental Home and School Fonds, Bob Stewart Archives.

59 Woman's Missionary Society, *Annual Report ... 1898–99*, xciii.

60 For a deeper discussion of the regulation of white women who entered into cross-racial alliances with men, see Velma Demerson's autobiographical book, *Incorrigible* (Waterloo: Wilfrid Laurier University Press, 2004).

61 J.E. Starr to E.S. Strachan, September 1887, Oriental Home and School Fonds, Bob Stewart Archives.

62 For more on the relationship between mission work and social order, see Talal Asad, *Genealogies of Religion: Discipline and Reasons of Power in Christianity and Islam* (Baltimore: Johns Hopkins University Press, 1993).

63 Woman's Missionary Society, Twenty-Second Annual Report of the Woman's Missionary Society of the Methodist Church of Canada, 1902–1903 (Toronto: The Ryerson Press, 1903), lxxxiv.

64 Mariana Valverde, *The Age of Light, Soap, and Water: Moral Reform in English Canada, 1885–1925* (Toronto: McClelland and Stewart, 1991), 105.

65 Minutes of the Oriental Home and School Advisory Committee, November 1898, Oriental Home and School Fonds, 1896–1914, MS-2439, BCA.

66 See Chapter 7 for a discussion of the courts' use of this doctrine.

67 Although the Home was run by women and, thus, the term "maternalistic" might seem more appropriate, the connotations associated with maternalism and motherhood fall short of the mark here. The spirit of paternalism, as it has been applied to men's power and authority over both children and *adult* women, seems more appropriate.

68 "Elsie" is a name given to Quai Shing by those who ran the Home. Her case is one of four analyzed in Chapter 6.

69 Minutes of the Oriental Home and School Advisory Committee, March 1899, Oriental Home and School Fonds, 1896–1914, MS-2439, BCA.

70 Ibid.

71 "Record 72," Oriental Home Register, Oriental Home and School Fonds, Bob Stewart Archives, 30.

72 Ibid.

73 Minutes of the Oriental Home and School Advisory Committee, November 1898, Oriental Home and School Fonds, 1896–1914, MS-2439, BCA.

74 Ibid., January 1899.

75 Ibid., May 1908.

76 Ibid.

77 Alison Bashford and Carolyn Strange, "Isolation and Exclusion in the Modern World: An Introductory Essay," in *Isolation: Places and Practices of Exclusion*, ed. Alison Bashford and Carolyn Strange (New York: Routledge, 2003), 6.

78 Ibid., emphasis in original.

79 "Record 47," Oriental Home Record Book and Register, 1886–1929 (hereafter Oriental Home Record Book), Oriental Home and School Fonds, Bob Stewart Archives, 21

80 For more on confinement as prevention, see Bashford and Strange, "Isolation and Exclusion," 7.

81 Bashford and Strange make clear that, by "the twentieth century, an array of legally mandated exclusionary practices classified and contained not only the bad, the sick and the mad but those deemed racially inferior, the intellectually unfit and, importantly, the *potentially* dangerous." See Bashford and Strange, "Isolation and Exclusion," 3, emphasis in original.

82 "Record 42 and 43," Oriental Home Record Book, Oriental Home and School Fonds, Bob Stewart Archives, 19.

83 "Record 191," Oriental Home Record Book, Oriental Home and School Fonds, Bob Stewart Archives, 67

84 In the following chapter, I discuss how prostitution was seen as a risk not only to the women who were viewed as victims of this trade but also to white men.

85 Pascoe, *Relations of Rescue*, 53.

86 In Bashford and Strange, *Isolation*.

87 Oriental Home Register, Oriental Home and School Fonds, Bob Stewart Archives.

88 Bashford and Strange, "Isolation and Exclusion," 6.

89 Minutes of the Oriental Home and School Advisory Committee, December 1913, Oriental Home and School Fonds, 1896–1914, MS-2439, BCA.

CHAPTER 2: PILLARS OF DOMESTICITY AND THE "CHINESE PROBLEM"

Epigraph: Derek Chang, "Marked in Body, Mind, and Spirit": Home Missionaries and the Remaking of Race and Nation," in *Race, Nation, and Religion in the Americas*, ed. Henry Goldschmidt and Elizabeth McAlister, 133–56 (New York: Oxford University Press, 2004), 137.

1 "Celestial Bliss: Two Fond Chinese Hearts United Last Evening," *British Colonist*, August 28, 1889.

2 Marilyn Lake and Henry Reynolds, *Drawing the Global Colour Line: White Men's Countries and the International Challenge of Racial Inequality* (Cambridge: Cambridge University Press, 2008), 23.

3 Ibid., 23.

4 Renisa Mawani, *Colonial Proximities: Cross Racial Encounters and Juridical Truths in British Columbia, 1871–1921* (Vancouver: UBC Press, 2009), 26.

5 Ibid., 109 (emphasis in original).

6 Royal Commission on Chinese Immigration, *Report on the Royal Commission on Chinese Immigration: Report and Evidence* (Ottawa: Royal Commission on Chinese Immigration, 1885), vii (emphasis added).

7 Ibid., 1–2.

8 Ibid., xi.

9 As Lake and Reynolds observe in their discussion of Chinese migration, "nineteenth-century migration created new identities and new ways of being in the world. Opponents of Chinese migration forged a sense of transnational community, identifying white men under siege, men whose sovereign right of self-government was threatened, not just by the Chinese, but by distant metropolitan centres of power." See Lake and Reynolds, *Drawing the Global Colour Line*, 28.

10 Report on the Royal Commission on Chinese Immigration, xxxix.

11 Ibid., liii.

12 Ibid., vii.

13 Ibid.

14 Ibid.

15 For a more detailed discussion of the threat of prostitution to family life, see Joan Sangster, *Regulating Girls and Women: Sexuality, Family, and the Law in Ontario, 1920–1960* (Don Mills: Oxford University Press 2001), esp. chap. 4.

16 *Report of the Royal Commission on Chinese and Japanese Immigration: Session 1902* (Ottawa: S.E. Dawson, 1902), 22.

17 Ibid., 23.
18 Ibid., 24.
19 Ibid., 25.
20 Ibid., 27.
21 Ibid., 26.
22 As Joseph Henning argues in his discussion of Japanese mission work, "the only alternative to Christian missions was perpetual heathenism. These beliefs gave purpose and power to the missionaries. They, and they alone, had been chosen; only they could convert and civilize the heathen." See Joseph M. Henning, *Outposts of Civilization: Race, Religion, and the Formative Years of American-Japanese Relations* (New York: New York University Press, 2000), 40.
23 *Report of the Royal Commission on Chinese and Japanese Immigration*, 38.
24 Ibid., 29.
25 For a more detailed discussion of these measures, see Roy Miki, *Redress: Inside the Japanese Canadian Call for Justice* (Vancouver: Raincoast Books, 2004); Patricia Roy, *A White Man's Province: British Columbia Politicians and Chinese and Japanese Immigrants, 1858–1914* (Vancouver: UBC Press, 1989); Peter Ward, *White Canada Forever: Popular Attitudes and Public Policy Toward Orientals in British Columbia* (Montreal and Kingston: McGill-Queen's University Press, 1990).
26 For more on moral geographies, see Lawrence J. Taylor, "Moral Entrepreneurs and Moral Geographies on the US/Mexico Border," *Social and Legal Studies* 19, 3 (2010): 299–310.
27 Bryan Hogeveen, "Discontinuity and/in the Early Twentieth Century Ontario Juvenile Court," *Journal of Historical Sociology* 20, 4 (2007): 613.
28 Ibid.
29 Twenty Second Annual Report of the Woman's Missionary Society of the Methodist Church, Canada, 1902–1903 (Toronto: William Briggs, 1903).
30 Amy Kaplan, "Manifest Domestici," *American Literature* 70, 3 (1998): 581–82.
31 Ibid., 582.
32 J.E. Starr to E.S. Strachan, September 1887, Oriental Home and School Fonds, United Church BC Conference Archives (hereafter Bob Stewart Archives).
33 Writing of the American Baptist Home Mission Society (ABHMS), Derek Chang argues: "Even as movements toward segregation, disfranchisement, and exclusion called on a somatic, or biological definition of race to demarcate the boundaries of citizenship ... the ABHMS articulated an alternative vision of the nation in which Christianity stood as the primary standard for inclusion ... Although missionaries rejected the growing movement toward restriction and exclusion, they often found themselves caught in a process that required the delineation of social and religious hierarchies. Conversion was predicated on the 'inevitably pejorative nature of missionary constructions of heathenism' at the core of evangelical calls for social and religious uplift and transformation. The emphasis on *difference* threatened ultimately to undermine missionaries' more egalitarian aims." See Chang, "Marked in Body, Mind, and Spirit," 135.
34 *Report of the Royal Commission on Chinese and Japanese Immigration*, 36.
35 Ibid., 37.
36 See, for instance, Peggy Pascoe, *Relations of Rescue: The Search for Female Moral Authority in the American West, 1874–1939* (New York: Oxford University Press, 1990); Maina Chawla Singh, *Gender, Religion, and "Heathen Lands": American Missionary Women in South Asia (1860s–1940s)* (New York: Garland, 2000).
37 J.E. Starr to E.S. Strachan, September 1887.
38 Report on the Royal Commission on Chinese Immigration, lxxxii.

39 J.E. Starr to E.S. Strachan, September 1887.
40 Ibid.
41 These familial metaphors will be taken up more fully in the next chapter.
42 J.E. Starr to E.S. Strachan, September 1887.
43 Ibid.
44 Forty Third Annual Report of the Woman's Missionary Society of the Methodist Church of Canada, 1923–1924 (Toronto: The Ryerson Press, 1924), cxx.
45 "Daisy," Victoria Oriental Home Register and Biography, 1888–1908 (hereafter Oriental Home Register), Oriental Home and School Fonds, Bob Stewart Archives.
46 For more on sacred performances of religion, see Talal Asad, Genealogies of Religion: Discipline and Reasons of Power in Christianity and Islam (Baltimore: Johns Hopkins University Press, 1993), 53.
47 Oriental Home Register, Oriental Home and School Fonds, Bob Stewart Archives.
48 Minutes of the Oriental Home and School Advisory Committee, December 1903, Oriental Home and School Fonds, 1896–1914, MS-2439, British Columbia Archives (hereafter BCA).
49 Minutes from the Advisory Committee of Japanese (Oriental) Missions, January 1913, Methodist Church BC Conference Fonds, 1908–1923, Bob Stewart Archives.
50 Homi Bhabha, The Location of Culture (London: Routledge, 1994), 122.
51 Ibid., 125–26.
52 Minutes from the Advisory Committee of Japanese (Oriental) Missions, July 1918, Methodist Church BC Conference Fonds, 1908–1923, Bob Stewart Archives.
53 Minutes of the Oriental Home and School Advisory Committee, August 1914, Oriental Home and School Fonds, 1896–1914, MS-2439, BCA.
54 Norman Knowles, "Religious Affiliation, Demographic Change and Family Formation among British Columbia's Chinese and Japanese Communities: A Case Study of Church of England Missions, 1861–1942," Canadian Ethnic Studies 27, 2 (1995): 64.
55 Barbara Riley, "Six Saucepans to One: Domestic Science vs. the Home in British Columbia, 1900–1930," in British Columbia Reconsidered: Essays on Women, ed. Gillian Creese and Veronica Strong-Boag, 119–42 (Vancouver: Press Gang, 1992).
56 This intention arose out of a proposal that was introduced at the General Conference of the Methodist Church in 1878. See "The Woman's Missionary Society of the Methodist Church of Canada," Missionary Outlook 1, 5 (1881): 13.
57 A. Sutherland, "A Woman's Missionary Society," Missionary Outlook 1,1 (1881): 3.
58 Ibid., 3–4.
59 "Woman's Work," Missionary Outlook 1, 4 (1881): 10.
60 "The Woman's Missionary Society of the Methodist Church of Canada," Missionary Outlook 1, 5 (1881): 54.
61 Ibid.
62 Ibid.
63 Constitution from the Eighth Annual Report of the Woman's Missionary Society of the Methodist Church, Canada, 1888–89 (Toronto: William Briggs, 1889), 165.
64 Joseph M. Henning, Outposts of Civilization: Race, Religion, and the Formative Years of American-Japanese Relations (New York: New York University Press, 2000), 48, 49.
65 Constitution from the Eighth Annual Report of the Woman's Missionary Society of the Methodist Church, 172–73 (emphasis added).
66 Ibid. (emphasis added).
67 Ibid.

68 Ibid.

69 J.E. Starr to E.S. Strachan, September 1887.

70 For a more comprehensive discussion of the house itself, see Chapter 4, this volume.

71 J.E. Starr to E.S. Strachan, September 1887.

72 Ibid.

73 Chang, "Marked in Body, Mind, and Spirit," 137.

74 J.E. Starr to E.S. Strachan, September 1887.

75 Ibid. Gardiner would later be implicated in a number of very public court cases, which is the subject of Chapter 5, this volume.

76 J.E. Starr to E.S. Strachan, September 1887.

77 Ibid.

78 See Pascoe, *Relations of Rescue*. For a deeper discussion of white women's moral regulatory potential in British Columbia, see Adele Perry, *On the Edge of Empire, Gender, Race, and the Making of British Columbia, 1849–1871* (Toronto: University of Toronto Press, 2001), 139.

79 Pascoe, *Relations of Rescue*.

80 Here, I am borrowing from Althusser to underscore how the space of the Home functioned ideologically to "call" some and to exclude others. See Louis Althusser, *Lenin and Philosophy and Other Essays* (New York: Monthly Review Press, 2001), especially the chapter entitled "Ideology and Ideological State Apparatuses (Notes towards an Investigation)."

81 J.E. Starr to E.S. Strachan, September 1887.

82 Ibid.

Chapter 3: Crossing the Threshold

1 "Build New Chinese Girls' Mission Home," *British Colonist*, April 3, 1908.

2 "Rescue Home Doing a Remarkable Work," *British Colonist*, April 12, 1908.

3 Alison Blunt, "Cultural Geography: Cultural Geographies of Home," *Progress in Human Geography*, 29 2005): 506.

4 Shelley Mallett, "Understanding Home: A Critical Review of the Literature," *Sociological Review* 52, 1 (2004): 62–89.

5 Michel Foucault, "Nietzsche, Genealogy, History," in *The Essential Foucault*, ed. Paul Rabinow and Nikolas Rose (New York: The New Press, 2003), 351.

6 Peggy Pascoe, *Relations of Rescue: The Search for Female Moral Authority in the American West, 1874–1939* (New York: Oxford University Press, 1990), xvi.

7 Henry Lefebvre, *The Production of Space* (Oxford: Blackwell, 1991).

8 James S. Duncan and David Lambert, "Landscapes of Home," in *A Companion to Cultural Geography*, ed. James S. Duncan, Nuala C. Johnson and Richard H. Schein, 382–403 (Malden: Blackwell, 2004).

9 "Home," *Merriam-Webster.com* (Merriam-Webster, 2015), http://www.merriam-webster.com/dictionary/home.

10 Pascoe, *Relations of Rescue*, 6.

11 J.E. Starr to E.S. Strachan, September 1887, Oriental Home and School Fonds, United Church BC Conference Archives (hereafter Bob Stewart Archives).

12 Ibid.

13 Ibid.

14 Adele Perry, *On the Edge of Empire, Gender, Race, and the Making of British Columbia, 1849–1871* (Toronto: University of Toronto Press, 2001), 21–36.

15 Minutes of the Oriental Home and School Advisory Committee, November 1898, Oriental Home and School Fonds, 1896–1914, MS-2439, British Columbia Archives (hereafter BCA).

16 The numbering system in Victoria changed sometime after 1905, thus the new address was 732 Cormorant Street. "History of Japanese in Oriental Home, Victoria BC," WMS, Bob Stewart Archives, 1959.

17 "Minutes of the Oriental Home and School Advisory Committee," November 1909, Oriental Home and School Fonds, 1896–1914, MS-2439, BCA.

18 The Home closed its doors during the Second World War when its residents were moved to Saskatchewan as part of the Japanese Canadian internment process. By this time, the Home only housed Japanese women and children.

19 See, for instance, William Morgan, *The Abrams Guide to American House Styles* (New York: Harry N. Abrams, 2004).

20 Martin Segger, *Victoria: A Primer for Regional History in Architecture* (Watkins Glen: The American Life Foundation and Study Institute, 1979).

21 Morgan, *Abrams Guide to American House Styles.*

22 Woman's Missionary Society, Annual Report of the Woman's Missionary Society of the Methodist Church of Canada, 1907–1908 (Toronto: The Ryerson Press, 1908), xciii.

23 Sherene Razack, "When Place Becomes Race," in *Race, Space, and the Law*, ed. Sherene Razack (Toronto: Between the Lines, 2002), 9.

24 "Metonymy," *Merriam-Webster.com* (Merriam-Webster, 2015), http://www.merriam-webster. com/dictionary/metonymy.

25 Robert Young, *Colonial Desire: Hybridity in Theory, Culture and Race* (New York: Routledge, 1995), 98.

26 Woman's Missionary Society, Annual Report of the Woman's Missionary Society of the Methodist Church of Canada, 1916–1917 (Toronto: The Ryerson Press, 1917), xcix.

27 Minutes of the Oriental Home and School Advisory Committee," August 1909, Oriental Home and School Fonds, 1896–1914, MS-2439, BCA.

28 Ibid.

29 Ibid.

30 "Joe" is a pseudonym.

31 Records 80, 81, and 82, Oriental Home Record Book and Register, 1886–1929, Oriental Home and School Fonds, Bob Stewart Archives, 32–35.

32 Joan Sangster, writing on the Toronto Elizabeth Fry Society (EFT), explains that "maternalism is a flexible and fluid ideological concept that underpins and justifies a wide variety of political and social agendas" (231). Further, she explains that EFT reformers saw "women's familial roles as 'essential to the social order' and believed their socialization as women and mothers gave them 'special insights in reform campaigns directed at women'" (231–32). See Joan Sangster, "Reforming Women's Reformatories: Elizabeth Fry, Penal Reform and the State, 1950–70," *Canadian Historical Review* 85, 2 (2004): 227–52.

33 "Jeanie" is a pseudonym.

34 Minutes of the Oriental Home and School Advisory Committee, May 1901, Oriental Home and School Fonds, 1896–1914, MS-2439, BCA.

35 Ibid.

36 Woman's Missionary Society, Twenty-Second Annual Report of the Woman's Missionary Society of the Methodist Church of Canada, 1902–1903 (Toronto: The Ryerson Press, 1903), lxxxv.

37 Minutes of the Oriental Home and School Advisory Committee, April 1902, Oriental Home and School Fonds, 1896–1914, MS-2439, BCA.

38 Ibid. (emphasis added).
39 For more on how mothering was distinguished as a Western trait, see Alison Diduck, "Legislating Ideologies of Motherhood," *Social and Legal Studies* 2 (1993): 461–85.
40 Woman's Missionary Society, *Annual Report of the Woman's Missionary Society of the Methodist Church of Canada, 1896–1897* (Toronto: The Ryerson Press, 1897), lxxiv (emphasis added).
41 Ibid., Annual Report of the Woman's Missionary Society of the Methodist Church of Canada, 1898–1899 (Toronto: The Ryerson Press, 1899), xxviii (emphasis added).
42 Rosemary Gagan, *A Sensitive Independence* (Montreal and Kingston: McGill-Queen's University Press, 1992), 174.
43 Woman's Missionary Society, *Annual Report ... 1898–1899*, xxviii.
44 Ibid., *Annual Report ... 1902–1903*, lxxxiv (emphasis added).
45 Ibid., Annual Report of the Woman's Missionary Society of the Methodist Church of Canada, 1904–1905 (Toronto: The Ryerson Press, 1905), lxxvi.
46 Ibid., Annual Report of the Woman's Missionary Society of the Methodist Church of Canada, 1906–1907 (Toronto: The Ryerson Press, 1907), lxxxviii.
47 Ibid., Annual Report of the Woman's Missionary Society of the Methodist Church of Canada, 1912–1914 (Toronto: The Ryerson Press, 1914), xcviii.
48 Ibid., Annual Report of the Woman's Missionary Society of the Methodist Church of Canada, 1909–1910 (Toronto: The Ryerson Press, 1910), lxxi.
49 Veronica Strong-Boag, "Daughters of the True North 1900–1995," *Beaver* 74, 6 (1995): 29–41.
50 Woman's Missionary Society, Annual Report of the Woman's Missionary Society of the Methodist Church of Canada, 1923–1924 (Toronto: The Ryerson Press, 1924), cxix.
51 Ibid. (emphasis added).
52 Ibid.
53 For a detailed analysis of women's roles in "child neglect," See Karen J. Swift, "An Outrage to Common Decency: Historical Perspectives on Child Neglect," *Child Welfare* 74, 1 (1995): 71–91.
54 Woman's Missionary Society, *Annual Report ... 1916–1917*, xcviii.
55 Alison Diduck, "Legislating Ideologies of Motherhood," *Social and Legal Studies* 2 (1993): 466.
56 "Abby" is a pseudonym.
57 Oriental Home and School Record Book, Record 75, pp. 30–31, Oriental Home and School Fonds, Bob Stewart Archives.
58 Woman's Missionary Society, Annual Report of the Woman's Missionary Society of the Methodist Church of Canada, 1920–1921 (Toronto: The Ryerson Press, 1921), cxxiv.
59 For a discussion of Victoria Chung, who stayed in the Home and went on to become a medical doctor, see John Price and Ningping Yu, "A True Trailblazer: Victoria Chung Broke the Mould for Women and Chinese Canadians," *Times Colonist*, October 23, 2011.
60 Woman's Missionary Society, *Annual Report ... 1920–1921*, cxxiv.
61 J.E. Starr to E.S. Strachan, September 1887, Oriental Home and School Fonds, Bob Stewart Archives.
62 Woman's Missionary Society, Annual Report of the Woman's Missionary Society of the Methodist Church of Canada, 1895–1896 (Toronto: The Ryerson Press, 1896), 24.
63 Ibid., Annual Report ... 1916–1917, xcviii.
64 Here, I am indebted to the work of Michel Foucault on "docile bodies." See Michel Foucault, *Discipline and Punish: The Birth of the Prison* (New York: Random House, 1995), 136.
65 Woman's Missionary Society, Annual Report of the Woman's Missionary Society of the Methodist Church of Canada, 1911–1912 (Toronto: The Ryerson Press, 1912), lxxxvi.

66 Ibid., Annual Report of the Woman's Missionary Society of the Methodist Church of Canada, 1899–1900 (Toronto: The Ryerson Press, 1900), xciv.

67 Ibid.

68 Woman's Missionary Society, *Annual Report ... 1899–1900,* xciii.

69 Ibid., xciv.

70 Minutes of the Oriental Home and School Advisory Committee, July 1905, Oriental Home and School Fonds, 1896–1914, MS-2439, BCA.

71 Ibid., April 1913, Oriental Home and School Fonds, 1896–1914, MS-2439, BCA.

72 Ibid., June 1897, Oriental Home and School Fonds, 1896–1914, MS-2439, BCA.

73 Woman's Missionary Society, *Annual Report ... 1899–1900,* xciv.

74 Ibid., Annual Report of the Woman's Missionary Society of the Methodist Church of Canada, 1913–1914 (Toronto: The Ryerson Press, 1914), xcvii.

75 *Victoria Daily Times,* December 26, 1895.

76 Minutes of the Oriental Home and School Advisory Committee, May 1896, Oriental Home and School Fonds, 1896–1914, MS-2439, BCA.

77 Ibid., August 1896, Oriental Home and School Fonds, 1896–1914, MS-2439, BCA (the "*Guardian*" probably refers to the *Christian Guardian,* a weekly Methodist newspaper, and the *Outlook* may refer to the British publication *Church Missionary Outlook,* which was published from 1841 to 1972).

78 Minutes of the Oriental Home and School Advisory Committee, June 1897, Oriental Home and School Fonds, 1896–1914, MS-2439, BCA.

79 Ibid., January 1898, Oriental Home and School Fonds, 1896–1914, MS-2439, BCA.

80 Pascoe, *Relations of Rescue.*

81 Alan Hunt, *Governing Morals: A Social History of Moral Regulation* (Cambridge: Cambridge University Press, 1999), 95.

82 Minutes of the Oriental Home and School Advisory Committee, May 1911, Oriental Home and School Fonds, 1896–1914, MS-2439, BCA.

83 Ibid.

84 Minutes of the Oriental Home and School Advisory Committee, March 1912, Oriental Home and School Fonds, 1896–1914, MS-2439, BCA.

85 "Minutes of the Oriental Home and School Advisory Committee," June, 1907, Oriental Home and School Fonds, 1896–1914, Record Number MS-2439, British Columbia Archives.

86 Ibid.

87 Minutes of the Oriental Home and School Advisory Committee, November, 11 and 21, 1908, Oriental Home and School Fonds, 1896–1914, Record Number MS-2439, British Columbia Archives.

88 See Chapter 6 (this volume) for a discussion of some of these cases.

89 Lee Mong Kow is the subject of one of the court cases discussed in Chapter 5.

90 Timothy J. Stanley, "LEE MONG KOW," in *Dictionary of Canadian Biography,* vol. 15, University of Toronto/Université Laval, 2003–, http://www.biographi.ca/en/bio/lee_mong_kow_15E.html (viewed June 26, 2014).

91 Pascoe, *Relations of Rescue,* 94.

92 Denise Chong, *The Concubine's Children: Portrait of a Family Divided* (Toronto: Penguin, 1994).

93 In the book *Jin Guo,* from which her story is taken, Margaret Chan gives her birth year as 1902. However, the records of the Home indicate she was only eleven years old at the

time, giving her birthday as April 1906. If her birth year was indeed 1902, she was likely fifteen years old when she was admitted in April 1917. It is possible that she hoped she would be treated better in the Home if she was thought to be younger because younger women were often offered more educational opportunities. See Women's Book Committee Chinese Canadian National Council, *Jin Guo: Voices of Chinese Canadian Women* (Toronto: Women's Press, 1992), 28.

94 Women's Book Committee Chinese Canadian National Council, *Jin Guo*.
95 Michiko Midge Ayukawa, *Hiroshima Immigrants in Canada, 1891–1941* (Vancouver: UBC Press, 2008), 40–42.
96 Ibid., 41.
97 Minutes of the Oriental Home and School Advisory Committee, March 1900, Oriental Home and School Fonds, 1896–1914, MS-2439, BCA.
98 Woman's Missionary Society, Annual Report of the Woman's Missionary Society of the Methodist Church of Canada, 1919–1920 (Toronto: The Ryerson Press, 1920), cxi.
99 Pascoe, *Relations of Rescue*, 94.
100 "Agreement," in Miscellaneous, Oriental Home and School Fonds, Bob Stewart Archives.
101 Ibid.
102 For more on belonging and religious affiliation, see Norman Knowles, "Religious Affiliation, Demographic Change and Family Formation among British Columbia's Chinese and Japanese Communities: A Case Study of Church of England Missions, 1861–1942," *Canadian Ethnic Studies* 27, 2 (1995): 59–80.
103 Alison Marshall, *The Way of the Bachelor: Early Chinese Settlement in Manitoba* (Vancouver: UBC Press, 2011).
104 According to Norman Knowles, these programs were "designed to introduce Japanese women to the basics of Christianity and Canadian techniques in everything from parenting to sewing ... The success, however, reflected less an acceptance of Christianity than a desire to escape the isolation and loneliness of domesticity." Kindergartens were especially appealing as they provided inexpensive forms of day care and education. See Knowles, "Religious Affiliation," 506.
105 Alison Blunt, "Cultural Geography," 506.

CHAPTER 4: OUTSIDE THE WALLS OF THE HOME

Note: Portions of this chapter have appeared as "Marriage, Morals, and Men: Re/defining Victoria's Chinese Rescue Home," *BC Studies* 177 (2013): 65–84.

1 For a discussion of spaces of exception, see Etienne Balibar, "At the Borders of Citizenship: A Democracy in Translation," *European Journal of Social Theory* 13, 3 (2010): 315–22.
2 While court records are not available for the cases discussed here, a more thorough discussion of other court proceedings is provided in the following chapter. Given this chapter's reliance on news accounts, it is important to note that I do not view newspapers as neutral sources. Their actions, whether they took the form of reporting or exposé, were practices of power. Newspapers not only produced accounts of these cases but also shaped public opinion about them and, more specifically, about what constituted appropriate cross-racial contact (such as was to be found within the Home). Conceived in this way, newspapers might thus be considered as active texts, as both shaping and being shaped by public opinion and sentiment. See Dorothy Smith, *Texts, Facts, and Femininity: Exploring the Relations of Ruling* (London: Routledge, 1990).

3 Both of Vrooman Gardiner's parents were missionaries for the American Board of Commissioners for Foreign Missions (ABCFM) in China.

4 J.E. Starr to E.S. Strachan, September 1887, Oriental Home and School Fonds, United Church BC Conference Archives (hereafter Bob Stewart Archives).

5 "Police Court" *British Colonist,* January 18, 1888.

6 Ibid.

7 "Police Committee Inquiry," *British Colonist,* February 20, 1887.

8 Ibid.

9 Ibid.

10 Ibid.

11 Thornton Fell is discussed in more detail in Chapter 5 as he was not only Gardiner's attorney but also Home's.

12 Ibid.

13 "Police Committee Inquiry," *British Colonist,* February 27, 1887.

14 Ibid.

15 Ibid.

16 Ibid.

17 Ibid.

18 Ibid.

19 Ibid.

20 Ibid.

21 "Seeming Impossibilities," *British Colonist,* May 13, 1886.

22 "Trafficking in Girls," *Daily Times,* May 30, 1888.

23 "The Chinese Case: The 'Times' Charge against Prof. Menzies of Selling Chinese Girls," *British Colonist,* June 1, 1888.

24 "'Professor' Menzies: Left the City Thursday Morning – A Few More Incidents," *Daily Times,* June 1, 1888.

25 "The 'Menzies' Affair' (a)," *British Colonist,* June 2, 1888 (emphasis in original).

26 See David Pritchard and Dan Berkowitz, "How Readers' Letters May Influence Editors and News Emphasis: A Content Analysis of 10 Newspapers, 1948–1978," *Journalism Quarterly* 68, 3 (1991): 388–95.

27 Elsewhere, I argue that media is part of the rhizome, or dense network, of surveillance and regulation that produces racialized bodies as objects of democratized surveillance. Evidence of the power of such interconnections in this case were found in the ongoing dialogue between the newspapers, the Home, the courts, the police, and the "concerned citizen." See Shelly Ikebuchi Ketchell, "Carceral Ambivalence: Japanese Canadian 'Internment' and the Sugar Beet Program during WWII," *Surveillance and Society* 7, 1 (2009): 21–35.

28 "The 'Menzies' Affair (b)," *British Colonist,* June 2, 1888.

29 "The Menzies Affair," *British Colonist,* June 5, 1888.

30 "'Professor' Menzies: An Investigation to be Held on Monday Next," *Daily Times,* June 2, 1888.

31 "'Prof' Menzies Case: An Investigation before the Police Committee about Menzies," *Daily Times,* June 5, 1888.

32 Habeas corpus cases will be discussed in more detail in Chapter 5.

33 "'Prof' Menzies Case."

34 Ibid.

35 Ibid.

36 "Board of Aldermen." *British Colonist,* June 7, 1888.

37 See Lawrence J. Taylor, "Moral Entrepreneurs and Moral Geographies on the US/Mexico Border," *Social and Legal Studies* 19, 3 (2010): 299–310.
38 "Trafficking in Girls," *Daily Times*, May 30, 1888.
39 Ibid.
40 Ibid.
41 Ibid.
42 Ibid.
43 Ibid.
44 Ibid.
45 Ibid.
46 Ibid.
47 "The Menzies Affair," *British Colonist*, July 4, 1888.
48 "Traffic in Chinese," *British Colonist*, July 4, 1888
49 Ibid.
50 Ibid.
51 Ibid.
52 Ibid, emphasis added.
53 "The Chinese Matter," *British Colonist*, July 6, 1888.
54 "The Colonist's Gardnerphobia," *Daily Times*, July 4, 1888, (emphasis added).
55 Ibid.
56 Ibid.
57 "Traffic in Chinese," *British Colonist*, July 7, 1888.
58 "The Menzies Apologist." *Daily Times*, July 6, 1888.
59 Ibid.
60 Ibid.
61 "Chinese Matter."
62 "Traffic in Chinese," *British Colonist*, July 7, 1888.
63 Cathy Converse, *Mainstays: Women Who Shaped BC* (Victoria: Horsdal and Schubart, 1998), 33–34.
64 "The Chinese Affair," *British Colonist*, July 8, 1888 (emphasis added).
65 "Menzies Affair."
66 "Editorial Comments," *British Colonist*, July 13, 1888.
67 Ibid.
68 Ibid.
69 Ibid.
70 Ibid.
71 "The Chinese 'Home,'" *British Colonist*, July 13, 1888.
72 "Chinese Matter"; and "Traffic in Chinese," *British Colonist*, July 7, 1888.
73 "Editorial Comments."
74 "Letter from Rev. J.E. Starr," *British Colonist*, July 13, 1888.
75 Ibid.
76 Ibid. (emphasis in original).
77 Ibid.
78 Ibid. (emphasis added).
79 It should be noted here that, although the age of the young women was mentioned, within the courts their age was not a topic of concern. It is possible that the increased press attention was attributable to the youth of the young women. However, this was not a point of law as marriage laws at the time only required young women to be twelve years

old to marry. This would not change in British Columbia until 1911, when the age was increased to sixteen.

80 "Is It a Conspiracy?," *Victoria Times*, July 27, 1888.

81 "The Menzies' Case," *British Colonist*, August 3, 1888; "The Menzies Case," *British Colonist*, August 4, 1888.

82 "The Menzies Case," *British Colonist*, August 21, 1888.

83 "Elizabeth" is a pseudonym.

84 Royal Commission on Chinese and Japanese Immigration, *Report of the Royal Commission on Chinese and Japanese Immigration*, sessional paper no. 54, session 1902 (Ottawa: S.E. Dawson, 1902), 38.

85 "Bev" is a pseudonym.

86 Minutes of the Oriental Home and School Advisory Committee, January and March 1901, Oriental Home and School Fonds, 1896–1914, MS-2439, British Columbia Archives (hereafter BCA).

87 Ibid.

88 "The Menzies Case," *Victoria Times*, August 21, 1888.

89 For more on Chinese testimony, see Reginald Good, "Regulating Indian and Chinese Civic Identities in British Columbia's 'Colonial Contact Zone,' 1858–1887," *Canadian Journal of Law and Society* 26, 1 (2011): 69–88.

90 Royal Commission on Chinese Immigration, *Report on the Royal Commission on Chinese Immigration: Report and Evidence* (Ottawa: Royal Commission on Chinese Immigration, 1885), lxxxvii.

91 "The Menzies Case," *British Colonist*, August 22, 1888.

92 Ibid.

93 "Burlesque," *Merriam-Webster.com* (Merriam-Webster, 2015), http://www.merriam-webster. com/dictionary/burlesque.

94 For a compelling discussion of racial burlesque, see Renisa Mawani, *Colonial Proximities: Cross Racial Encounters and Juridical Truths in British Columbia, 1871–1921* (Vancouver: UBC Press, 2009), esp. chap. 1.

95 "The Menzies Case," *British Colonist*, August 22, 1888.

96 Ibid.

97 Ibid.

98 Ibid.

99 Ibid.

100 Ibid. (emphasis added).

101 Ibid.

102 Ibid.

103 "The Menzies Case," *British Colonist*, August 28, 1888.

104 Ibid, emphasis added.

105 Ibid.

CHAPTER 5: ROOFS, RAFTERS, AND REFUGE

1 "Habeas Corpus," *Irwin Law's Canadian Online Legal Dictionary* (Irwin Law 2009–2010) http://www.irwinlaw.com/cold.

2 Constance Backhouse, *Colour-Coded: A Legal History of Racism in Canada, 1900–1950* (Toronto: University of Toronto Press, 1999), 274.

3　"In re AH GWAY, ex parte CHIN SU," in *British Columbia Reports, Being Reports of Cases Determined in the Supreme and County Courts and in Admiralty, and on Appeal in the Full Court, Law Society of British Columbia* (Victoria: The Colonist Printing and Publishing Company, 1893), vol. 8.

4　Woman's Missionary Society, Annual Report of the Woman's Missionary Society of the Methodist Church of Canada, 1895–1896 (Toronto: The Ryerson Press, 1896), 22.

5　"The Chinese Work in Victoria," *Missionary Outlook* 7, 3 (1887): 2.

6　Ibid.

7　Minutes of the Oriental Home and School Advisory Committee, January 1898, Oriental Home and School Fonds, 1896–1914, MS-2439, British Columbia Archives (hereafter BCA).

8　Ibid., November 1897, Oriental Home and School Fonds, 1896–1914, MS-2439, BCA.

9　Ibid.

10　"In re QUAI SHING, An Infant," in *British Columbia Reports, Being Reports of Cases Determined in the Supreme and County Courts and in Admiralty, and on Appeal in the Full Court, Law Society of British Columbia* (Victoria: The Colonist Printing and Publishing Company, 1898), 6: 86–87.

11　Minutes of the Oriental Home and School Advisory Committee, 1898, Oriental Home and School Fonds, 1896–1914, MS-2439, BCA.

12　"In re FONG YUK and the CHINESE IMMIGRATION ACT," in *British Columbia Reports, Being Reports of Cases Determined in the Supreme and County Courts and in Admiralty, and on Appeal in the Full Court, Law Society of British Columbia* (Victoria: The Colonist Printing and Publishing Company, 1901), 8: 120.

13　"In re AH GWAY, ex parte CHIN SU," in *British Columbia Reports, Being Reports of Cases Determined in the Supreme and County Courts and in Admiralty, and on Appeal in the Full Court, Law Society of British Columbia* (Victoria: The Colonist Printing and Publishing Company, 1895), 2: 264.

14　Ibid.

15　"In re QUAI SHING," 7:87.

16　"Choy Wan's Guardian." *British Colonist*, September 7, 1895.

17　Ibid.

18　"Mayors Listed by Name," *City of Victoria* (City of Victoria 2012). http://www.victoria.ca/EN/main/departments/legislative-services/archives/faqs/mayors-name.html

19　"921 Foul Bay Road, Oak Bay Community Heritage Register," *Heritage Oak Bay* (Corporation of the District of Oak Bay 2012–2015). https://www.oakbay.ca/our-community/history/heritage/heritage-sites/921-foul-bay-road.

20　"In re AH GWAY," vol. 8.

21　Ibid.

22　It should be noted here that Begbie was a strong advocate of continued Chinese immigration. He testified to the "industry, economy, sobriety, and law-abidingness" of the Chinese before the Royal Commission in 1885. He was a strong believer in the importance of Chinese labour, claiming that he did not see "how people would get on here at all without Chinamen [*sic*]." See Royal Commission on Chinese Immigration, *Report on the Royal Commission on Chinese Immigration: Report and Evidence* (Ottawa: Royal Commission on Chinese Immigration, 1885), 75 and 71.

23　Begbie, in fact, is a clear example of how the language of race was drawn from a transnational context. Renisa Mawani argues that Begbie "drew on Britain's overseas experiences to make sense of the new and unfamiliar racial exigencies facing the young colony, including the 'problem' of Chinese migration." See Renisa Mawani, *Colonial Proximities: Cross Racial Encounters and Juridical Truths in British Columbia, 1871–1921* (Vancouver: UBC Press, 2009), 24.

24 "In re AH GWAY," 8:345.

25 Ibid. (emphasis added).

26 See Walder G.W. White, "A Comparison of Some Parental and Guardian Rights," *Canadian Journal of Family Law* 3 (1980): 219–49.

27 Mary Ann Mason, *From Father's Property to Children's Rights: The History of Child Custody in the United States* (New York: Columbia University Press, 1994), xii.

28 Ibid., 6.

29 Ibid., 14.

30 Michael H. Cramer, "Public and Political: Documents of the Woman's Suffrage Campaign in British Columbia, 1871–1917 – The View from Victoria," in *British Columbia Reconsidered: Essays on Women*, ed. Gillian Creese and Veronica Strong-Boag (Vancouver: Press Gang Publishers, 1992), 66.

31 Ibid.

32 Ibid.

33 "Little Choy Wan." *British Colonist*, September 5, 1895.

34 Ibid.

35 "In re AH GWAY," 8:345 (emphasis added).

36 Timothy J. Stanley, "LEE MONG KOW," in EN:UNDEF: public_citation_publication, vol. 15 (University of Toronto/Université Laval, 2003–). http://www.biographi.ca/en/bio/lee_mong_kow_15E.html.

37 "Chinese Child Poisoned," *Daily Colonist*, October 21, 1896.

38 "The City," *British Colonist*, September 26, 1897.

39 "In re QUAI SHING," 6:96.

40 Ibid., 6:87.

41 Ibid., 6:89

42 Ibid., 6:90.

43 Ibid.

44 Ibid., 6:92 (emphasis added).

45 Ibid., 6:94.

46 "Wants the Child" *British Colonist*, July 11, 1900.

47 Timothy J. Stanley, "CHANG TOY (Chen Cai in Mandarin), known also as Chan Doe Gee (Chen Daozhi) and Chan Chang-Jin, but generally as Sam Kee (San Ji), in EN:UNDEF:public_citation_publication, vol. 15 (University of Toronto/Université Laval, 2003). http://www.biographi.ca/en/bio/chang_toy_15E.html.

48 "In RE SOY KING, AN INFANT," in *British Columbia Reports, Being Reports of Cases Determined in the Supreme and County Courts and in Admiralty, and on Appeal in the Full Court, Law Society of British Columbia* (Victoria: The Colonist Printing and Publishing Company, 1900), 7: 292.

49 Ibid., 7:291.

50 Ibid. (emphasis added).

51 "In re AH GWAY," 8:345.

52 "In re QUAI SHING," 6:88.

53 Sara Ahmed, *Strange Encounters: Embodied Others in Post-Coloniality* (New York: Routledge, 2000), 39.

54 Ibid., 37.

55 Ibid., 30.
56 For a deeper discussion of structures of domination, see Michael Omi and Howard Winant, *Racial Formation in the United States from the 1960s to the 1990s* (New York: Routledge, 1994).
57 Ahmed, *Strange Encounters*, 55.
58 "In re QUAI SHING," 6:88 (emphasis added).
59 Ahmed, *Strange Encounters*, 21 (emphasis in original).
60 Ibid., 21–22.
61 "In re AH GWAY," 8:346.
62 Ibid.
63 "In re QUAI SHING," 6:87.
64 Ibid., 6:88.
65 Ibid.
66 White, "Comparison of Some Parental and Guardian Rights," 237.
67 For more on the uses of *parens patriae* in juvenile delinquency and the origins of the doctrine, see Ian Grant "The 'Incorrigible' Juvenile: History and Prerequisites of Reform in Ontario," *Canadian Journal of Family Law* 4, 3 (1984): 293–318; Marge Reitsma-Street, "More Control Than Care: A Critique of Historical and Contemporary Laws for Delinquency and Neglect of Children in Ontario," *Canadian Journal of Women and the Law* 3, 2 (1989–90): 510–30; Lawrence B. Custer, "The Origins of the Doctrine of Parens Patriae," *Emory Law Journal* 23 (1978): 195–208.
68 Mason, *From Father's Property to Children's Rights*, 101.
69 Dorothy Chunn, *From Punishment to Doing Good: Family Courts and Socialized Justice in Ontario, 1880–1940* (Toronto: University of Toronto Press, 1992), 45–46.
70 "In re SOY KING," 8:292.
71 Ibid., 8:295.
72 Ibid., 8:296.
73 Ahmed, *Strange Encounters*, 37.
74 Cited in "In re SOY KING," 7:296.
75 Record 201, Oriental Home Register and Biography, 1888–1908, Oriental Home and School Fonds, United Church BC Conference Archives (hereafter Bob Stewart Archives), 72.
76 Although a newspaper account claimed that the child was turned over to Mong Kow Lee on September 6, record books from the Home do not show her being discharged until September 10.
77 "Choy Wan's Case." *British Colonist*, September 8, 1895.
78 Ahmed, *Strange Encounters*, 89, emphasis in original.
79 Ibid.
80 Ibid.
81 "The City," *British Colonist*, September 19, 1895.
82 Ibid.
83 John McLaren, "Race and the Criminal Justice System in British Columbia, 1892–1920: Constructing Chinese Crimes," in *Essays in the History of Canadian Law: In Honour of R.C.B. Risk*, ed. G. Blaine Baker and Jim Phillips (Toronto: University of Toronto Press, 1999), 427, 423.
84 Ian Haney López, *White by Law: The Legal Construction of Race* (New York: New York University Press, 1996), 10–13.
85 Backhouse, *Colour-Coded*, 274.

86 Shah makes a similar argument that Chinese were threats to white families in general and to the "American Standard of Living" in particular. Also relevant here is Mawani's (2009, 105–11) discussion of Chinese as threats to white families (Mawani, *Colonial Proximities*, 105–11). See Nayan Shah, *Contagious Divides: Epidemics and Race in San Francisco's Chinatown* (Berkeley: University of California Press, 2001).

87 Alan Hunt, *Governing Morals: A Social History of Moral Regulation* (Cambridge: Cambridge University Press, 1999), 32–33.

88 "In re QUAI SHING," 6:95.

89 Ibid., 6:344.

90 Ibid.

91 Ibid.

92 "Choy Wan's Guardian." *British Colonist*, September 7, 1895, 7.

93 Ibid.

94 See, for instance, Mawani, *Colonial Proximities*.

95 "Choy Wan's Guardian."

96 "The City," *British Colonist*, July 26, 1896.

97 Sadiah Qureshi, "Displaying Sara Baartman, the 'Hottentot Venus,'" *History of Science* 42 (2004): 235.

98 Ibid.

99 Ibid., 236.

100 Ibid., 238.

101 "In re QUAI SHING," 6:94.

102 Ibid.

103 Ibid.

104 Ibid.

105 Ibid.

106 Ibid., 6:95

107 Ibid.

108 Ibid.

109 "Little Quai Shing," *Daily Colonist*, February 10, 1898.

110 "In re QUAI SHING," 6:87.

111 "The City" *British Colonist*, September 26, 1897.

112 Ibid., 96 (emphasis added).

113 Ibid.

114 White, "Comparison of Some Parental and Guardian Rights," 223.

115 Ibid., 96.

116 Cited in "In re SOY KING,"7:296.

CONCLUSION: RACE, GENDER AND NATIONAL IMAGININGS

1 For a more detailed discussion of the relationship between citizenship and nationalist discourses, see Benedict Anderson, *Imagined Communities: Reflections on the Origin and Spread of Nationalism* (London: Verso, 1983).

2 See Jeffrey Weeks, *Sexuality and Its Discontents* (London: Routledge, 1985).

3 For a detailed discussion of the reproduction of race, class, and gender in the domestic realm, see Evelyn Nakano Glenn, "From Servitude to Service Work: Historical Continuities in the Racial Division of Paid Reproductive Labor," *Signs: Journal of Women in Culture and Society* 18, 1 (1992): 1–43.

4   "Caution Young Women" *British Colonist,* July 8, 1909.
5   Ibid.
6   Bruce L. Berg, *Qualitative Research Methods for the Social Sciences* (Boston: Pearson Education, Inc., 2009), 318.
7   Weeks, *Sexuality and Its Discontents,* 10.
8   For a broader discussion of white slavery, see Renisa Mawani, *Colonial Proximities: Cross Racial Encounters and Juridical Truths in British Columbia, 1871–1921* (Vancouver: UBC Press, 2009), 114.
9   CBC, "Summary Report: Consulting the Public on Marriages of Convenience," Citizenship and Immigration Canada (Government of Canada, 2011), http://www.cic.gc.ca/english/department/consultations/marriagefraud/index.asp#tphpidtphp.
10 David McKie, "Marriages of Convenience Problems Persist," CBC.ca (CBC 2010), http://www.cbc.ca/news/politics/marriages-of-convenience-problems-persist-1.876101.
11 CBC, "Summary Report."
12 CBC News, "Arranged Marriage Breaks Down at Toronto Airport," CBC.ca (CBC News 2011), http://www.cbc.ca/news/canada/toronto/arranged-marriage-breaks-down -at-toronto-airport-1.1088938; and CBC News, "Immigrant Marriage Fraud Crackdown Urged," CBC.ca (CBC News 2010), http://www.cbc.ca/news/canada/toronto/immigrant-marriage-fraud-crackdown-urged-1.973627.
13 Geraldine Pratt, "From Registered Nurse to Registered Nanny: Discursive Geographies of Filipina Domestic Workers in Vancouver, BC," *Economic Geography* 75, 3 (1999): 226, 216.
14 Abigail B. Bakan and Daiva Stasiulis, "Foreign Domestic Worker Policy in Canada and the Social Boundaries of Modern Citizenship," *Science and Society* 58, 1 (1994): 10.
15 Ibid., 15.
16 Ibid.
17 Miu Chang Yan and Sean Lauer, "Social Capital and Ethno-Cultural Diverse Immigrants: A Canadian Study on Settlement House and Social Integration," *Journal of Ethnic and Cultural Diversity in Social Work* 17, 3 (2008): 229–50.
18 Louise W. Knight, "Biography's Window on Social Change: Benevolence and Justice in Jane Addams's 'A Modern Lear,'" *Journal of Women's History* 9, 1 (1997): 113.
19 Yan and Lauer, "Social Capital and Ethno-Cultural Diverse Immigrants," 236.

Appendix: Sources and Methodology

1   Joy Parr, "Gender History and Historical Practice," *Canadian Historical Review* 76, 3 (1995): 365.
2   Frances Henry and Carol Tator, *Discourses of Domination: Racial Bias in the Canadian English-Language Press* (Toronto: University of Toronto Press, 2002), 25.
3   Marianne Jorgenson and Louise Phillips, *Discourse Analysis as Theory and Method* (London: Sage 2002) 5–7.
4   Ibid., 65.
5   Norman Fairclough, "Discourse, Social theory, and Social research: The Discourse of Welfare Reform," *Journal of Sociolinguistics* 4, 3 (2000): 176.
6   Jorgenson and Phillips, *Discourse Analysis,* 61.

Bibliography

PRIMARY SOURCES

Archival Sources

British Columbia Archives (BCA)
Oriental Home and School Fonds, 1896–1914, MS-2439, British Columbia Archives.

City of Victoria
Councillors Listed by Name, http://www.victoria.ca/EN/main/departments/legislative
-services/archives/faqs/councillors-name.html.
Mayors Listed by Name, http://www.victoria.ca/EN/main/departments/legislative-services/
archives/faqs/mayors-name.html.

Heritage Oak Bay
Oak Bay Community Heritage Register

Library and Archives Canada
"New Chinese Home, Victoria, British Columbia," accession number 1979–282 NPC,
item number 132, reproduction copy number C-012600

*United Church BC Conference Archives (Bob Stewart Archives), University of British
Columbia, Vancouver, BC*
Annual Reports of the Woman's Missionary Society of the Methodist Church of
Canada
Methodist Church BC Conference Fonds
Missionary Outlook
Oriental Home Register, Oriental Home and School Fonds

Jurisprudence
"In re AH GWAY, ex parte CHIN SU." *British Columbia Reports,* The Law Society of British Columbia, Victoria: The Colonist Printing and Publishing Company. 1893.
"In re FONG YUK and the CHINESE IMMIGRATION ACT." *British Columbia Reports,* The Law Society of British Columbia, Victoria: The Colonist Printing and Publishing Company. 1901.
"In re QUAI SHING, An Infant." *British Columbia Reports,* The Law Society of British Columbia, Victoria: The Colonist Printing and Publishing Company. 1898.
"In RE SOY KING, AN INFANT" *British Columbia Reports,* The Law Society of British Columbia, Victoria: The Colonist Printing and Publishing Company. 1900.

Newspapers
British Colonist
Daily Colonist
Victoria Daily Times (previously *Daily Times)*
Victoria Times

Printed Reports and Reference Material
Constitution from the Eighth Annual Report of the Woman's Missionary Society of the Methodist Church, Canada, 1888–89. Toronto: William Briggs, 1889.
Report of the Royal Commission on Chinese and Japanese Immigration. Sessional Paper No. 54, Session 1902. Ottawa: Printed by Order of Parliament by SE. Dawson, Printer to the King's Most Excellent Majesty, 1902.
Report on the Royal Commission on Chinese Immigration: Report and Evidence. Ottawa: Royal Commission on Chinese Immigration, 1885.

SECONDARY SOURCES

Adachi, Ken. *The Enemy That Never Was: A History of Japanese Canadians.* Toronto: McClelland and Stewart, 1991.
Adilman, Tamara. "A Preliminary Sketch of Chinese Women and Work in British Columbia, 1858–1950." In *British Columbia Reconsidered: Essays on Women,* ed. Gillian Creese and Veronica Strong-Boag, 309–39. Vancouver: Press Gang, 1992.
Ahmed, Sara. *Strange Encounters: Embodied Others in Post-Coloniality.* New York: Routledge, 2000.
Allerfeldt, Kristofer. "Race and Restriction: Anti-Asian Immigration Pressures in the Pacific North-West of America during the Progressive Era, 1885–1924." *History* 88, 289 (2003): 53–73. http://dx.doi.org/10.1111/1468-229X.00251.
Althusser, Louis. *Lenin and Philosophy and Other Essays.* New York: Monthly Review Press, 2001.
Anderson, Benedict. *Imagined Communities.* London: Verso, 1983.
Anderson, Kay. *Vancouver's Chinatown: Racial Discourse in Canada, 1875–1980.* Montreal and Kingston: McGill-Queen's University Press, 1991.
Anzaldua, Gloria. *Borderlands/La Frontera: The New Mestiza.* San Francisco: Aunt Lute Books, 1987.
Archives, BC. *BC Archives.* 2010. http://www.bcarchives.gov.bc.ca/exhibits/timemach/galler02/images/chdia4m2.jpg (viewed 10 27, 2010).

Asad, Talal. *Genealogies of Religion: Discipline and Reasons of Power in Christianity and Islam*. Baltimore: Johns Hopkins University Press, 1993.

Ayukawa, Michiko Midge. *Hiroshima Immigrants in Canada 1891–1941*. Vancouver: UBC Press, 2008.

–. "Good Wives and Mothers: Japanese Picture Brides in Early Twentieth-Century British Columbia." *BC Studies*, 105/106 (1995): 103–18.

Backhouse, Constance. *Colour-Coded: A Legal History of Racism in Canada, 1900–1950*. Toronto: University of Toronto Press, 1999.

Bakan, Abigail B., and Daiva Stasiulis. "Foreign Domestic Worker Policy in Canada and the Social Boundaries of Modern Citizenship." *Science and Society* 58, 1 (1994): 7–33.

Balibar, Etienne. "At the Borders of Citizenship: A Democracy in Translation." *European Journal of Social Theory* 13, 3 (2010): 315–22. http://dx.doi.org/10.1177/1368431010371751.

Barman, Jean, and Jan Hare. *Good Intentions Gone Awry: Emma Crosby and the Methodist Mission on the Northwest Coast*. Vancouver: UBC Press, 2006.

Bashford, Alison. "Cultures of Confinement: Tuberculosis, Isolation and the Sanatorium." In *Isolation: Places and Practices of Exclusion*, ed. Carolyn Strange and Alison Bashford, 133–50. New York: Routledge, 2003. http://dx.doi.org/10.4324/9780203405222_chapter_9.

Bashford, Alison, and Carolyn Strange. "Isolation and Exclusion in the Modern World: An Introductory Essay." In *Isolation: Places and Practices of Exclusion*, ed. Alison Bashford and Carolyn Strange, 1–20. New York: Routledge, 2003. http://dx.doi.org/10.4324/9780203405222_chapter_1.

BC GenWeb. 1901 Census of Victoria Statistics. 10 06, 2009. http://www.rootsweb.ancestry.com/~canbc/1901vic_cen/stats.htm (viewed 04 04, 2011).

BC Historic Craigflower Manor, Victoria, British Columbia. Shangaan Webservices Inc. 1998–2010. http://britishcolumbia.com/things-to-do-and-see/attractions/craigflower-manor/ (accessed May 16th, 2015).

Berg, Bruce L. *Qualitative Research Methods for the Social Sciences*. Boston: Pearson Education, Inc, 2009.

Bhabha, Homi. *The Location of Culture*. London: Routledge, 1994.

Blumer, Herbert. "Race Prejudice as a Sense of Group Position." *Pacific Sociological Review* 1, 1 (1958): 3–7. http://dx.doi.org/10.2307/1388607.

Blunt, Alison. "Cultural Geography: Cultural Geographies of Home." *Progress in Human Geography* 29, 4 (2005): 505–15. http://dx.doi.org/10.1191/0309132505ph564pr.

–. *Domicile and Diaspora: Anglo-Indian Women and the Spatial Politics of Home*. Malden: Blackwell, 2005. http://dx.doi.org/10.1002/9780470712740.

–. "Imperial Geographies of Home: British Domesticity in India, 1886–1925." *Transactions of the Institute of British Geographers* 24, 4 (1999): 421–40. http://dx.doi.org/10.1111/j.0020-2754.1999.00421.x.

Briggs, Laura, Gladys McCormick, and J.T. Way. "Transnationalism: A Category of Analysis." *American Quarterly* 60, 3 (2008): 625–48. http://dx.doi.org/10.1353/aq.0.0038.

Burton, Antoinette. *Burdens of History: British Feminists, Indian women, and Imperial Culture, 1865–1915*. Chapel Hill: University of North Carolina Press, 1994.

Cauthers, Janet. *Victorian Tapestry: Impressions of Life in Victoria, BC, 1880–1914*. Victoria: Provincial Archives, 1978.

CBC News. *Arranged Marriage Breaks Down at Toronto Airport*. 03 18, 2011. http://www.cbc.ca/news/canada/toronto/arranged-marriage-breaks-down-at-toronto-airport-1.1088938 (viewed May 16th, 2015).

–. *Immigrant Marriage Fraud Crackdown Urged.* 07 16, 2010. http://www.cbc.ca/news/canada/toronto/story/2010/07/16/immigration-marriage-fraud541.html (viewed 04 01, 2011).

Chang, Derek. ""Marked in Body, Mind, and Spirit": Home Missionaries and the Remaking of Race and Nation." In *Race, Nation, and Religion in the Americas,* ed. Henry Goldschmidt and Elizabeth McAlister, 133–50. New York: Oxford University Press, 2004. http://dx.doi.org/10.1093/0195149181.003.0006.

Chari, Sharad. "Critical Geographies of Racial and Spatial Control." *Geography Compass* 2, 6 (2008): 1907–21. http://dx.doi.org/10.1111/j.1749-8198.2008.00169.x.

Chong, Denise. *The Concubine's Children: Portrait of a Family Divided.* Toronto: Penguin Group, 1994.

Chunn, Dorothy. *From Punishment to Doing Good: Family Courts and Socialized Justice in Ontario, 1880–1940.* Toronto: University of Toronto Press, 1992.

Chunn, Dorothy, and Shelley Gavigan. "Social Control: Analytical Tool or Analytical Quagmire?" In *Moral Regulation and Governance in Canada: History, Context and Critical Issues,* ed. Amanda Glasbeek, 11–30. Toronto: Canadian Scholars' Press, 2006.

Citizenship and Immigration Canada. *National Online Consultation Launched to Gather Views on Impact of Marriage Fraud.* 09 27, 2010. http://www.cic.gc.ca/english/department/media/releases/2010/2010-09-27.asp (viewed 04 04, 2011).

–. Summary Report: Consulting the Public on Marriages of Convenience. 03 25, 2011. http://www.cic.gc.ca/english/department/consultations/marriagefraud/index.asp#tphpidtphp (viewed 04 10, 2011).

City of Victoria. *Mayors and Councillors.* 2015. http://www.victoria.ca/EN/main/departments/legislative-services/archives/faqs.html (viewed May 16th, 2015).

Con, Harry, Ronald J. Con, Graham Johnson, Edgar Wickberg, and William E. Wilmott, *From China to Canada: A History of the Chinese Communities in Canada.* Toronto: McClelland and Stewart, 1982.

Converse, Cathy. *Mainstays: Women Who Shaped BC.* Victoria: Horsdal and Schubart, 1998.

Cramer, Michael H. "Public and Political: Documents of the Woman's Suffrage Campaign in British Columbia, 1871–1917: The View from Victoria." In *British Columbia Reconsidered: Essays on Women,* ed. Gillian Creese and Veronica Strong-Boag, 55–72. Vancouver: Press Gang, 1992.

Custer, Lawrence B. "The Origins of the Doctrine of Parens Patriae." *Emory Law Journal* 23 (1978): 195–208.

Dean, Mitchell. "'A Social Structure of Many Souls': Moral Regulation, Government, and Self-Formation." In *Moral Regulation and Governance in Canada: History, Context and Critical Issues,* ed. Amanda Glasbeek, 277–98. Toronto: Canadian Scholars' Press, 2006.

Demerson, Velma. *Incorrigible.* Waterloo: Wilfrid Laurier University Press, 2004.

Diduck, Alison. "Legislating Ideologies of Motherhood." *Social and Legal Studies* 2, 4 (1993): 461–85. http://dx.doi.org/10.1177/096466399300200406.

Domosh, Mona. "Geography and Gender: Home, Again?" *Progress in Human Geography* 22, 2 (1998): 276–82. http://dx.doi.org/10.1191/030913298676121192.

–. "Toward a Feminist Historiography of Geography." *Transactions of the Institute of British Geographers* 16, 1 (1991): 95–104. http://dx.doi.org/10.2307/622908.

Dubinsky, Karen. "Telling Stories about Dead People." In *On the Case: Explorations in Social History,* ed. Franca Iacovetta and Wendy Mitchinson, 359–66. Toronto: University of Toronto Press, 1989.

Dunae, Patrick A. ""Making the 1891 Census in British Columbia." *Histoire sociale/Social History* 31, 62 (1998): 223–39.

Duncan, James S., and David Lambert. "Landscapes of Home." In *A Companion to Cultural Geography*, ed. James S. Duncan, Nuala C. Johnson, and Richard H. Schein, 382–403. Malden: Blackwell, 2004.

Fairclough, Norman. "Discourse, Social Theory, and Social Research: The Discourse of Welfare Reform." *Journal of Sociolinguistics* 4, 2 (2000): 163–95. http://dx.doi.org/10.1111/1467-9481.00110.

Fanon, Frantz. *Black Skin, White Masks*. New York: Grove Press, 1967.

FindLaw Legal Dictionary. *Parens patriae*. FindLaw Legal Dictionary. 1996. dictionary.lp.findlaw.com (viewed December 31, 2009).

Foucault, Michel. *Discipline and Punish: The Birth of the Prison*. New York: Random House, 1995.

–. "Nietzsche, Genealogy, History." In *The Essential Foucault*, ed. Paul Rabinow and Nikolas Rose, 351–69. New York: The New Press, 2003.

–. "Technologies of the Self." In *The Essential Foucault*, ed. Paul Rabinow and Nikolas Rose, 145–69. New York: The New Press, 2003.

–. "Truth and Power." In *The Essential Foucault*, ed. Paul Rabinow and Nikolas Rose, 300–18. New York: The New Press, 2003.

Gagan, Rosemary. *A Sensitive Independence*. Montreal and Kingston: McGill-Queen's University Press, 1992.

Geiger, Andrea. *Subverting Exclusion: Transpacific Encounters with Race, Caste, and Borders, 1885–1928*. New Haven: Yale University Press, 2011.

George, Rosemary Marangoly. "Homes in the Empire, Empires in the Home." *Cultural Critique* 26 (1993–94): 95–127.

Glasbeek, Amanda. "Introduction." In *Moral Regulation and Governance in Canada: History, Context and Critical Issues*, ed. Amanda Glasbeek, 1–9. Toronto: Canadian Scholars' Press Inc, 2006.

Glenn, Evelyn Nakano. "From Servitude to Service Work: Historical Continuities in the Racial Division of Paid Reproductive Labor." *Signs* 18, 1 (1992): 1–43. http://dx.doi.org/10.1086/494777.

Goldberg, David Theo. *The Racial State. Maiden*. Blackwell, 2002.

Good, Reginald. "Admissibility of Testimony from Non-Christian Indians in the Colonial Municipal Courts of Upper Canada/Canada West." *The Windsor Yearbook of Access to Justice* 23, 1 (2005): 55–94.

–. "Regulating Indian and Chinese Civic Identities in British Columbia's 'Colonial Contact Zone,' 1858–1887." *Canadian Journal of Law and Society* 26, 1 (2011): 69–88. http://dx.doi.org/10.3138/cjls.26.1.069.

Gowans, Georgina. "Imperial Geographies of Home: Memsahibs and Miss-Sahibs in India and Britain, 1915–1947." *Cultural Geographies* 10, 4 (2003): 424–41. http://dx.doi.org/10.1191/1474474003eu2830a.

Grant, Ian. "The 'Incorrigible' Juvenile: History and Prerequisites of Reform in Ontario." *Canadian Journal of Family Law* 4, 3 (1984): 293–318.

Green, Valerie. *Upstarts and Outcasts: Victoria's Not-So-Proper Past*. Victoria: Horsdal and Schubart, 2000.

Gregory, Derek. "Imaginative Geographies." *Progress in Human Geography* 19, 4 (1995): 447–85. http://dx.doi.org/10.1177/030913259501900402.

Gregson, Harry. *A History of Victoria 1842–1970*. Victoria: Morriss, 1970.

Hall, Catherine Naledi. *White, Male and Middle Class: Explorations in Feminism and History*. Cambridge: Polity Press, 1992.

Halliday, Paul D. *Habeas Corpus: From England to Empire*. Cambridge: Belknap Press of Harvard University Press, 2010.

Handa, Amita. "Modest and Modern: Women as Markers of the Indian Nation State." In *Feminisms and Womanisms: A Woman's Studies Reader*, ed. Althea and Silva-Wayne, Susan Prince, 171–78. Toronto: Woman's Press, 2004.

Henning, Joseph M. *Outposts of Civilization: Race, Religion, and the Formative Years of American-Japanese Relations*. New York: New York University Press, 2000.

Henry, F., and C. Tator. *Discourses of Domination: Racial Bias in the Canadian English-Language Press*. Toronto: University of Toronto Press, 2002.

Hier, Sean P. "Probing the Surveillant Assemblage: On the Dialectics of Surveillance Practices as Processes of Social Control." *Surveillance and Society* 1, 3 (2003): 399–411.

Hogeveen, Bryan. "Discontinuity and/in the Early Twentieth Century Ontario Juvenile Court." *Journal of Historical Sociology* 20, 4 (2007): 605–21. http://dx.doi.org/10.1111/j.1467-6443.2007.00325.x.

Houston, Susan E. "Victorian Origins of Juvenile Delinquency: A Canadian Experience." *History of Education Quarterly* 12, 3 (1972): 254–80. http://dx.doi.org/10.2307/367514.

Humphreys, Danda. "The Pendray House." *Focus Online: Victoria's Magazine of People, Ideas and Culture*. 09 2010. http://www.focusonline.ca/?q=node/84 (viewed 11 11, 2010).

Hunt, Alan. *Governing Morals: A Social History of Moral Regulation*. Cambridge: Cambridge University Press, 1999.

Iacovetta, Franca, and Wendy Mitchinson. "Social History and Case Files Research." In *On the Case: Explorations in Social History, by Franca Iacovetta*, ed. Franca Iacovetta, 3–21. Toronto: University of Toronto Press, 1998.

Irwin Law Inc. *Habeas Corpus*. 2009–2010. http://www.irwinlaw.com/cold (viewed 8 15, 2010).

Jacobs, Jane M. "A Geography of Big Things." *Cultural Geographies* 13, 1 (2006): 1–27. http://dx.doi.org/10.1191/1474474006eu3540a.

Johnston, Hugh J.M. *The Pacific Province: A History of British Columbia*. Vancouver: Douglas and McIntyre, 1996.

Jorgenson, Marianne, and Louise Phillips. *Discourse Analysis as Theory and Method*. London: Sage, 2002.

Kaplan, Amy. "Manifest Domesticity." *American Literature* 70, 3 (1998): 581–606. http://dx.doi.org/10.2307/2902710.

Ketchell, Shelly Ikebuchi. "Carceral Ambivalence: Japanese Canadian "Internment" and the Sugar Beet Program during WWII." *Surveillance and Society* 7, 1 (2009): 21–35.

Klempa, Lois, and Rosemary Doran. *Certain Women Amazed Us: The Women's Missionary Society, Their Story, 1864–2002*. Toronto: Women's Missionary Society, 2002.

Knight, Louise W. "Biography's Window on Social Change: Benevolence and Justice in Jane Addams's 'A Modern Lear.'" *Journal of Women's History* 9, 1 (1997): 111–38. http://dx.doi.org/10.1353/jowh.2010.0191.

Knowles, Norman. "Religious Affiliation, Demographic Change and Family Formation among British Columbia's Chinese and Japanese Communities: A Case Study of Church of England Missions, 1861–1942." *Canadian Ethnic Studies* 27, 2 (1995): 59–80.

Kobayashi, A., and L. Peake. "Racism Out of Place: Thoughts on Whiteness and an Antiracist Geography in the New Millennium." *Annals of the Association of American Geographers* 90, 2 (2000): 392–403. http://dx.doi.org/10.1111/0004-5608.00202.

Lai, David Chuenyan. *Chinese Community Leadership: Case Study of Victoria in Canada.* Toh Tuck Link: World Scientific Publishing, 2010. http://dx.doi.org/10.1142/9789814295185.

–. *The Forbidden City within Victoria.* Victoria: Orca, 1991.

Lake, Marilyn, and Henry Reynolds. *Drawing the Global Colour Line: White Men's Countries and the International Challenge of Racial Inequality.* Cambridge: Cambridge University Press, 2008. http://dx.doi.org/10.1017/CBO9780511805363.

Lefebvre, Henry. *The Production of Space.* Oxford: Blackwell, 1991.

Legg, Stephen. "Gendered Politics and Nationalised Homes: Women and the Anticolonial Struggle in Delhi, 1930–47." *Gender, Place and Culture* 10, 1 (2003): 7–27. http://dx.doi.org/10.1080/0966369032000052630.

Leontidou, Lila, Hastings Donnan, and Alex Afouxenidis. "Exclusion and Difference along the EU Border: Social and Cultural Markers, Spatialities and Mappings." *International Journal of Urban and Regional Research* 29, 2 (2005): 389–407. http://dx.doi.org/10.1111/j.1468-2427.2005.00591.x.

López, Haney. *Ian F. White by Law: The Legal Construction of Race.* New York: New York University Press, 1996.

Makabe, Tomoko. *The Canadian Sansei.* Toronto: University of Toronto Press, 1998.

Mallett, Shelley. "Understanding Home: A Critical Review of the Literature." *Sociological Review* 52, 1 (2004): 62–89. http://dx.doi.org/10.1111/j.1467-954X.2004.00442.x.

Mamdani, Mahmood. *Good Muslim, Bad Muslim: America, the Cold War, and the Roots of Terror.* New York: Pantheon, 2004.

Mar, Lisa Rose. *Brokering Belonging: Chinese in Canada's Exclusion Era, 1885–1945.* New York: Oxford University Press, 2010. http://dx.doi.org/10.1093/acprof:oso/9780199733132.001.0001.

Marshall, Alison. *The Way of the Bachelor: Early Chinese Settlement in Manitoba.* Vancouver: UBC Press, 2011.

Mason, Mary Ann. *From Father's Property to Children's Rights: The History of Child Custody in the United States.* New York: Columbia University Press, 1994.

Mawani, Renisa. "Cleansing the Conscience of the People: Reading Head Tax Redress in Multicultural Canada." *Canadian Journal of Law and Society* 19, 2 (2004): 127–51. http://dx.doi.org/10.1017/S0829320100008164.

–. *Colonial Proximities: Cross Racial Encounters and Juridical Truths in British Columbia, 1871–1921.* Vancouver: UBC Press, 2009.

–. "Cross Racial Encounters and Juridical Truths: (Dis)Aggregating Race in British Columbia's Colonial Contact Zone." *BC Studies* 156 2008: 141–71.

McClintock, Anne. *Imperial Leather: Race, Gender and Sexuality in the Colonial Contest.* New York: Routledge, 1995.

McKie, David. *Marriages of Convenience Problems Persist.* November 10, 2010. http://www.cbc.ca/news/politics/story/2010/11/07/david-mckie-marriages-of-convenience.html (viewed 4 01, 2011).

McLaren, John. "Race and the Criminal Justice System in British Columbia, 1892–1920: Constructing Chinese Crimes." In *Essays in the History of Canadian Law: In Honour of R.C.B. Risk*, ed. G. Blaine Baker and Jim Phillips, 398–442. Toronto: University of Toronto Press, 1999.

Meen, Sharon. "Colonial Society and Economy." In *The Pacific Province: A History of British Columbia*, ed. Hugh J.M. Johnston, 97–132. Vancouver: Douglas and McIntyre, 1996.

Melman, Billie. *Women's Orients: English Women and the Middle East, 1718–1918.* London: Macmillan Academic and Professional, 1992.

Miki, Roy. *Redress: Inside the Japanese Canadian Call for Justice.* Vancouver: Raincoast Books, 2004.

Miles, Robert. *Racism.* London: Routledge, 1989.

Morgan, William. *The Abrams Guide to American House Styles.* New York: Abrams, 2004.

Myers, Tamara. *Montreal's Modern Girls and the Law, 1869–1945.* Toronto: University of Toronto Press, 2006.

Ng, Wing Chung. *The Chinese in Vancouver, 1945–80: The Pursuit of Identity and Power.* Toronto: University of Toronto Press, 1999.

Omi, Michael, and Howard Winant. *Racial Formation in the United States From the 1960s to the 1990s.* New York: Routledge, 1994.

Parr, Joy. "Gender History and Historical Practice." *Canadian Historical Review* 76, 3 (1995): 354–76. http://dx.doi.org/10.3138/CHR-076-03-03.

Pascoe, Peggy. *Relations of Rescue: The Search for Female Moral Authority in the American West, 1874–1939.* New York: Oxford University Press, 1990.

Perry, Adele. "'Fair Ones of a Purer Caste': White Women and Colonialism in Nineteenth-Century British Columbia." *Feminist Studies* 23, 3 (1997): 501–25. http://dx.doi.org/10.2307/3178383.

–. "Metropolitan Knowledge, Colonial Practice, and Indigenous Womanhood: Missions in Nineteenth Century British Columbia." In *Contact Zones: Aboriginal and Settler Women in Canada's Colonial Past,* ed. Katie Pickles and Myra Rutherdale, 109–30. Vancouver: UBC Press, 2005.

–. *On the Edge of Empire, Gender, Race, and the Making of British Columbia, 1849–1871.* Toronto: University of Toronto Press, 2001.

Pethick, Derek. *Summer of Promise: Victoria 1864–1914.* Victoria: Sono Nis, 1980.

Pratt, Geraldine. "From Registered Nurse to Registered Nanny: Discursive Geographies of Filipina Domestic Workers in Vancouver, BC." *Economic Geography* 75, 3 (July 1999): 215–36. http://dx.doi.org/10.2307/144575.

Price, John. *Orienting Canada: Race, Empire and the Transpacific.* Vancouver: UBC Press, 2011.

–. "'Orienting' the Empire: Mackenzie King and the Aftermath of the 1907 Race Riots." *BC Studies* 156 (2007/08): 53–81.

Price, John, and Ningping Yu, "A True Trailblazer: Victoria Chung Broke the Mould for Women and Chinese Canadians," *Times Colonist,* October 23, 2011.

Pritchard, David, and Dan Berkowitz. "How Readers' Letters May Influence Editors and News Emphasis: A Content Analysis of 10 Newspapers, 1948–1978." *Journalism Quarterly* 68, 3 (1991): 388–95. http://dx.doi.org/10.1177/107769909106800309.

Qureshi, Sadiah. "Displaying Sara Baartman, The 'Hottentot Venus.'" *History of Science* 42 (2004): 233–57.

Razack, Sherene. *Casting Out: Race and the Eviction of Muslims From Western Law and Politics.* Toronto: University of Toronto Press, 2008.

–. "When Place Becomes Race." In *Race, Space, and the Law,* ed. Sherene Razack. 1–20. Toronto: Between the Lines, 2002.

Reitsma-Street, Marge. "More Control Than Care: A Critique of Historical and Contemporary Laws for Delinquency and Neglect of Children in Ontario." *Canadian Journal of Women and the Law* 3, 2 (1989–90): 510–30.

Reksten, Terry. *"More English Than the English": A Very Social History of Victoria.* Victoria: Orca, 1986.

Riley, Barbara. "Six Saucepans to One: Domestic Science vs. the Home in British Columbia, 1900–1930." In *British Columbia Reconsidered: Essays on Women*, ed. Gillian Creese and Veronica Strong-Boag, 119–42. Vancouver: Press Gang, 1992.

Roy, Patricia. *A White Man's Province: British Columbia Politicians and Chinese and Japanese Immigrants, 1858–1914*. Vancouver: UBC Press, 1989.

–. *The Oriental Question: Consolidating a White Man's Province, 1914–41*. Vancouver: UBC Press, 2003.

Ruggiero, Kristin. "Houses of Deposit and the Exclusion of Women in Turn-of-the-Century Argentina." In *Isolation: Places and Practices of Exclusion*, ed. Carolyn Strange and Alison Bashford, 119–32. New York: Routledge, 2003.

Rutherdale, Myra. *Women and the White Man's God: Gender and Race in the Canadian Mission Field*. Vancouver: UBC Press, 2003.

Said, Edward. *Orientalism: Western Representations of the Orient*. London: Routledge and Kegan Paul, 1978.

Sangster, Joan. "Reforming Women's Reformatories: Elizabeth Fry, Penal Reform and the State, 1950–70." *Canadian Historical Review* 85, 2 (2004): 227–52. http://dx.doi.org/10.3138/CHR.85.2.227.

–. *Regulating Girls and Women: Sexuality, Family, and the Law in Ontario, 1920–1960*. Don Mills: Oxford University Press, 2001.

Segger, Martin. *A Primer for Regional History in Architecture. Watkins Glen*. Victoria: The American Life Foundation and Study Institute, 1979.

Semple, N. *The Lord's Dominion: The History of Canadian Methodism*. Montreal and Kingston: McGill-Queen's University Press, 1996.

Semple, Rhonda Ann. *Missionary Women: Gender, Professionalism and the Victorian Idea of Christian Mission*. Woodbridge: Boydell Press, 2003.

Shah, Nayan. *Contagious Divides: Epidemics and Race in San Francisco's Chinatown*. Berkeley: University of California Press, 2001.

–. *Stranger Intimacy: Contesting Race, Sexuality and the Law in the North American West*. Berkeley: University of California Press, American Crossroads Series, 2011.

Sibley, David. *Geographies of Exclusion: Society and Difference in the West*. London: Routledge, 1995. http://dx.doi.org/10.4324/9780203430545.

Singh, Maina Chawla. *Gender, Religion, and "Heathen Lands": American Missionary Women in South Asia, 1860s–1940s*. New York: Garland, 2000.

Smith, Dorothy. *Texts, Facts, and Femininity: Exploring the Relations of Ruling*. London: Routledge, 1990. http://dx.doi.org/10.4324/9780203425022.

Stanley, Timothy. *Contesting White Supremacy: School Segregation, Anti-Racism, and the Making of Chinese Canadians*. Vancouver: UBC Press, 2001.

– "LEE MONG KOW," in *Dictionary of Canadian Biography*, vol. 15, University of Toronto/Université Laval 2003–, viewed 06 26, 2014, http://www.biographi.ca/en/bio/lee_mong_kow_15E.html.

– "CHANG TOY (Chen Cai in Mandarin), known also as Chan Doe Gee (Chen Daozhi) and Chan Chang-Jin, but generally as Sam Kee (San Ji) in *Dictionary of Canadian Biography*, vol. 15, University of Toronto/Université Laval, 2003–, viewed 06 26, 2014, http://www.biographi.ca/en/bio/chang_toy_15E.html.

Stasiulis, Daiva. "Feminist Intersectional Theorizing." In *Race and Ethnic Relations in Canada*, ed. Peter S. Li, 347–98. Don Mills: Oxford University Press, 1999.

Steyn, M., and D. Conway. "Introduction: Intersecting Whiteness, Interdisciplinary Debates." *Ethnicities* 10, 3 (2010): 283–91. http://dx.doi.org/10.1177/1468796810372309.

Stoler, Ann Laura. "Colonial Archives and the Arts of Governance." *Archival Science* 2, 1–2 (2002): 87–109. http://dx.doi.org/10.1007/BF02435632.

—. *Race and the Education of Desire: Foucault's History of Sexuality and the Colonial Order of Things*. Durham, NC: Duke University Press, 1995.

—. "Sexual Affronts and Racial Frontiers: European Identities and the Cultural Politics of Exclusions in Colonial Southeast Asia." *Comparative Studies in Society and History* 34, 3 (1992): 514–51. http://dx.doi.org/10.1017/S001041750001793X.

Strange, Carolyn. "Stories of Their Lives: The Historian and the Capital Case File." In *On the Case: Explorations in Social History*, ed. Franca Iacovetta, 25–48. Toronto: University of Toronto Press, 1998.

Strong-Boag, Veronica. "Daughters of the True North, 1900–1995." *Beaver* 74, 6 (1995): 29–41.

Swift, Karen J. "An Outrage to Common Decency: Historical Perspectives on Child Neglect." *Child Welfare* 74, 1 (1995): 71–91.

Taylor, Lawrence J. "Moral Entrepreneurs and Moral Geographies on the US/Mexico Border." *Social and Legal Studies* 19, 3 (2010): 299–310. http://dx.doi.org/10.1177/0964663910372182.

Terry, Jennifer. "Theorizing Deviant Historiography." *differences* 3, 2 (1991): 55–74.

Tuchman, G. *Making News: A Book in the Construction of Reality*. New York: The Free Press, 1978.

Tuori, Salla, and Salla Peltonen. "Feminist Politics: An Interview with Sara Ahmed." *NORA* 15, 4 (2007): 257–64. http://dx.doi.org/10.1080/08038740701691941.

Twine, France Winddance, and Charles Gallagher. "The Future of Whiteness – A Map of the 'Third Wave.'" *Ethnic and Racial Studies* 31, 1 (2008): 4–24. http://dx.doi.org/10.1080/01419870701538836.

Valverde, Mariana. *The Age of Light, Soap, and Water: Moral Reform in English Canada, 1885–1925*. Toronto: McClelland and Stewart, 1991.

VancouverIsland.com. *Historic Craigflower Manor, Victoria, British Columbia*. 2010. http://www.vancouverisland.com/attractions/?id=62 (viewed 10 10, 2010).

viHistory. *Victoria Municipal Census of 1871*. n.d. http://vihistory.ca/content/census/1871/census1871.php?show=y (viewed 10 13, 2014).

—. *viHistory Maps*. 2006. http://vihistory.uvic.ca/content/about/about.php (viewed 10 12, 2010).

Ward, Peter. *White Canada Forever: Popular Attitudes and Public Policy toward Orientals in British Columbia*. Montreal and Kingston: McGill-Queen's University Press, 1990.

Weeks, Jeffrey. *Sexuality and Its Discontents*. London: Routledge, 1985. http://dx.doi.org/10.4324/9780203407462.

White, Walder G.W. "A Comparison of Some Parental and Guardian Rights." *Canadian Journal of Family Law* 3 (1980): 219–49.

Whiteley, Marilyn Färdig. *The Life and Letters of Annie Leake Tuttle: Working for the Best*. Waterloo: Wilfrid Laurier University Press, 1999.

Wishart, David. "The Selectivity of Historical Representation." *Journal of Historical Geography* 23, 2 (1997): 111–8. http://dx.doi.org/10.1006/jhge.1996.0044.

Women's Book Committee Chinese Canadian National Council. *Jin Guo: Voices of Chinese Canadian Women*. Toronto: Women's Press, 1992.

Yan, Miu Chung, and Sean Lauer. "Social Capital and Ethno-Cultural Diverse Immigrants: A Canadian Study on Settlement House and Social Integration." *Journal of Ethnic & Cultural Diversity in Social Work* 17, 3 (2008): 229–50. http://dx.doi.org/10.1080/15313200802258125.

Young, Robert. *Colonial Desire: Hybridity in Theory, Culture and Race*. New York: Routledge, 1995.

Index

as threat to white women, 188; use Home for own purposes, 104; white women challenge rights of, 109

Chinese Mission Home (San Francisco). See San Francisco: Chinese rescue missions in

Chinese Rescue Home: ambivalence of white community towards, 132, 138, 147; approach to, 7–29, 183, 186, 190–92, 198–99; closing of, 191–92, 212n18; as domain of women, 30; future research on, 13, 191–92; impetus for, 4; Jennie Menzies's attacks on, 129–34; location of, 37–38, 39(f), 40; mandates and goals of, 6–7, 22, 101; name change of, 45, 87, 153; national scope of work done by, 42; vs residential schools, 32–33; roles of white women in, 40; shift in objectives and demographics of, 12, 48, 191; sources for study of, 11–12, 14–16, 57, 83, 183, 191, 197–98, 199; as understudied, 184. See also admission to Home, factors in; buildings, Home's; escape attempts; matrons, Home's; recruitment strategies, Home's; residents, Home's; workers, Home's

Chinese women: as both included and excluded in nation and Home, 19–21, 24, 73, 103, 171, 183, 185; convert to Christianity for non-faith reasons, 24, 113; as domestic delinquents, 9, 57–61; framed in terms of particular discourses, 18; immigration of, 34–35, 110; missing voices of, 13, 191; motivations for learning English domestic skills, 44; numbers of, 205n11; as promiscuous or as prostitutes, 4, 27, 34–35, 53–55, 60, 174, 176; as rebellious, 128; state and public's shifting interest in fate of, 120, 124; as threat, 53–55; unable to attain whiteness, 28, 103; as victims or as vulnerable, 27, 51, 60, 94–95, 126, 167. See also residents, Home's

Chong, Denise, 110

Choy Wan case, 159; discourse of stranger in, 168–70; free will as factor in, 155;

Home portrays itself as orphanage in, 153; race as factor in, 173–74; summary of, 150

Christian church, prostitution of, 146

Christian community, Royal Commission (1902) testimony of, 42, 61–64, 69, 140

Christianity, 70–74; architecture reflects values of, 90; Chinese and Japanese women as members of family of, 28, 68, 73, 94, 95, 103, 187; conversion by Chinese and Japanese community for non-faith reasons, 24, 113, 140, 215n104; as cure for threats posted by Chinese and Japanese women, 55; domesticity encompasses values of, 78; equated with citizenship, 105–6, 190, 204n73; equated with morality, 63, 209n22; as guaranteeing partial entry into nation, 66, 67, 70–71; immigration as price for global dominance of, 185; racism of, 21. See also family; marriage; religion

Chunn, Dorothy, 167

church archives, 15

churches, intervention by, 24. See also Christianity; religion

citizenship: challenges posed by Chinese and Japanese women to, 9; cultural vs global, 26–27; equated with Christianity, 105–6, 190, 204n73; equated with whiteness, 190, 204n73; goal of Home, 187; measures of residents' candidacy for, 72–74; as projected on bodies of Asian women, 24. See also assimilation; nation

Citizenship and Immigration Canada, 193

civil policing. See public, general: polices cross-racial contact

civilization, legitimization of white settlement through, 32. See also assimilation

class: domestication as process of, 187; as factor in habeas corpus cases, 159–60, 161, 174, 179; immigration as problem of, 63, 64; Victoria's hierarchy of, 36, 37; white women's benevolent work as mark of higher, 43

Printed and bound in Canada by Friesens

Set in Garamond Pro by Apex CoVantage, LLC.

Copy editor: Joanne Richardson

Proofreader: Sophie Pouyanne

Indexer: Marnie Lamb

Cartographer: Eric Leinberger